30-Day Whole Foods Cookbook

Transform the Way You Eat with 250 Whole Food
Recipes Free of Gluten, Dairy, and Refined Sugar with
30-Day Meal Plan to Reset Your Body

By Danilo Angelo

Table of Content

Introduction

Chapter 1: Why Whole Food   2
Benefits of Whole Food   3
Why Should You Choose Whole Food?   4

Chapter 2: Program Rules for Whole Food   6
Guidelines and Plannings   7
Rules of Whole Food   9
Food to Eat   11
Food to Avoid   12
Exceptions   14
Shopping and Pantry List   15
FAQs   16

Chapter 3: 30-Day Meal Plan   17
What to Do After 30 Days   20

Chapter 4 Eggs

Kale and Bacon Frittata   21
Bistro Endive and Egg Salad   21
Bacon, Spinach, and Tomato Breakfast Salad   22
Mushroom and Spinach Frittata   22
Eggs Florentine   23
Sausage and Mushroom Frittata   23
Fried Eggs with Green Beans and Mushrooms   24
Sweet Potato Breakfast Stacks   24
Spinach and Tomato Frittata   25
Shakshuka   25
Green Omelet   26
Scrambled Eggs with Smoked Salmon   27
Pesto-Pepper Frittata with Butternut Squash   27
Scrambled Egg Breakfast Tacos   28

Chapter 5 Salads

Cilantro-Lime Pork Salad	29
Chicken Taco Salad	29
Steak Fajita Salad	30
Fattoush Salad	30
Oregano Chicken and Kale Salad	31
Cucumber and Tomato Salad	31
Curried Chicken Salad	31
Balsamic Peach Arugula Salad	32
Lemon Mediterranean Chicken Salad	32
Salmon Potato Salad	33
Orange Tuna, Snow Pea, and Broccoli Salad	33
Thai Chicken Larb Salad	33
Fruity Chicken Salad	34
Red Potato Salad with Chicken Sausage	34
Pork Greek Salad	34
Chimichurri Pork and Cabbage Salad	35
Ahi Mango Poke	35
Mango and Shrimp Salad	36
Chicken Romaine Salad	36
Ground Beef Taco Salad	37
Beef and Broccoli Salad	37
Steak Salad with Charred Onions	38
Greek Turkey Meatball Salad	38
Spicy Chicken, Watermelon, and Spinach Salad	39
Carne Asada Salad	39

Chapter 6 Soups and Stews

Chicken and Carrot Stew	40
Mexican Pork Shoulder Stew	40
Slow Cooker Beef Fajita Soup	41
Italian Chicken Sausage Soup	41
Hot and Sour Shrimp Soup	41
Italian Chicken Vegetable Soup	42
Thyme Chicken Zoodle Soup	42
Beef and Pepper Soup	42
Lush Pork Loin Stew	43
Kale and Chicken Sausage Stew	43
Almond Chicken and Sweet Potato Stew	43
Vegetable Soup with Basil Pesto	44
Beef and Vegetable Stew	44
Potato and Green Soup	45
Cauliflower Soup with Sausage and Spinach	45
Spiced Moroccan Meatball Stew	46
Pork and Green Chile Stew	46

Mexican Chicken Soup   47
Pork and Napa Cabbage Soup   47
Sweet Potato Pork Stew   48
Butternut Squash Apple Soup   48
Chicken Avocado Soup   49
Turnip Leek Soup   49

5-Minute Sugar Snap Peas   50
Sweet Potato Cauliflower Mash   50
Easy Zucchini Noodles   50
Garlic Kale   50
Mashed Sweet Potatoes   51
Roasted Cauliflower   51
Garlic and Herb Stuffed Portobello Mushrooms   51
Lime-Garlic Zucchini Ribbons   52
Garlicky Green Beans with Almonds   52
Beet and Red Cabbage Salad   52
Roasted Brussels Sprouts with Lemon Tahini   53
Chile Lime Roasted Sweet Potatoes   53
Balsamic Roasted Root Vegetables   53
Roasted Parsnips with Lemon and Dill   54
Kale and Butternut Squash Salad   54
Curried Carrot Sweet Potato Soup   54
Mustard Brussels Sprout Slaw   55
Greek Lemon Potatoes   55
Pistachio Kale Salad   55
Thai Red Curry Cauliflower   56
Red Cabbage with Bacon and Apple   56
Grilled Romaine with Lemon Tahini Dressing   56
Hasselback Zucchini with Basil   57
Dukkah Brussels Sprouts   57
Carrots with Fennel and Shallots   58
Creamy Broccoli Soup   58
Sautéed Greens with Pine Nuts   59
Almond Green Beans   59

Russian Beef Stew   60
Asian Beef Zoodle Soup   60
Pineapple Beef Kabobs   61
Beef Stuffed Bell Peppers   61
Basil Sirloin Medallions with Carrots   62
Beef, Zucchini, and Mushroom Stir-Fry   62

Chapter 7 Vegetables and Sides

Chapter 8 Red Meat

Onion-Braised Beef Brisket	63
Tunisian Lamb and Squash Stew	63
Beef Short Ribs Braised with Mushrooms	64
Black Pepper Beef and Cabbage Stir-Fry	64
Hearty Hamburger Soup	65
Grilled Steaks with Garlic-Shallot Purée	65
Steak Fajita Bowls with Vegetables	66
Sweet Potato Beef Chili	66
Beef and Broccoli Stir-Fry	67
Tender Pot Roast	67
Classic Borscht	68
Mici	68
Catalina Beef Tacos	69
Mongolian Beef and Mixed Greens	69
Indian Pepper Steak Stir-Fry	70
Grilled Skirt Steak	70
Thyme Lamb Chops and Fingerlings	71
Asian Beef with Mushrooms and Snow Peas	71
Authentic Picadillo	72
Lamb Loaves with Apricots and Cauliflower	72
Rosemary Beef Eye of Round Roast	73
Hot Roast Beef	73
Thai Coconut Beef Curry with Green Beans	74
Balsamic Roast Beef and Veggies	74
Cuban-Style Beef and Peppers	75
Beef Brisket Braised with Potatoes	75
Beef Stroganoff with Coconut Cream	76
Mushroom Stuffed Beef Roulade	77
Seared Sirloin Steak	78

Chapter 9 Pork

Pork Carnitas	79
Applesauce Pork Chops	79
Pork Lettuce Wraps with Peach Salsa	80
Apricot Stuffed Pork Chops	80
Green Chile Pork	81
Cider Pulled Pork	81
Pork Chops with Parsnip Purée	82
Green Pork Curry with Asparagus	82
Pork Scaloppini with Mushrooms	83
Rosemary Pork Chops with Red Potatoes	83
Basil Pork and Cauliflower Curry	84
Sausage Potato Hash	84
Apple Pork Chops and Spinach	85

Lemon-Tarragon Grilled Pork Rib Chops	85
Grilled Pork Chops with Watermelon Salad	86
Potato, Sausage, and Kale Soup	86
Coriander Crusted Pork Tenderloin	87
Roasted Pork with Butternut Squash	87
Pork with Sweet Potato Colcannon	88
Pork and Bell Pepper Stir-Fry	88
Pork Chops with Mashers and Pepita Pesto	89
Cider-Brined Roasted Pork	90
Spice-Crusted Roast Pork Tenderloin	91
Banger Sausage Patties with Sweet Potatoes	92
Chili Verde Pork	93

Chapter 10 Poultry

Asian Chicken Curry	94
Creamy Spinach Artichoke Chicken	95
Mojo Roast Chicken	95
Chicken and Artichoke Stew	96
Comforting Chicken Fricassée	96
Thai Lemon Curry Chicken Bowls	97
Chicken with Mushrooms and Sweet Potatoes	97
Roasted Pepper Chicken	98
Garlic Herb Chicken and Veggies	98
Sticky Apricot Drumsticks	98
Greek Lemon Chicken and Potatoes	99
Chipotle Chicken Thighs with Tomatoes	99
Piri Piri Chicken	100
Spanish Chicken Cauliflower Skillet	100
Green Chile Chicken Stew	101
Sweet Potato and Chicken Hash	101
Lemony Chicken with Green Beans	101
Crispy Chicken Schnitzel	102
Chicken Cacciatore	102
Chicken Meatballs with Creamy Tomato Sauce	103
Salsa Verde Chicken	103
Grapefruit Chicken	104
Rosemary Whole Chicken	104
Butter Chicken	105
Lemon and Oregano Chicken with Parsnips	105
Lemon and Herb Roast Chicken and Vegetables	106
Slow-Cooker Five-Spice Chicken Wings	106

Turkey Meatballs with Spaghetti Squash 107
Onion Chicken Meatballs 107
Turmeric Chicken Thighs 108
Smoky Spanish Chicken Meatballs 109
Braised Chicken with Artichoke and Olives 109
Balsamic Turkey Tenderloins with Peppers 110
Chicken Stir Fry 110
Italian-Style Chicken with Fennel 111
Turkey Stuffed Bell Peppers 111
Stir-Fried Chicken and Bok Choy 112
Garlic Chicken Primavera 112

Broiled Shrimp with Pine Nuts 113
Pan-Seared Scallops with Orange Sauce 113
Cod in Tomato and Pepper Sauce 114
Lemon Dill Salmon 114
Cod en Papillote 114
Sweet and Sour Snapper 115
Shrimp and Fish Cakes 115
Baked Fish en Papillote 116
Jamaican Jerk Salmon with Mango Salsa 116
Citrus-Ginger Glazed Halibut 117
Baked Cod with Mushrooms 117
Harissa Salmon Fillets 118
Basil Roasted Salmon with Broccoli 118
Mexican Tuna Boats 119
Ahi Tuna Steaks with Mango Salsa 119
Asian Shrimp Zucchini Noodles 119
Shrimp Mashed Potatoes 120
Pineapple Salmon 120
Fish Vegetable Stir-Fry 121
Garlic Mussels in Spicy Tomato Sauce 121
per with Shiitake Mushrooms 122
Thai Red Curry Shrimp 122
Salmon with Cauliflower and Spinach Salad 123
Easy Shrimp Scampi 123
Citrus Almond Cod with Spinach 124
Sea Scallops with Ginger-Blueberry Sauce 125
Cassava Crusted Calamari 125
Cod with Olive Relish and Pilaf 126

Chapter 11 Fish and Shellfish

Chapter 12 Sauces and Dressings

Italian Dressing	127
Sunflower Seed Curry Sauce	127
Balsamic Vinaigrette	127
Avocado Green Goddess Dressing	127
Cumin and Tomato Pineapple Sauce	128
Cashew Cauliflower Alfredo	128
Herb and Garlic Chimichurri Sauce	128
Carrot and Tomato Sauce	129
Almond Lime Satay Sauce	129
Asian Orange Dressing	129
Hollandaise Sauce	130
Cider-Mustard Vinaigrette	130
Lemon Dressing	130
Buffalo Sauce	131
Ginger Curry Sauce	131

Chapter 13 Basics

Homemade Mayonnaise	132
Basic Cauliflower Rice	132
Beef Bone Broth	132
Creamy Ranch Dressing	133
Sriracha	133
Ketchup	133
Clarified Butter	134
Chicken Bone Broth	134

Chapter 14 Drinks

Citrus Zinger	135
Rosemary Raspberry Smash	135
Iced Mango Mint Green Tea	135
Blood Orange Paloma	136
White Tea Sangria	136
Basil Peach Agua Fresca	136

Appendix 1: Measurement Conversion Chart	137
Appendix 2: Recipe Index	138

Introduction

You are what you eat, and true enough, many people in our modern, fast-paced world are unhealthy as they tend to overindulge in greasy, processed, calorie-dense foods for the sake of convenience. You can reset your body by accepting a 30 Days Whole Food. In just 30 days, you'll change your habits, learn about proper nutrition, reset your metabolism, and genuinely enjoy what REAL food tastes like.

While some types of carbohydrates are healthy and good for you, there has been a tendency over the last century to consume them in excess. Worse still, an increasing amount of the food we consume is processed and highly refined. It leads to many people's health being impacted negatively, while they remain blissfully unaware and continue eating meals that are making them sick. Adverse effects can include low energy levels, random unexplained aches in the body, weight gain/difficulty losing weight, or even certain conditions, such as skin problems or problems with digestion. These may be explained through your diet, as you may be eating more wrong foods than the appropriate options.

An excellent way to get back on track is to go through a total reboot. Fix your diet by changing it completely, taking away all the unhealthy options and begin eating the right foods, foods that have been proven to provide proper sustenance and aid our body's function, especially when consumed in the appropriate quantities. It is not to say that a person cannot treat themselves now and again, but for now, it will be best to cut as much unhealthy food from your life as possible, to better find out where you are in terms of nutrition and diet.

Chapter 1: Why Whole Food

The whole food diet is an approach to reducing the amount of packaged, processed, and premade foods consumed. By replacing these less nutritious ingredients that make up a large portion of most diets with nutrient-rich, colorful, filling, and whole tasty ingredients as detailed in this 30-day plan, you'll see improvements in your overall health and energy levels.

Benefits of Whole Food

Why should you or anyone else follow a Whole Food diet? Well, there's a massive list of advantages of the Whole Food diet, the significant benefits include the following:

- **Clearer and brighter skin, healthy fingernails, and healthy hair:** Once you start to cut down unhealthy and processed foods from your diet, the appearance and condition of your skin, fingernails, and hair will improve drastically.

- **Increased energy:** It has been suggested that the Whole Food can triple a person's energy. This is because you are fueling your body with 100% pure natural energy. However, this increase in energy is not going to happen instantly. You will feel tired and lack energy during the first week of the Whole Food, but after your body adjusts itself to the Whole Food diet, you soon will feel a boost in energy.

- **The Whole Food will help you lose weight:** Since you are getting rid of sugar, dairy, wheat, and junk food from your diet, it will certainly help burn some fat.

- **Improve the quality of sleep.** The Whole Food has been proven to help to improve and to regulate the hormones in your body. It helps with how your body sleeps and improve your sleeping patterns.

- **Mental clarity and better focus:** When you are consuming whole food, fresh meats, and organic vegetables, it will help you stay healthy, focused, and energized throughout the day.

- **The Whole Food can help fight certain diseases:** Multiple diseases such as diabetes, cerebral palsy, or certain psychological disorders can be eliminated while being on a Whole Food diet. Patients with such diseases and disorders have shown an improvement from these chronic diseases while on the Whole Food diet.

Why Should You Choose Whole Food?

- **It's not as challenging as people perceive think it.** Changing your diet is easy. Do you know what's difficult? Fighting off cancer. Giving birth. Losing a loved one. Choosing to drink black coffee pales in comparison to those. It's only thirty days, and these thirty days will allow you to get used to eating healthier and improve your lifestyle for the rest of your life.

- **There are no accidents in diets.** There are no "oops" moments when it comes to eating, unless someone shoved food in your mouth and forced you to swallow. Do not consider slipping up, as making excuses for yourself may cause you to have failed even before truly beginning.

- **Similarly, you always have a choice when you eat.** Even if there's a celebration, or a special occasion, whatever you eat is your choice. You could choose to eat healthy, or you could choose to give in to peer pressure like a high school kid. You choose.

- **Becoming healthier requires effort.** Putting more thoughts in your meals, planning groceries, finding out what's in your restaurant's food, all this needs time and effort. We have laid out the rules and what you need to do, but it's up to you to put it into action.

- **It may sound intimidating, but you can do this.** Tell your loved ones that you are undergoing this challenge, and they can serve as your support group when it comes to eating healthy.

Chapter 2: Program Rules for Whole Food

Since Whole Food is not just a diet for losing weight, but a way to switch to a healthy lifestyle, it has several essential rules which are strictly obligatory. If you cannot follow them all; then, do not start the program. If you break even just one of them during the clearance, you should start your whole food challenge from the beginning.

- The ingredients should not contain any artificial flavors

- There should be no artificial preservatives, sweeteners, and colors.

- There should be no use of hydrogenated fats

- There should be no antibiotic use on animals providing meat. Also, avoid synthetic nitrates

- Consider wild-caught seafood

- No any kind of alcohol – even as an additive to food

- No smoking – during the whole month

- No measuring. You are prohibited from weighing or doing any other measurements of your body during the diet. Weigh and measure the waist size on the first day of the program and then at the last one, but not in the middle of the diet.

- No calories counting

- Three meals a day is an ideal option, although dried fruits and nuts as snacks are not prohibited. But in reasonable quantities!

- All cleaning elements and products need to have ingredients that are safe for the environment.

Also, a critical thing to remember when doing the whole food diet is to check the label on each product you purchase as a lot of prepacked goods have additives or added sugar that you might not be aware of.

Let's say, bacon (Naked Bacon, Pederson's Natural Farms and US Wellness Meats are Whole Food compliant), sausages (Chicken & Apple Sausage are Whole Food compliant), mayonnaise (Chipotle Lime Mayo and Ranch Dressing are Whole Food compliant) etc. You might be shocked at the ingredients included in the foods that you once ate. The levels of sodium, sugar, and additives that have names you cannot even pronounce could be preventing you from maintaining a healthy weight. Becoming conscious about every bite you put in your mouth can help you achieve the healthy weight you desire and stay that way!

Guidelines and Plannings

Here are some tips to make your Whole Food journey as pleasant as possible.

- Make up your mind, be aware of all possible difficulties and start when you are fully committed.

- Plan, plan, and plan one more time. Carefully prepare your first-week meal plan. Then go for the next ones.

- Clear out your fridge off all foods that do not match with the Whole Food challenge.

- Plan your meals and go shopping according to it. If you are busy, keep one day aside to create your meal plan for the rest of the week. Take your lunch to the office.

- Do not cook something you should cook, but something that will make you happy and keep entertained throughout the month (check our recipes below, there are many decent ones to choose from)

- Have emergency snacks in your bag, car, office, parents' house. This could be some nuts or fruits.

- Before starting your Whole Food journey, check out all the coming events such as birthdays and parties. The temptation is great. So keep your food-related socializing events at a minimum.

- Involve your friends, family, or housemates – it is always good to go on a diet with company, not alone.

- And most importantly, never give up!

Rules of Whole Food

The four general rules to follow on the Whole Food diet are:

No cheating

To get the most out of the Whole food program, it is highly recommended that you don't cheat. The Whole Food is all-or-nothing, so plan ahead – especially if it's around holidays, birthdays, traveling or socializing where you have no control over any available foods and drinks.

If you are a busy person, it's a good idea to have prepared meals in advance. Meals such as soups, stews, and salads can be stored in your refrigerator until ready to eat.

Don't weigh yourself.

Daily weighing in and measuring your body is not allowed on the Whole Food. The Whole Food diet encourages gradual and safe weight loss. You're not going to find any dramatic change in your weight if you check the scale each day. Instead, weigh and measure yourself before and after the Whole Food diet.

Don't recreate unhealthy foods or drinks.

Many people think that recreating a Whole Food cheesecake is fine as long as the ingredients are Whole Food compliant.

However, you must avoid recreating unhealthy food and drinks even if you are using Whole Food compliant ingredients. This can contribute to unintentional weight gain, physical illness, mental illness, and psychological disorders. Trying to recreate unhealthy food into healthy ones will defeat the purpose of the Whole Food, and will only waste your time, energy, and money.

My advice for you is to keep an open mind about new recipes and ingredients. If you restrict yourself to a few meals, you will quickly tire out your taste buds and your patience. Luckily for you, in this book, you will find a diverse set of recipes that you can enjoy each day.

Avoid certain food items.

The main rule of the Whole Food diet is to not consume any items from the following food groups:

- Any form of alcohol
- Any form of sugar or sweetener
- Any form of baked goods such as cakes, cupcakes, cheesecakes, cookies
- Dairy
- Processed foods
- Junk food

- Candies and sweets
- Pasta
- Grains
- Starchy foods
- Instant gravy mixes and sauces
- Processed meats
- Legumes
- Processed snacks

You will find a fully comprehensive list in the "Whole Food Foods to Avoid" section.

Food to Eat

1. **Fruits:** Fruits are important in the Whole 30 diets; It helps to fulfill your sugar carving. It contains vitamins, minerals, fiber, and antioxidants. Fruits help to stay hydrated during the summer months.

2. **Best choices:** Apples, bananas, figs, grapefruit, lemons, cherries, berries, grapes, pineapples etc.

3. **Vegetables:** Vegetables are low in calories and rich in fiber, which is very beneficial for maintaining your cholesterol level. Frozen vegetables are also the best option in the Whole Food diets. Frozen fruits are low cost and also find sometimes more nutrients compared to fresh ones.

4. **Best choices:** Brussels sprouts, carrot, broccoli, cauliflower, kale, eggplant, mushrooms, onion, potatoes, spinach, tomatoes, zucchini, etc.

5. **Unprocessed Meats:** During Whole Food diet, your body needs a massive amount of proteins. Unprocessed meat is the best source of protein.

6. **Best choices:** Grass-fed beef, organic chicken and pork, etc.

7. **Seafood:** Whole Food diets recommend seafood, which contains omega-3 fatty acids. This helps to improve your brain and heart health.

8. **Best choices:** Wild-caught fish, sardines, salmon, herring, etc.

9. **Eggs:** Eggs are the best choice for your breakfast; it is the best when it comes to the source of healthy protein.

10. **Fats:** You can use good and healthy fat during the Whole Food diet.

11. **Best choices:** Coconut oils, avocado oils, olive oils, raw nuts, organic ghee, etc.

12. **Coffee:** You can add coffee into your Whole 30 diet. Don't add milk into coffee and add a dash of cinnamon into tour coffee to sweeten lightly.

Food to Avoid

The more crucial aspect of the diet, however, is what the participant should avoid eating during the challenge. Getting rid of the following foods and drinks for the duration of the challenge will help reset yourself, allowing you to resist cravings, improve your metabolism, and get used to a healthier diet. Being able to do this successfully will undoubtedly be a step towards living a better, healthier life.

1. **Dairy:** Avoid dairy products during the Whole 30 diets except ghee. You should avoid cheese, sour cream, butter, yogurt, milk, kefir, etc.

2. **Added sugar:** During Whole Food diet, all types of sugar are prohibited for 30 days, whether it is artificial or real. You can avoid maple syrup, agave, honey, stevia, splenda, xylitol, etc. Check labels of any packaged product to ensure that they contain no added sugar.

3. **Grains:** Grains are a source of carbohydrates, and as such, you should try to eliminate them from your diet. Avoid all grains during Whole 30 diet even it is gluten-free. You should avoid wheat, oats, corn, millet, sorghum, quinoa, sprouted grains, bulgur, rice, amaranth, buckwheat, rye, etc. Make sure to read the labels of any packaged product to ensure that you are not unwittingly consuming grain.

4. **Legumes:** During 30 days, you should not allow consuming any type of beans and soy. You should strictly avoid peas, lentils, peanut butter, lentils, chickpeas and soy like tofu, soy sauce, miso, tempeh, etc. Remember to check the label for bean products, as soy lecithin is a common component in many commercial foods.

5. **Alcohol:** Any types of alcohol are strictly avoided during 30 day's diet plans. Even you cannot use alcohol for cooking purposes. In addition to this, do not make use of tobacco products as well.

6. **Junk Foods:** Eliminate baked goods, treats, and junk food, even when they have "approved" ingredients. Trying to mimic processed junk foods by contorting them in ways that conform to the whole food diet is not what living a healthy whole food lifestyle is all about. There is such a thing as following the letter of the law while violating the spirit of the law, and this is one of those examples. Stay away from the types of foods that lead you down the path of unhealthy eating and suboptimal living. Embrace the whole food lifestyle and don't try to "hack" it or "game" it. The point of the challenge is to cleanse your diet, and though certain treats may be from ingredients on the approved list, this defeats the purpose of the diet.

7. **Eliminate Monosodium Glutamate and other additives.** These additives include sulfites and carrageenan in addition to the aforementioned MSG.

Remember that the reason that you are removing these foods from your diet for the next thirty days is that you are trying to reset your palate and get yourself used to eating healthy. If you continue to indulge, then you will continue to crave these things and will have a harder time when it comes to eating properly. If you are not sure whether or not you should eat something, better leave it out to be safe. After all, you are only removing it 100% from your diet for only thirty days.

Exceptions

Though rules were mentioning what should be avoided 100%, there are certain exceptions.

- **Ghee or clarified butter.** This is the only type of dairy you may consume.

- **Fruit juice.** Some products use fruit juice as a sweetener, which is permissible.

- **Some legumes.** Green beans and snow peas are allowed.

- **Vinegar.** Most types of vinegar are permitted, such as white, red wine, balsamic, apple cider, and rice vinegar.

- **Coconut aminos.** These are allowed even if they may have coconut nectar as a listed ingredient.

- **Salt.** You may wonder why this is in the exception list, but iodized salt contains sugar as well, and as salt is crucial and thus unavoidable, it is an exception to the no added sugar rule.

Shopping and Pantry List

I remind you that all foods should be natural (organic is not a must, but the best option). Avoid factory-made products as they usually contain harmful substances such as Pasta MSG, sulfites, or added sugar.

Protein:

- Beef /Lamb /Pork
- Beef steak /Pork joint
- Chicken /Chicken breast /Turkey
- Salmon /Shrimp /Scallops / Seafood /Eggs

Vegetables:

- Acorn squash / Asparagus / Pumpkin /Zucchini
- Beetroots / Broccoli /Brussels sprouts /Butternut squash
- Cabbage /Carrots /Cauliflower / Celery /Cucumber /Eggplant
- Green beans /Lettuce / Mushrooms /Onion / /Peppers / Garlic
- Radish /Spinach /Sweet potato/ Tomato /Turnip

Fruits:

- Apples /Apricots /Bananas / Blackberries /Blueberries / Cherries /Dates /Grapefruits Grapes /Kiwi /Melon /Oranges/ Pears /Plums /Raspberries / Strawberries /Watermelon

Oil:

- Coconut Oil /Ghee /Extra virgin olive oil /Clarified butter

Store Cupboard:

- Almonds /Cashews /Hazelnuts / Pistachios / Walnuts /Coconut
- Almond, Coconut milk, / Almond, Coconut flour /Olives
- Coconut water /Coffee / Mustard/Tahini /Vinegar / Herbs & Spices

FAQs

1. **What is the Whole Food?**

   The Whole Food is a diet where you eliminate certain food groups from your diet for 30 days to reset your body and reevaluate your relationship with food.

2. **What can I eat during the Whole Food?**

   You can eat real whole food such as meat, seafood, eggs, vegetables, fruit, fats, oils, nuts, and seeds. Natural, unprocessed, and organic food is heavily encouraged on the Whole Food.

3. **What can I not eat during the Whole Food?**

   For 30-days, you cannot eat any forms of sugar or sweetener, alcohol, grains, dairy, legumes, and any food that contains carrageenan, MSG, or sulfites.

4. **Will I lose weight on the Whole Food?**

   Most people on the Whole Food will lose weight, but the sole purpose of the Whole Food is not to lose weight but to remove foods and food groups that negatively affect your health.

5. **Can the Whole Food cure diseases and illnesses?**

   Many people on the Whole Food claim that the Whole Food challenge helped prevent, improved, or cured illnesses such as:

   High blood pressure / Type 1 Diabetes/ Type 2 Diabetes / High Cholesterol /Asthma / Allergies / Skin Conditions / Infertility / Bipolar Disorders / Depression / Leaky Gut Syndrome / Joint Pain and other illnesses.

6. **Can I have a Cheat Day during the Whole Food challenge?**

   No, for a successful Whole Food diet, you must be strict not to eat any "cheat" or "junk" foods. Zero exceptions.

7. **Can I adjust the Whole Food diet?**

   No, one is forcing you not to eat the restricted foods. However, you may not experience all the benefits after the 30-day diet is up.

8. **If I mess up, do I have to reset back to day one?**

   Most of the time, yes. If you eat birthday cake, drink alcohol, or something sugary, you should think about restarting the Whole Food challenge.

9. **What if I am vegan?**

   Meat is highly encouraged on the Whole Food, but you can still have a successful Whole Food by incorporating Whole Food compliant vegan sources such as nuts and seeds.

Chapter 3: 30-Day Meal Plan

	Breakfast	Lunch	Dinner
1	Scrambled Egg Breakfast Tacos	Oregano Chicken and Kale Salad	Citrus Almond Cod with Spinach
2	Leftover cod with your favorite side	Basil Sirloin Medallions with Carrots	Creamy Spinach Artichoke Chicken
3	Leftover chicken with your favorite side	Sweet and Sour Snapper	Beef Stuffed Bell Peppers
4	Leftover beef with your favorite side	Mojo Roast Chicken	Pork with Sweet Potato Colcannon
5	Leftover pork and sweet potato with your favorite side	Cilantro-Lime Pork Salad	Shrimp and Fish Cakes
6	Leftover cakes with your favorite side	Beef Stroganoff with Coconut Cream	Rosemary Whole Chicken
7	Leftover chicken with your favorite side	Pork Scaloppini with Mushrooms	Asian Shrimp Zucchini Noodles
8	Leftover noodles with your favorite side	Beef Short Ribs Braised with Mushrooms	Cider-Brined Roasted Pork
9	Leftover pork with your favorite side	Grapefruit Chicken	Catalina Beef Tacos

10	Leftover beef tacos with your favorite side	Fish Vegetable Stir-Fry	Turmeric Chicken Thighs
11	Leftover chicken thighs with your favorite side	Beef and Broccoli Salad	Lemon and Oregano Chicken with Parsnips
12	Leftover chicken and parsnips with your favorite side	Thyme Lamb Chops and Fingerlings	Cod with Olive Relish and Pilaf
13	Leftover cod with your favorite side	Chipotle Chicken Thighs with Tomatoes	Spice-Crusted Roast Pork Tenderloin
14	Leftover pork tenderloin with your favorite side	Salmon with Cauliflower and Spinach Salad	Butter Chicken
15	Leftover chicken with your favorite side	Onion-Braised Beef Brisket	Lemony Chicken with Green Beans
16	Leftover chicken and green beans with your favorite side	Basil Pork and Cauliflower Curry	Mongolian Beef and Mixed Greens
17	Leftover beef with your favorite side	Turkey Meatballs with Spaghetti Squash	Basil Roasted Salmon with Broccoli
18	Leftover salmon and broccoli with your favorite side	Salmon Potato Salad	Apple Pork Chops and Spinach
19	Leftover pork chops with your favorite side	Ahi Tuna Steaks with Mango Salsa	Braised Chicken with Artichoke and Olives
20	Leftover chicken with your favorite side	Indian Pepper Steak Stir-Fry	Asian Chicken Curry

21	Leftover chicken with your favorite side	Thai Red Curry Shrimp	Balsamic Roast Beef and Veggies
22	Leftover beef and veggies with your favorite side	Greek Turkey Meatball Salad	Shrimp Mashed Potatoes
23	Leftover shrimp and potatoes with your favorite side	Asian Beef with Mushrooms and Snow Peas	Roasted Pepper Chicken
24	Leftover chicken with your favorite side	Lemon-Tarragon Grilled Pork Rib Chops	Pineapple Salmon
25	Leftover salmon with your favorite side	Beef Brisket Braised with Potatoes	Grilled Pork Chops with Watermelon Salad
26	Leftover salad with your favorite side	Lemon Dill Salmon	Pork Lettuce Wraps with Peach Salsa
27	Leftover pork lettuce wraps with your favorite side	Spicy Chicken, Watermelon, and Spinach Salad	Pork Carnitas
28	Leftover pork carnitas with your favorite side	Garlic Herb Chicken and Veggies	Cod in Tomato and Pepper Sauce
29	Leftover cod with your favorite side	Cuban-Style Beef and Peppers	Ginger Snapper with Shiitake Mushrooms
30	Leftover snapper and mushrooms with your favorite side	Balsamic Turkey Tenderloins with Peppers	Tender Pot Roast

What to Do After 30 Days

After the monthly detox program, the second chapter of your Whole Food 30-day challenge begins – you have to reinstate those products that were eliminated from the diet slowly. Each group of products must be entered separately from the other. You can start with any, but the best is to choose dairy and milk products. So, on the first day after your one-month diet has finished, you start eating dairy products. You eat them throughout the day, and then for four days, you again go back to the whole food diet. It is a time to observe your condition.

You have to note any unpleasant symptoms that have not been seen all month, and now they have appeared again after the first day of reintroduction. It can be anything: bloating and diarrhea, itchy skin and queasiness, headache, and increased blood pressure. Anything that makes you feel bad.

If you did not notice any unpleasant symptoms within four days after the first "milk day," go on to reinstate into the diet, the second group of excluded foods, for example, legumes.

Theoretically, you can return all the excluded products. However, if you seriously approach to tracking your health after introducing a product group into the diet, you will find that not all of them are consumed by your body normally.

In addition, there are groups of products that you should never consume, like harmful vegetable oils, trans fats, sugar.

Chapter 4: Eggs

Kale and Bacon Frittata

Prep time: 10 minutes | Cook time: 40 minutes

Serves 4

4 slices bacon, thinly sliced
8 large eggs
¼ cup full-fat coconut milk
¼ cup finely chopped kale stems
Kosher salt and freshly

ground black pepper, to taste
½ red bell pepper, diced
1 shallot, diced
1 large Roma (plum) tomato, thinly sliced

1. Preheat the oven to 325°F (163°C).
2. Place the bacon slices in a 10-inch oven-safe nonstick or cast-iron skillet and set it over medium heat. Cook, turning the bacon once or twice, until golden brown and slightly crispy, about 6 minutes. Transfer to paper towels to drain excess grease and set aside. Pour off all but 2 tablespoons of the rendered bacon fat in the skillet.
3. In a medium bowl, whisk together the eggs and coconut milk until thoroughly combined and smooth. Set aside.
4. Return the skillet to medium heat, add the kale stems, and season with salt and black pepper. Cook, stirring, until slightly softened, 3 to 4 minutes. Add the bell pepper and shallot and cook, stirring, for 2 minutes more, until softened. Pour the egg mixture into the pan and add the bacon. Gently stir to evenly distribute the ingredients.
5. Top with the tomato slices and transfer the pan to the oven. Cook for 20 to 25 minutes, until a toothpick or cake tester inserted into the center comes out clean. Serve immediately.

Bistro Endive and Egg Salad

Prep time: 10 minutes | Cook time: 20 minutes

Serves 2

4 cups packed curly endive
1½ tablespoons extra-virgin olive oil
1 tablespoon apple cider vinegar
1 teaspoon Whole Food-compliant Dijon mustard
¼ teaspoon minced

garlic
Salt and black pepper, to taste
4 slices Whole Food-compliant bacon, cut into ¼-inch pieces
2 teaspoons white vinegar
4 large eggs

1. Wash and dry the endive. Place in a shallow salad bowl and chill until needed.
2. Combine the oil, apple cider vinegar, mustard, and garlic in a small jar with a lid. Season with salt and pepper. Cover and shake vigorously to combine. Set aside.
3. Cook the bacon in a small amount of water in a small skillet over medium-high heat for 5 minutes. Drain the bacon and dry the skillet. Return the bacon to the dry skillet and cook over medium heat until browned and crisp.
4. Meanwhile, fill a wide saucepan with 3 inches of water. Add the white vinegar and 1 teaspoon salt. Bring to a boil over high heat. Crack each egg into a separate small bowl or cup. Gently pour each egg into the boiling water. Remove the pan from the heat, cover, and let sit until the whites are firm but the yolks are still runny, about 4 minutes. Remove the poached eggs from the skillet with a slotted spoon and place on a paper towel-lined plate to drain.
5. Drizzle the endive with the vinaigrette, tossing to coat well. Divide the endive between two plates. Top each with two poached eggs and sprinkle with the bacon. Season with pepper and serve immediately.

Bacon, Spinach, and Tomato Breakfast Salad

Prep time: 10 minutes | Cook time: 15 minutes
Serves 2

6 cups baby spinach (about 6 ounces / 170 g)
1 ripe avocado, halved, pitted, peeled, and sliced
½ cup grape or cherry tomatoes, halved
4 slices Whole Food-compliant bacon
1 small shallot, finely chopped
3 tablespoons extra-

virgin olive oil
2 tablespoons red wine vinegar
¼ teaspoon dry mustard
⅛ teaspoon black pepper
2 teaspoons white vinegar
1 teaspoon salt
4 large eggs
Sliced green onions (optional)

1. Divide the spinach, avocado, and tomatoes between two serving bowls.
2. Cook the bacon until browned and crisp in a large skillet over medium heat. Drain the bacon on paper towels, reserving 3 tablespoons of the drippings in the skillet. Crumble the bacon and set aside.
3. Cook the shallot in the reserved bacon drippings over medium heat, stirring frequently, until tender, about 3 minutes. Remove from the heat; whisk in the oil, red wine vinegar, dry mustard, and pepper.
4. Meanwhile, fill a wide saucepan with 3 inches of water. Add the white vinegar and salt and bring to a boil over high heat. Crack each egg into a separate small bowl. Gently slide each egg into the boiling water. Remove the pan from the heat, cover, and let sit for 3 minutes for very soft yolks or 5 minutes for firm yolks. Remove the cooked eggs from the pan with a slotted spoon and place on a paper towel-lined plate to drain.
5. Top each bowl of the spinach mixture with two poached eggs and divide the crumbled bacon and the dressing evenly between them. If desired, sprinkle with green onions.

Mushroom and Spinach Frittata

Prep time: 10 minutes | Cook time: 10 minutes
Serves 2 or 3

2 medium leeks (white and light green parts only)
6 large eggs, lightly beaten
1 tablespoon full-fat coconut milk
2 teaspoons fresh thyme, finely chopped, or ½ teaspoon dried thyme, crushed
¼ teaspoon salt
¼ teaspoon red

pepper flakes
2 tablespoons extra-virgin olive oil
1½ cups sliced fresh mushrooms
1 (about 6-ounce / 170-g) bag baby spinach, roughly chopped
1 clove garlic, minced
2 tablespoons thinly sliced green onions

1. Trim the roots and wilted leaves from the leeks. Cut the leeks in half lengthwise, then cut them crosswise into ¼-inch-thick pieces. Rinse well with cold water. Drain and dry the leeks and set aside.
2. Preheat the broiler. In a medium bowl, combine the eggs, coconut milk, thyme, salt, and red pepper flakes; set aside.
3. Heat the olive oil in a large oven-safe skillet over medium heat; add the leeks and mushrooms and cook, stirring frequently, until softened, 5 to 8 minutes. Add the spinach and garlic and let the spinach wilt for 30 seconds.
4. Pour the egg mixture into the skillet and cook over medium heat. As the egg mixture sets, run a spatula around edge of skillet, lifting the cooked egg so the uncooked egg flows underneath. Cook until the egg is beginning to set (the surface will still be moist).
5. Transfer the pan with the eggs to the oven and broil 4 to 5 inches from the heat (or bake in the preheated oven for 1 to 3 minutes), until the top is set and lightly browned. Top with the green onions. Cut into wedges and serve hot, directly out of the pan.

Eggs Florentine

Prep time: 10 minutes | Cook time: 30 minutes

Serves 6

1 tablespoon ghee, plus more for greasing
1 shallot, finely chopped
½ red bell pepper, diced
Kosher salt and freshly ground black pepper, to taste
3 cups loosely packed

baby spinach, finely chopped
11 large eggs
½ cup full-fat coconut milk
4 ounces (113 g) no-sugar-added smoked salmon, thinly sliced into ribbons

1. Preheat the oven to 325°F (163°C). Grease a 12-cup muffin tin with ghee and set it on a rimmed baking sheet to catch any spills.
2. In a large nonstick skillet, melt the ghee over medium heat. Add the shallot and bell pepper, season with a pinch each of salt and black pepper, and cook, stirring, until the vegetables are slightly softened, about 3 minutes. Add the spinach and cook, stirring, until wilted, about 2 minutes. Taste and adjust the salt and pepper as desired. Remove the pan from the heat.
3. In a large bowl, whisk together the eggs and coconut milk until thoroughly combined and smooth.
4. Using a spoon, distribute the vegetable mixture evenly among the prepared muffin cups. Divide the sliced salmon evenly over the vegetables, then ladle the egg mixture over the top. Bake until a toothpick or cake tester inserted into the center of an egg cup comes out clean, about 25 minutes.
5. Serve immediately, or let cool, transfer to an airtight container, and store in the refrigerator for up to 4 days.

Sausage and Mushroom Frittata

Prep time: 10 minutes | Cook time: 15 minutes

Serves 4

8 large eggs
¾ teaspoon salt
⅛ teaspoon black pepper
8 ounces (227 g) ground pork
1 teaspoon Italian seasoning, crushed
¼ teaspoon smoked paprika
⅛ teaspoon fennel seeds
⅛ teaspoon red

pepper flakes
2 tablespoons extra-virgin olive oil
2 cups sliced white or cremini mushrooms
2 cloves garlic, minced
3 cups roughly chopped arugula
1 cup chopped tomato
¼ cup sliced green onions
Whole Food-compliant hot sauce (optional)

1. Preheat the broiler. In a medium bowl, beat the eggs with ½ teaspoon of the salt and the black pepper; set aside.
2. In a medium bowl, combine the pork, Italian seasoning, paprika, fennel seeds, red pepper flakes, and remaining ¼ teaspoon salt; mix well.
3. Heat the olive oil in a large oven-safe skillet over medium heat. Add the pork mixture and cook, stirring frequently, until the meat is browned. Add the mushrooms and garlic. Cook, stirring, until the mushrooms are tender, 3 to 4 minutes. Stir in the arugula and cook until wilted, about 1 minute. Pour the egg mixture into the skillet. As the mixture sets, run a spatula around the edge of the skillet, lifting the egg mixture so the uncooked egg flows underneath. Cook until almost set, 2 to 3 minutes more.
4. Place the skillet under the broiler, 4 to 6 inches from the heat, and broil for 1 to 2 minutes, until the top is set.
5. To serve, top the frittata with the tomato and green onions. Cut into quarters and serve hot, directly from the skillet. Pass hot sauce alongside, if desired.

Fried Eggs with Green Beans and Mushrooms

Prep time: 10 minutes | Cook time: 15 minutes
Serves 2

6 tablespoons extra-virgin olive oil	1 teaspoon salt
2 cups sliced fresh mushrooms	4 cups arugula
12 ounces (340 g) fresh green beans, trimmed and cut into 2-inch pieces	6 large eggs
	½ teaspoon grated lemon zest
	1 tablespoon fresh lemon juice
1 sprig fresh thyme	2 tablespoons finely chopped shallot
1 clove garlic, minced	Black pepper, to taste

1. Heat 2 tablespoons of the olive oil in a large nonstick skillet over high heat. Add the mushrooms and cook, stirring occasionally, until just beginning to brown, about 3 minutes. Reduce the heat to medium and stir in the green beans, thyme, garlic, and ½ teaspoon of the salt. Cook, stirring frequently, for 2 minutes. Cover and cook, stirring once or twice, until the beans are crisp-tender, about 5 minutes. Remove and discard the thyme.
2. Spread the arugula on a large platter or in a large shallow bowl. Top with the hot vegetables. Let stand until the arugula wilts, about 5 minutes.
3. Meanwhile, wipe out the skillet. Heat 2 tablespoons of the oil in the skillet over medium-high heat. Fry the eggs in the hot oil until the whites are set and the yolks are cooked to your desired doneness, flipping the eggs if desired.
4. In a small bowl, whisk together the lemon zest and juice, the remaining 2 tablespoons oil, and the shallot.
5. Toss together the wilted arugula and vegetables. Drizzle with the dressing and top with the fried eggs. Sprinkle with the remaining ½ teaspoon salt and black pepper to taste.

Sweet Potato Breakfast Stacks

Prep time: 5 minutes | Cook time: 20 minutes
Serves 2

2 tablespoons extra-virgin olive oil	vinegar
	4 large eggs
1 medium sweet potato, peeled and cut into eight ½-inch-thick rounds	1 clove garlic, minced
	4 cups baby spinach
¼ teaspoon salt	4 slices Whole Food-compliant bacon, cooked until crisp
¼ teaspoon black pepper	Whole Food-compliant hot sauce, for serving
2 teaspoons white	

1. Heat 1 tablespoon of the olive oil in a large skillet over medium heat. Add the sweet potato rounds in a single layer and cook until fork-tender and browned on both sides, 3 to 5 minutes per side. Remove the sweet potatoes from the skillet and sprinkle with ⅛ teaspoon of the salt and ⅛ teaspoon of the pepper.
2. Meanwhile, fill a wide saucepan with 3 inches of water. Add the vinegar and bring to a boil over high heat. Crack each egg into a separate small bowl. Gently slide each egg into the boiling water. Remove the pan from the heat, cover, and let sit for 3 minutes for very soft yolks or 5 minutes for firm yolks. Remove the cooked eggs from the pan with a slotted spoon and place on a paper towel-lined plate to drain.
3. Heat the remaining 1 tablespoon oil in the large skillet over medium heat. Add the garlic and cook, stirring, until fragrant, about 30 seconds. Stir in the spinach and cook, stirring, until wilted, about 1 minute. Stir in the remaining ⅛ teaspoon salt and ⅛ teaspoon pepper.
4. On each plate, top four of the cooked sweet potato rounds with spinach, bacon, and two poached eggs. Serve with hot sauce for drizzling.

Spinach and Tomato Frittata

Prep time: 10 minutes | Cook time: 10 to 15 minutes

Serves 2

6 large eggs, beaten
¼ teaspoon salt
¼ teaspoon black pepper
2 tablespoons cooking fat
½ onion, diced
1 cup diced seeded tomato (plus a few slices for topping the frittata)
1 (about 9-ounce / 255-g) bag baby spinach, roughly chopped
Grated zest and juice of ¼ lemon

1. Set the oven to broil.
2. In a mixing bowl, whisk the eggs with the salt and pepper.
3. Heat a large oven-safe skillet over medium heat. Add the cooking fat to the pan and swirl to coat the bottom. When the fat is hot, add the onion and tomato and cook, stirring, until softened, 2 to 3 minutes. Add the spinach and let it wilt for 30 seconds. Add the eggs and fold them into the vegetables with a rubber spatula. Cook, without stirring to let the eggs set on the bottom and sides of the pan, until the eggs are firm and still appear wet, 3 to 4 minutes. Lay a few tomato slices on top. Drizzle the lemon juice and sprinkle the lemon zest over the top.
4. Transfer the pan with the eggs to the oven and broil 4 to 6 inches from the heat (or bake in the preheated oven) for 3 to 5 minutes, until the top is golden brown. Cut into slices and serve hot out of the pan.

Shakshuka

Prep time: 10 minutes | Cook time: 25 minutes

Serves 2

2 tablespoons extra-virgin olive oil
½ cup chopped onion
1 cup chopped red bell pepper
4 cloves garlic, minced
1 (28-ounce / 794-g) can Whole Food-compliant fire-roasted crushed tomatoes
1 to 2 tablespoons Whole Food-compliant harissa
1 teaspoon ground cumin
½ teaspoon salt
6 large eggs
Black pepper, to taste
3 tablespoons chopped fresh parsley

1. Heat the oil in a large skillet over medium heat. Add the onion and cook, stirring, until slightly wilted, about 2 minutes. Add the bell pepper and garlic and cook, stirring, until the onion and pepper are tender, 4 to 5 minutes more. Add the tomatoes, harissa, cumin, and salt; bring to a boil. Reduce the heat to low and simmer, stirring occasionally, until the sauce has thickened, 10 to 15 minutes.
2. Use the back of a spoon to make six depressions in the sauce. Crack one egg into a small bowl and carefully slide the egg into one depression in the sauce. Repeat with the remaining eggs. Cook, covered, until the egg whites are completely cooked and the yolks begin to thicken but are not hard, 6 to 8 minutes. Remove from the heat. Season with black pepper and sprinkle with the parsley before serving.

Green Omelet

Prep time: 10 minutes | Cook time: 45 minutes
Serves 2

Charred Tomatillo Salsa:

3 cloves garlic, unpeeled
4 tomatillos, husked, rinsed, and dried
1 medium poblano chile, stemmed, seeded, and quartered
½ small onion, cut into thin wedges

2 tablespoons snipped fresh cilantro
1 tablespoon fresh lime juice
½ teaspoon coarse salt
¼ teaspoon ground cumin

Omelet:

4 teaspoons extra-virgin olive oil
2 green onions, thinly sliced
½ cup thin bite-size strips green bell pepper
6 large eggs

2 tablespoons water
¼ teaspoon coarse salt
¼ teaspoon black pepper
1 cup coarsely chopped baby spinach

1. Make the salsa: Wrap the garlic in aluminum foil. Place the packet on a rack in the lower third of the oven. Adjust top oven rack to 4 or 5 inches from the broiler. Preheat the broiler. Line a baking pan with foil and combine the tomatillos, poblano, and onion on the pan. Place the pan on the top oven rack and broil for 8 to 10 minutes, turning the tomatillos once or twice, until the tomatillos and poblano skins are charred. Place the pan on a wire rack. Bring the foil up and around vegetables to fully enclose them. Let stand until cool. Change the oven setting to 400°F (205°C). Roast the garlic for 10 minutes more, then set on a wire rack to cool. Using a sharp knife, peel the skin off the cooled poblano quarters. Peel the cooled garlic. In a food processor, combine the poblano, tomatillos, onion, and garlic. Pulse until finely chopped. Transfer to a medium bowl. Stir in the cilantro, lime, juice, salt, and cumin.
2. Make the omelet: Heat 2 teaspoons of the olive oil in an 8-inch ceramic nonstick skillet with flared sides over medium heat. Add the green onions, reserving some of the green tops for garnish, and the bell pepper and cook, stirring occasionally, until the pepper is crisp-tender, 3 to 5 minutes. Transfer the bell pepper mixture to a small bowl.
3. Meanwhile, in a 2-cup glass measure, beat the eggs, water, salt, and black pepper until well combined. In the same skillet, heat 1 teaspoon of the olive oil over medium heat. Add half the egg mixture to the skillet. Cook and stir the eggs, pushing the cooked portion toward the center with a spatula and allowing the uncooked egg to flow under, until the eggs are set and have formed an even layer in the skillet. Spoon half the bell pepper mixture and half the spinach over one side of the egg. Fold the opposite side over the filling. Transfer the omelet to a serving plate and keep warm. Repeat with the remaining olive oil, egg mixture, bell pepper mixture, and spinach to make a second omelet.
4. Spoon ¼ cup of the charred tomatillo salsa over each omelet. Top with the reserved green onion.

Scrambled Eggs with Smoked Salmon

Prep time: 5 minutes | Cook time: 10 minutes
Serves 3 or 4

8 large eggs
2 tablespoons ghee or grass-fed butter
4 ounces (113 g) no-sugar-added smoked

salmon, thinly sliced into ribbons
2 tablespoons finely chopped fresh chives
Freshly ground black pepper, to taste

1. In a medium bowl, whisk the eggs vigorously until smooth.
2. In an 8-inch nonstick skillet, melt the ghee over medium-low heat, about 1 minute. Pour in the eggs and, using a spatula, gently drag the eggs from the outer edges of the pan toward the center. Cook, repeating this motion, until the eggs are only slightly runny, about 2 minutes. Add the salmon and cook, continuing to drag the eggs toward the center, until the eggs are cooked to the desired consistency, about 1 minute more.
3. Garnish with the chives, season with pepper, and serve immediately.

Pesto-Pepper Frittata with Butternut Squash

Prep time: 10 minutes | Cook time: 15 minutes
Serves 2

1 cup firmly packed fresh basil leaves
¼ cup pine nuts or chopped walnuts, toasted
3 cloves garlic, chopped
1 tablespoon nutritional yeast (optional)
¼ teaspoon coarse salt
¼ teaspoon black pepper

4 tablespoons extra-virgin olive oil
1 small red or green bell pepper, cut into thin bite-size strips
¼ cup very thinly sliced onion
6 large eggs
⅓ cup thawed frozen puréed butternut squash

1. Preheat the oven to 375°F (190°C).
2. In a food processor, combine the basil, nuts, garlic, nutritional yeast (if using), ⅛ teaspoon of the salt, and ⅛ teaspoon of the black pepper. Cover and pulse until very finely chopped. With the food processor running, pour 3 tablespoons of the oil through the feed tube, processing until well combined and nearly smooth.
3. Heat the remaining 1 tablespoon oil in an oven-safe 6-inch nonstick skillet with flared sides over medium heat. Add the bell pepper and onion and cook, stirring occasionally, until the vegetables are tender, about 5 minutes. Meanwhile, in a medium bowl, whisk together the eggs, squash, remaining ⅛ teaspoon salt, and remaining ⅛ teaspoon black pepper.
4. Reduce the heat under the skillet to medium-low. Add the egg mixture and cook, without stirring, until the eggs begin to set. Cook, stirring, for 1 minute more. Remove the skillet from the heat. Spoon half the pesto in mounds onto the egg mixture; fold gently to partially mix the pesto into the egg. Spread the egg mixture into an even layer.
5. Transfer to the oven and bake for 6 to 9 minutes, until completely set. Let sit for 5 minutes before serving. Cut into four wedges. Divide the wedges between two serving plates. Top evenly with the remaining pesto.

Scrambled Egg Breakfast Tacos

Prep time: 15 minutes | Cook time: 15 minutes

Serves 4

Sausage:

¼ cup apple cider
1 teaspoon kosher salt
1 teaspoon ground chipotle chile pepper
1 teaspoon dried sage, crushed, or 1 tablespoon finely chopped fresh sage

½ teaspoon dried thyme, crushed
½ teaspoon black pepper
½ teaspoon garlic powder
½ teaspoon onion powder
1 pound (454 g) ground pork

Eggs:

1 tablespoon clarified butter or ghee
8 large eggs
Kosher salt and black pepper, to taste
12 butterhead lettuce leaves

Whole Food-compliant pico de gallo or hot sauce
Chopped avocado (optional)
Fresh cilantro leaves (optional)

1. Make the sausage: In a large bowl, combine the apple cider, salt, chipotle, sage, thyme, black pepper, garlic powder, and onion powder. Add the ground pork and use your hands to thoroughly mix in the seasonings.
2. In a large skillet, cook the sausage over medium-high heat until browned, using a wooden spoon to break up the meat into small pieces as it cooks. Use a slotted spoon to transfer the sausage to a bowl. Pour off any fat remaining in the skillet and wipe out the skillet.
3. Make the eggs: Set the skillet in which you cooked the sausage over medium heat and add the butter. In a medium bowl, whisk the eggs just until the yolks are broken. Pour the eggs into the skillet. Cook, stirring often, until they reach the desired doneness. Season with salt and black pepper.
4. Divide the sausage and eggs among the lettuce leaves. Top with pico de gallo and, if desired, avocado and cilantro.

Chapter 5: Salads

Cilantro-Lime Pork Salad

Prep time: 20 minutes | Cook time: 5 hours
Serves 4

Pork:

2 teaspoons chili powder
½ teaspoon salt
¼ teaspoon ground cumin
¼ teaspoon black pepper
Dash cayenne pepper

1 Whole Food-compliant pork tenderloin (about 1¼ pounds / 567 g), trimmed
½ cup Whole Food-compliant chicken broth

Salad:

½ cup Whole Food-compliant mayonnaise
½ teaspoon grated lime zest
1 tablespoon fresh lime juice
2 tablespoons chopped fresh cilantro
6 cups chopped

butterhead lettuce
1 medium avocado, halved, pitted, peeled, and diced
1 cup grape tomatoes, halved
¼ cup sliced green onions

1. Make the pork: In a small bowl, combine the chili powder, salt, cumin, pepper, and cayenne; sprinkle over the pork. Add the pork to a slow cooker. Pour the broth around the pork.
2. Cover and cook on low for 5 to 6 hours or on high for 2½ to 3 hours. Transfer the pork to a cutting board; cut into ½-inch slices. Discard the cooking liquid.
3. Make the salad: In a small bowl, combine the mayonnaise, lime zest, lime juice, and cilantro. If the dressing is too thick, stir in water, 1 teaspoon at a time, to reach desired consistency. Arrange the lettuce on plates. Top with the pork, avocado, tomatoes, and green onions. Spoon the dressing on top. Season with additional pepper, if desired.

Chicken Taco Salad

Prep time: 15 minutes | Cook time: 5 hours
Serves 4

1 tablespoon minced fresh cilantro
1 teaspoon grated lime zest
¼ cup fresh lime juice
½ teaspoon salt
1 medium onion, cut into wedges
1½ pounds (680 g) bone-in chicken thighs, skin removed
1 tablespoon chili powder
1 teaspoon ground

cumin
2 tablespoons extra-virgin olive oil
8 cups torn romaine lettuce
1 medium tomato, chopped
1 avocado, halved, pitted, peeled, and thinly sliced
Chopped fresh cilantro, for serving (optional)

1. In a small bowl, combine the cilantro, lime zest, lime juice, and salt until well blended. Divide the lime juice mixture into two small bowls; set aside.
2. In a slow cooker, layer the onion and chicken thighs. To one of the bowls of the lime juice mixture, add the chili powder and cumin and pour over the chicken and onions. Cover and refrigerate the remaining lime juice mixture for the dressing.
3. Cover and cook on low for 5 to 6 hours or on high for 2½ to 3 hours. Transfer the chicken and onions to a cutting board. Using two forks, pull the chicken apart into large shreds.
4. Meanwhile, whisk the olive oil into the reserved lime juice mixture until well combined.
5. Layer the lettuce, chicken, onions, tomato, and avocado on serving plates. Drizzle with the dressing and top with cilantro, if desired.

Steak Fajita Salad

Prep time: 20 minutes | Cook time: 6 hours

Serves 6

2 beef flank steaks (1 pound / 454 g each)
¼ cup plus 1 tablespoon fresh lime juice
¼ cup plus 1 tablespoon avocado oil
¼ cup finely chopped shallots
2 cloves garlic, minced
1 teaspoon paprika
½ teaspoon ground cumin
1 medium red onion, cut into ½-inch-thick slices
3 medium red, green, or yellow bell peppers, quartered
1 medium avocado, halved, pitted, peeled, and chopped
¾ cup quartered cherry tomatoes or chopped seeded tomatoes
¼ cup thinly sliced green onion tops
⅛ teaspoon salt
⅛ teaspoon cayenne pepper
6 cups torn romaine lettuce
½ cup chopped fresh cilantro

1. Using a sharp knife, score the flank steaks on both sides with shallow diagonal cuts 1 inch apart. Place the steaks in a large shallow baking dish. In a small bowl, whisk together ¼ cup of the lime juice, ¼ cup of the oil, the shallots, garlic, paprika, and cumin. Pour over the steaks in the baking dish, turning to coat the steaks all over with the marinade. Cover and marinate at room temperature for 30 minutes, turning once. (For even more flavor, marinate the steaks, covered, in the refrigerator for up to 8 hours.)
2. Place the red onion slices in a slow cooker. Top with the marinated steaks. Top the steaks with the peppers. Cover and cook on low for 6 to 7 hours or on high for 3 to 3½ hours.
3. In a medium bowl, combine the remaining 1 tablespoon lime juice, remaining 1 tablespoon avocado oil, the avocado, tomatoes, green onion tops, salt, and cayenne.
4. Using a slotted spoon, transfer the peppers and onions to a cutting board; cut the peppers into thin strips. Transfer the steaks to the cutting board; thinly slice across the grain. Arrange the lettuce on six serving plates. Top with the beef, pepper strips, onion slices, guacamole, and cilantro.

Fattoush Salad

Prep time: 20 minutes | Cook time: 0 minutes

Serves 3 or 4

Vinaigrette:

¼ cup extra-virgin olive oil
Juice of ½ lemon
1 tablespoon red wine vinegar
1 garlic clove, finely chopped
1 teaspoon ground sumac
1 teaspoon dried parsley
¼ teaspoon kosher salt, plus more as needed
⅛ teaspoon freshly ground black pepper, plus more as needed

Salad:

2 heads romaine lettuce, coarsely chopped into 2-inch pieces
6 radishes, thinly sliced into rounds
3 Persian cucumbers, sliced into thin half-moons
2 vine-ripened tomatoes, cut into 1-inch pieces
½ red onion, thinly sliced
12 fresh mint leaves, thinly sliced
¼ cup loosely packed fresh parsley leaves, coarsely chopped

1. Make the vinaigrette: In a mason jar, combine the olive oil, lemon juice, vinegar, garlic, sumac, parsley, salt, and pepper. Cover tightly with a lid and shake until combined. Taste and adjust the salt and pepper as desired.
2. Make the salad: In a large bowl, combine the lettuce, radishes, cucumbers, tomatoes, onion, mint, and parsley. Drizzle the vinaigrette over the top and toss to coat. Let sit for 10 to 15 minutes before serving.

Oregano Chicken and Kale Salad

Prep time: 20 minutes | Cook time: 6 hours
Serves 6

Chicken:

3 bone-in, skin-on chicken breast halves
3 sprigs fresh oregano
2 teaspoons grated orange zest
2 cloves garlic, minced
1½ teaspoons dried oregano

½ teaspoon salt
½ teaspoon black pepper
¼ cup fresh orange juice
2 tablespoons extra-virgin olive oil

Dressing:

2 tablespoons red wine vinegar
1 tablespoon fresh orange juice
½ teaspoon salt
½ teaspoon black pepper

3 tablespoons extra-virgin olive oil
½ cup thinly sliced red onion
1 bunch kale, stems removed and torn into bite-size pieces

1. Make the chicken: Use your fingers to loosen the skin from the meat of the chicken but do not remove the skin. Place an oregano sprig underneath the skin of each breast half. In a small bowl, combine the orange zest, minced garlic, oregano, salt, and pepper; rub over the chicken. Place the chicken in a slow cooker. Drizzle with the orange juice, then the olive oil.
2. Cover and cook on low for 6 to 7 hours or on high for 3 to 3½ hours. Remove the chicken; let cool until easy to handle. Remove the chicken from the bones; discard the skin, bones, and herb sprigs. Use two forks to shred the chicken. Moisten the chicken with the cooking liquid.
3. Make the dressing: Meanwhile, in a small bowl, combine the vinegar, orange juice, salt, and pepper. Whisk in the olive oil. Add the onion; cover and let stand for at least 1 hour.
4. Place the kale in a large bowl. Drizzle with the dressing and toss to coat. Add the chicken and toss to combine (the kale will wilt slightly).

Cucumber and Tomato Salad

Prep time: 15 minutes | Cook time: 0 minutes
Serves 2 to 4

4 Persian cucumbers, diced
2 Roma (plum) tomatoes, diced
½ red onion, diced
¼ cup loosely packed fresh parsley leaves, finely chopped
2 tablespoons extra-

virgin olive oil
1 tablespoon fresh lemon juice
2 teaspoons ground sumac
Kosher salt and freshly ground black pepper, to taste

1. In a large bowl, combine the cucumbers, tomatoes, onion, parsley, olive oil, lemon juice, and sumac. Taste and season with salt and pepper as desired. Serve, or cover and refrigerate for 2 to 3 days.

Curried Chicken Salad

Prep time: 15 minutes | Cook time: 0 minutes
Serves 3 to 4

½ cup Whole Food-compliant mayonnaise
1 tablespoon fresh lime juice
2 tablespoons fresh cilantro
2 teaspoons Whole Food-compliant curry powder
¼ teaspoon salt
2 cups diced cooked chicken
½ medium apple, diced

1 celery stalk, finely diced
3 tablespoons finely diced red onion
¼ cup roughly chopped Whole Food-compliant dry-roasted cashews
Sliced green onions, shredded cabbage, shredded carrots, and/or chopped cashews (optional)

1. In a medium bowl, stir together the mayonnaise, lime juice, cilantro, curry powder, and salt. Add the chicken, apple, celery, and onion and toss to coat. Fold in the cashews. If desired, top the salad with green onions, cabbage, carrots, and/or additional cashews.

Balsamic Peach Arugula Salad

Prep time: 20 minutes | Cook time: 15 minutes
Serves 8

Peaches and Vegetables:

3 ripe peaches, peeled and sliced, or 1 (16-ounce / 454-g) bag frozen peaches, thawed
2 tablespoons clarified butter or ghee, melted
2 tablespoons balsamic vinegar

1 small red onion, thinly sliced into rings
2 teaspoons extra-virgin olive oil
¼ teaspoon salt
¼ teaspoon black pepper
24 thin asparagus spears, trimmed

Arugula Salad:

½ cup balsamic vinegar
3 (5-ounce / 142-g) containers baby arugula
3 tablespoons extra-

virgin olive oil
½ teaspoon salt
¼ teaspoon pepper
½ cup coarsely chopped roasted pistachios

1. Preheat the oven to 425°F (220°C). Line two large rimmed baking pans with parchment paper.
2. Make the peaches and vegetables: Arrange the peach slices on half of one pan; brush with the butter. Drizzle vinegar over the slices. Arrange the onion on the other half of the pan. Drizzle with 1 teaspoon olive oil. Sprinkle with ⅛ teaspoon each salt and pepper. Roast for 5 minutes.
3. Meanwhile, arrange the asparagus on the other pan. Drizzle with 1 teaspoon olive oil. Sprinkle with the remaining ⅛ teaspoon each salt and pepper. Add the asparagus to the oven. Stir the onions. Roast both pans 10 minutes more.
4. Make the arugula salad: Meanwhile, in a small saucepan, bring the vinegar to a boil over medium-high heat. Reduce the heat to medium-low and simmer until reduced by half, 8 to 10 minutes. Cool completely.
5. Place the arugula in an extra-large bowl. Drizzle with the olive oil and sprinkle with ½ teaspoon salt and ¼ teaspoon pepper; toss to coat.
6. Divide the arugula, asparagus, peaches, and onions among 8 salad plates. Drizzle the salads with about 1 teaspoon of the reduced vinegar. Sprinkle with the pistachios.

Lemon Mediterranean Chicken Salad

Prep time: 15 minutes | Cook time: 5 hours
Serves 4

Dressing:

½ cup extra-virgin olive oil
¼ cup fresh lemon juice
2 cloves garlic, minced

2 teaspoons Whole Food-compliant Italian seasoning
¼ teaspoon salt

Chicken and Salad:

1 pound (454 g) bone-in, skinless chicken thighs
1 medium red onion, cut into wedges
8 cups torn romaine lettuce

1 red bell pepper, chopped
1 medium cucumber, chopped
¼ cup sliced pitted Whole Food-compliant Kalamata olives

1. Make the dressing: In a small bowl, combine the olive oil, lemon juice, garlic, Italian seasoning, and salt until well blended; set aside.
2. Make the chicken: In a slow cooker, layer the chicken and onion. Pour half the dressing over the chicken and onions. Cover and refrigerate the remaining dressing.
3. Cover and cook on low for 5 to 6 hours or on high for 2½ to 3 hours. Transfer the chicken and onions to a cutting board. Using two forks, pull the chicken apart into large shreds.
4. Arrange the lettuce, chicken and onion, bell pepper, cucumber, and olives on serving plates. Drizzle with the reserved dressing.

Salmon Potato Salad

Prep time: 10 minutes | Cook time: 15 minutes
Serves 4

1½ pounds (680 g) baby yellow potatoes, halved
⅓ cup avocado oil
1 tablespoon Whole Food-compliant Dijon mustard
1 tablespoon fresh lemon juice
½ teaspoon salt
½ teaspoon black pepper
1 (6-ounce / 170-g) can salmon, drained
2 cups arugula
3 green onions, sliced
2 tablespoons snipped fresh chives
1 tablespoon minced fresh parsley

1. Place the potatoes in a medium pot and add enough cold water to cover. Bring to a low boil and cook until tender, about 15 minutes. Drain.
2. In a large bowl, whisk together the avocado oil, mustard, lemon juice, salt, and pepper. Add the potatoes, salmon, arugula, green onions, chives, and parsley. Gently toss until the potatoes are coated. Serve warm.

Orange Tuna, Snow Pea, and Broccoli Salad

Prep time: 10 minutes | Cook time: 0 minutes
Serves 4

Dressing:
1 teaspoon grated orange zest
3 tablespoons extra-virgin olive oil
3 tablespoons rice vinegar

Salad:
1 orange, peeled and cut into bite-size pieces
1 (12-ounce / 340-g) bag broccoli slaw
1 (8-ounce / 227-g) package fresh snow peas, trimmed and halved diagonally
2 (5-ounce / 142-g) cans water-packed wild albacore tuna, drained and broken into chunks

1. Make the dressing: In a small bowl, combine the orange zest, olive oil, and vinegar.
2. Make the salad: In a large bowl, combine the orange pieces with the broccoli slaw, snow peas, and tuna. Drizzle with the dressing and gently toss.

Thai Chicken Larb Salad

Prep time: 20 minutes | Cook time: 5 hours
Serves 4

½ cup Whole Food-compliant chicken broth
1½ pounds (680 g) boneless, skinless chicken thighs, cut into ½-inch pieces
½ cup minced shallots
1 stalk lemongrass, bruised
1 Thai chile pepper, seeded (if desired) and finely chopped
4 tablespoons fresh lime juice
3 teaspoons Whole Food-compliant fish sauce
½ teaspoon salt
2 green onions, thinly sliced
¼ cup chopped fresh mint, plus extra for serving
2 tablespoons chopped fresh cilantro, plus extra for serving
1 (5-ounce / 142-g) package mixed salad greens
2 medium carrots, peeled and cut into matchsticks
½ English cucumber, sliced

1. In a slow cooker, combine the broth, chicken, shallots, lemongrass, Thai chile, 2 tablespoons of the lime juice, 2 teaspoons of the fish sauce, and the salt.
2. Cover and cook on low for 5 to 6 hours or on high for 2½ to 3 hours. Remove and discard the lemongrass.
3. Use a slotted spoon to transfer the chicken to a medium bowl. (Discard the cooking liquid.) Add the remaining 2 tablespoons lime juice, remaining 1 teaspoon fish sauce, the green onions, mint, and cilantro to the chicken.
4. Top the greens with the chicken mixture, carrots, cucumber, and additional cilantro and mint. Serve.

Fruity Chicken Salad

Prep time: 10 minutes | Cook time: 0 minutes
Serves 2

Dressing:

2 tablespoons fresh orange juice
1 tablespoon white wine vinegar
¼ cup extra-virgin olive oil
⅛ teaspoon salt
⅛ teaspoon black pepper

Salad:

1 medium orange, peeled and white pith removed
6 cups chopped romaine lettuce
1½ cups coarsely chopped cooked chicken
¼ cup pomegranate seeds
¼ cup coarsely chopped roasted cashews
2 green onions, sliced

1. Make the dressing: In a small bowl, whisk together the orange juice, vinegar, olive oil, salt, and pepper.
2. Make the salad: Divide the orange into segments. Arrange the lettuce in serving bowls. Top with the orange segments, chicken, pomegranate seeds, cashews, and green onions. Drizzle with the dressing and serve.

Red Potato Salad with Chicken Sausage

Prep time: 20 minutes | Cook time: 5 hours
Serves 4

1½ pounds (680 g) small red potatoes, sliced ¼-inch thick
1 small sweet onion, chopped
2 stalks celery, chopped
1 green bell pepper, chopped
2 slices Whole Food-compliant bacon, chopped into 1-inch pieces
1 tablespoon olive oil
½ teaspoon salt
½ teaspoon black pepper
1½ packages (24 ounces / 680 g total) Whole Food-compliant chicken-apple sausage, halved
¼ cup Whole Food-compliant chicken broth
3 tablespoons cider vinegar
¼ cup chopped Whole Food-compliant dill pickles
3 tablespoons chopped fresh dill
6 cups baby spinach

1. In a slow cooker, combine the potatoes, onion, celery, bell pepper, bacon, olive oil, salt, and pepper. Add the sausages and broth. Cover and cook on low for 5 to 6 hours or on high for 2½ to 3 hours, until the potatoes are tender.
2. Remove the sausages from the slow cooker; cover to keep warm. Add the vinegar, pickles, and dill to the potato mixture in the cooker; toss to combine.
3. Divide the spinach among four serving bowls; top each with some of the potato mixture and three sausage halves.

Pork Greek Salad

Prep time: 10 minutes | Cook time: 10 minutes
Serves 4

Pork:

1 pound (454 g) ground pork
1 teaspoon Greek seasoning
½ cup thinly sliced red onion
½ cup sliced pitted Kalamata olives

Salad:

3 tablespoons red wine vinegar
1 or 2 cloves garlic, minced
1 teaspoon Greek seasoning
¼ cup extra-virgin olive oil
8 cups chopped romaine lettuce
1 medium cucumber, chopped

1. Cook the pork: In a large nonstick skillet, cook the pork and Greek seasoning over medium-high heat, stirring occasionally, until browned and crispy, 6 to 8 minutes. Turn off the heat. Stir in the red onion and olives. Let stand for 2 minutes to soften the onion.
2. Make the salad: Meanwhile, in a small bowl, combine the vinegar, garlic, and Greek seasoning. Whisk in the olive oil until well combined.
3. Layer the lettuce, cucumber, and pork in bowls. Drizzle with the dressing and serve.

Chimichurri Pork and Cabbage Salad

Prep time: 30 minutes | Cook time: 9 hours
Serves 6

1 teaspoon salt
1 teaspoon garlic powder
1 teaspoon ground cumin
1 teaspoon black pepper
2½ to 3 pounds (1.1 to 1.4 kg) boneless pork shoulder, trimmed and cut into 3 pieces
1 cup packed fresh cilantro, large stems removed, plus extra for serving
1 cup packed fresh flat-leaf parsley, large stems removed, plus extra for serving
¼ cup chopped shallots
3 cloves garlic, chopped

¼ cup plus 3 tablespoons extra-virgin olive oil
3 tablespoons white wine vinegar
¼ teaspoon red pepper flakes
8 cups coarsely shredded cored savoy or green cabbage
1 cup purchased shredded carrots
½ cup thinly sliced green onion tops
½ cup unsulfured golden raisins
3 tablespoons fresh lemon juice
3 tablespoons extra-virgin olive oil
½ cup chopped walnuts or pecans, toasted

1. In a small bowl, combine ½ teaspoon of the salt, the garlic powder, cumin, and pepper. Sprinkle all over the pork pieces; rub in with your fingers. Place the pork in a slow cooker. Add ½ cup water.
2. Cover and cook on low for 9 to 10 hours or on high for 4½ to 5 hours. Transfer the pork to a cutting board; cool for about 10 minutes. Using two forks, coarsely shred the pork; transfer to a large bowl.
3. Meanwhile, in a blender or food processor, combine the cilantro, parsley, shallots, garlic, ¼ cup of the olive oil, the vinegar, and red pepper flakes. Cover and blend or process until almost smooth. Pour over the shredded pork and stir to combine. Set aside.
4. In a large bowl, toss together the cabbage, carrots, green onion tops, and raisins. In a small bowl, whisk together the remaining 3 tablespoons olive oil, remaining ½ teaspoon salt, and the lemon juice. Pour over the cabbage salad and toss to coat. Stir in the pork. Sprinkle with the walnuts and additional cilantro and/or parsley.

Ahi Mango Poke

Prep time: 20 minutes | Cook time: 0 minutes
Serves 4

Dressing:

3 tablespoons coconut aminos
1 tablespoon rice vinegar
1 teaspoon olive oil

1 teaspoon grated fresh ginger
¼ teaspoon salt
⅛ teaspoon black pepper

Salad:

1½ pounds (680 g) sushi-grade ahi tuna, cut into bite-sized pieces
1 (5-ounce / 142-g) package baby spinach
1 ripe avocado, halved, pitted, peeled, and chopped
1 ripe mango, pitted, peeled, and chopped

1 small unpeeled cucumber, sliced
1 cup packaged shredded carrots, or 2 medium carrots, shredded
Black sesame seeds (optional)
Sliced green onions (optional)

1. Make the dressing: In a small bowl, stir together the dressing ingredients.
2. Make the salad: In a medium bowl, gently toss the tuna with 2 tablespoons of the dressing to coat. Let stand and marinate while you assemble the salads.
3. Divide the spinach among four plates. Arrange the avocado, mango, cucumber, and carrots on the spinach. Top with the marinated tuna and drizzle the salads with the remaining dressing. Top with black sesame seeds and sliced green onions, if desired, and serve.

Mango and Shrimp Salad

Prep time: 15 minutes | Cook time: 5 minutes
Serves 2

Dressing:

½ teaspoon grated lime zest
2 tablespoons fresh lime juice
¼ cup extra-virgin olive oil

1 tablespoon chopped fresh cilantro
2 teaspoons finely chopped seeded jalapeño
⅛ teaspoon salt

Salad:

1 tablespoon extra-virgin olive oil
8 ounces (227 g) peeled and deveined large shrimp
1 teaspoon chili powder
⅛ teaspoon salt
6 cups torn Bibb

lettuce leaves
1 medium ripe mango, peeled, pitted, and diced
1 medium ripe avocado, halved, pitted, peeled, and diced

1. Make the dressing: In a small bowl, combine the lime zest and juice. While whisking, drizzle in the olive oil until combined. Stir in the cilantro, jalapeño, and salt.
2. Make the salad: In a large skillet, heat the olive oil over medium-high heat. Add the shrimp, chili powder, and salt. Cook, stirring, until the shrimp are opaque, about 5 minutes.
3. Arrange the lettuce on serving plates. Top with the mango, avocado, and shrimp. Drizzle the salads with the dressing and serve.

Chicken Romaine Salad

Prep time: 20 minutes | Cook time: 4 hours
Serves 4

4 green onions
2½ pounds (1.1 kg) bone-in chicken thighs, skin removed
½ cup Whole Food-compliant chicken broth
3 cloves garlic, minced
1 medium red bell pepper, diced
2 stalks celery, thinly

sliced
1 tablespoon Whole Food-compliant Dijon mustard
2 tablespoons cider vinegar
½ cup Whole Food-compliant mayonnaise
1 (16-ounce / 454-g) package hearts of romaine, chopped

1. Thinly slice the green onions; separate the white bottoms from the green tops. In a slow cooker, combine the green onion whites, chicken, broth, and garlic.
2. Cover and cook on low for 4 hours or on high for 2 hours. Add the bell pepper and celery. Turn the slow cooker to high if using low setting. Cover and cook for 20 to 30 minutes, or until the pepper and celery are tender. Using a slotted spoon, transfer the chicken, pepper, and celery to a large bowl.
3. Let the chicken cool slightly. Remove the chicken from the bones; discard the bones. Use two forks to shred the chicken. Stir the mustard, vinegar, and mayonnaise into the shredded chicken.
4. Arrange the lettuce on four plates; top with the warm chicken salad. Sprinkle with the reserved sliced green onion tops.

Ground Beef Taco Salad

Prep time: 15 minutes | Cook time: 2 hours
Serves 6

1½ pounds (680 g) lean ground beef
1 medium white onion, diced
2 cloves garlic, minced
2 Anaheim chile peppers, seeded and finely chopped
1 tablespoon ground cumin
1 teaspoon dried oregano
1 teaspoon chili powder
1 teaspoon coriander
1 teaspoon salt
1 teaspoon black pepper
1 (10-ounce / 283-g) bag chopped romaine or 1 head romaine lettuce, chopped
3 green onions, sliced
2 tomatoes, diced
2 jalapeños, seeded if desired, and sliced
Whole Food-compliant salsa (optional)
¼ cup chopped fresh cilantro (optional)
2 limes, cut into wedges

1. In a large skillet, cook the beef, onion, and garlic over medium-high heat, stirring with a wooden spoon to break up the beef, until no longer pink, 5 to 8 minutes. Use a slotted spoon to transfer to a slow cooker. Add the Anaheim chiles, cumin, oregano, chili powder, coriander, salt, and pepper. Stir to combine.
2. Cover and cook on high for 2 hours.
3. Serve the taco meat on top of the chopped lettuce. Top servings with green onions, tomatoes, and jalapeños, along with salsa and cilantro, if desired. Serve with the lime wedges.

Beef and Broccoli Salad

Prep time: 15 minutes | Cook time: 15 minutes
Serves 4

1 pound (454 g) boneless beef sirloin steak or stir-fry meat
½ teaspoon salt
¼ teaspoon black pepper
2 teaspoons grated lemon zest
6 tablespoons Whole Food-compliant lemon-garlic dressing
3 cups broccoli florets
1 large orange or red bell pepper, seeded and thinly sliced
1 (9-ounce / 255-g) package spring mix/ baby spinach
¼ cup snipped fresh chives

1. Thinly slice the meat across the grain into bite-size pieces and season both sides with the salt, pepper, and lemon zest. In a medium bowl, toss the meat with 2 tablespoons of the dressing.
2. In a large bowl, combine the broccoli, bell pepper, and 3 tablespoons of the dressing. Toss to coat.
3. In a large skillet, cook the broccoli and bell pepper over medium-high heat, stirring, for 3 minutes. Return the vegetables to the large bowl. Add the meat to the hot skillet and cook, stirring, until slightly pink in center, 1 to 2 minutes. Add the vegetables to the skillet and stir to combine with the meat.
4. In a large bowl, toss the greens with the remaining 1 tablespoon dressing. Serve the meat and vegetables over the greens. Sprinkle the salad with the snipped chives.

Steak Salad with Charred Onions

Prep time: 15 minutes | Cook time: 20 minutes
Serves 4

Steak and Onions:

1 flank steak or skirt steak (16 to 20 ounces / 454 to 567 g)
1 tablespoon cumin seeds, lightly crushed
1 teaspoon salt

1 teaspoon black pepper
1 large onion
2 tablespoons extra-virgin olive oil

Dressing:

¾ cup Whole Food-compliant mayonnaise
Grated zest and juice of 1 lime
2 teaspoons Whole Food-compliant hot sauce
8 cups chopped

butterhead or iceberg lettuce
2 avocadoes, halved, pitted, peeled, and diced
Chopped fresh cilantro, for serving

1. Preheat a grill to medium-high heat or a grill pan over medium-high heat.
2. Grill the steak and onions: Season the steak with the cumin seeds, salt, and pepper. Cut the onion into ½-inch-thick slices. Drizzle the steak and onions with the olive oil.
3. Grill the steak and onion slices over direct heat, turning once, until the onion is lightly charred, 5 to 6 minutes, and the steak is cooked to desired doneness, 15 to 20 minutes for medium (160°F / 71°C). Remove the steak and onion and let rest for 5 minutes.
4. Make the dressing: Meanwhile, in a small bowl, combine the mayonnaise, lime zest and juice, and hot sauce.
5. Thinly slice the steak against the grain and coarsely chop the onions. Place the lettuce in a serving bowl and top with the steak and onions. Drizzle the dressing over the salad. Top with the avocado and cilantro.

Greek Turkey Meatball Salad

Prep time: 15 minutes | Cook time: 20 minutes
Serves 2

Meatballs:

1 large egg
¼ cup almond flour
3 cloves garlic, minced
1 teaspoon dried oregano, crushed

½ teaspoon salt
¼ teaspoon black pepper
8 ounces (227 g) ground turkey

Lemon-Avocado Salad:

½ small avocado, pitted and peeled
¼ cup unsweetened flax milk or Whole Food-compliant coconut milk
1 to 2 tablespoons fresh lemon juice
1 clove garlic, minced
¼ teaspoon salt
⅛ teaspoon black

pepper
2 tablespoons chopped fresh mint
1 (9-ounce / 255-g) bag hearts of romaine
½ English cucumber, sliced, slices quartered
⅔ cup drained roasted red pepper, patted dry and chopped

1. Make the meatballs: Preheat the oven to 400°F (205°C). Line a baking pan with parchment paper.
2. In a medium bowl, whisk the egg until lightly beaten. Stir in the almond flour, garlic, oregano, salt, and black pepper. Add the ground turkey and gently mix to combine. Shape the mixture into 8 meatballs and place on the pan. Bake for 18 to 20 minutes, until the internal temperature is 165°F (74°C).
3. Make the lemon-avocado salad: Meanwhile, in a blender combine the avocado, flax milk, lemon juice, garlic, salt, and black pepper. Cover and blend until smooth. Transfer the dressing to a small bowl and stir in the mint.
4. Arrange the romaine on serving plates. Top with the cucumber, roasted pepper, and meatballs. Drizzle with the dressing and serve.

Spicy Chicken, Watermelon, and Spinach Salad

Prep time: 15 minutes | Cook time: 10 minutes

Serves 2

Chicken:

2 boneless, skinless chicken breasts (about 6 ounces / 170 g each)
1 teaspoon red pepper flakes
½ teaspoon garlic powder
½ teaspoon salt
½ teaspoon black pepper
2 tablespoons extra-virgin olive oil

Salad:

4 cups baby spinach
2 cups chopped seedless watermelon
¼ cup finely chopped shallot
3 tablespoons extra-virgin olive oil
2 tablespoons red wine vinegar
½ teaspoon salt
½ teaspoon black pepper
⅓ cup roasted salted pistachios, chopped

1. Make the chicken: Place the chicken breasts between two pieces of plastic wrap and use the flat side of a meat mallet to flatten to a ¼-inch thickness. (You can ask your butcher to do this for you.) Combine the pepper flakes, garlic powder, salt, and pepper in a small bowl. Sprinkle the seasoning over the chicken.
2. Heat the olive oil in a large skillet over medium-high heat. Add the chicken and cook, turning once, until browned and cooked through, about 8 minutes. Place the chicken on a cutting board and let rest for 5 minutes. Thinly slice the chicken.
3. Make the salad: Combine the spinach, watermelon, and shallot in a large bowl. Drizzle with the olive oil and vinegar. Sprinkle with the salt and black pepper. Toss the salad to coat with the dressing.
4. Arrange the salad on two serving plates. Top with the sliced chicken, sprinkle with the pistachios, and serve.

Carne Asada Salad

Prep time: 20 minutes | Cook time: 4 hours

Serves 4

Steak:

1 cup fresh orange juice
¼ cup fresh lemon juice
¼ cup fresh lime juice
2 tablespoons olive oil
2 tablespoon minced jalapeño
6 cloves garlic, minced
1 tablespoon chopped fresh cilantro
¼ teaspoon salt
1 pound (454 g) flank or sirloin steak

Dressing:

1 avocado, halved, pitted, and peeled
3 tablespoons extra-virgin olive oil
1 tablespoon minced jalapeño
1 tablespoon fresh lime juice
2 tablespoons chopped fresh cilantro
⅛ teaspoon ground cumin
¼ teaspoon salt
½ cup water

Salad:

6 cups mixed salad greens
¼ cup sliced radishes
1 cup halved grape or cherry tomatoes
½ cup coarsely chopped green bell pepper
¼ cup sliced green onions

1. Make the steak: In a slow cooker, combine the orange, lemon, and lime juices, olive oil, jalapeño, garlic, cilantro, and salt. Place the steak in the slow cooker; turn to coat both sides.
2. Cover and cook for 4 hours on low or 2 hours on high, turning the steak once halfway through cooking. Transfer the steak to a cutting board; tent with foil while preparing the salad dressing.
3. Make the dressing: In a food processor, combine the avocado, olive oil, jalapeño, lime juice, cilantro, cumin, and salt. Process until smooth. Continue to process, slowly adding water until the dressing reaches the desired consistency.
4. Assemble the salad: Arrange the salad greens, radishes, tomatoes, and bell pepper on four serving plates. Slice the steak thinly and add to the salads. Drizzle with the avocado dressing and top with sliced green onions.

Chapter 6: Soups and Stews

Chicken and Carrot Stew

Prep time: 30 minutes | Cook time: 6 hours
Serves 4

1 medium onion, cut into wedges
2 cloves garlic, minced
4 slices Whole Food-compliant bacon, chopped
4 medium carrots, peeled and cut into 1-inch pieces
1 large leek, white part only, sliced
12 small red potatoes (about 12 ounces / 340 g)
Grated zest and juice of 1 lemon
½ cup Whole Food-compliant chicken broth
1 tablespoon tapioca flour

1 teaspoon salt
½ teaspoon coarsely ground black pepper
8 meaty bone-in chicken pieces (breast halves, thighs, and drumsticks), skin removed
2 tablespoons extra-virgin olive oil
2 teaspoons herbes de Provence
2 tablespoons Whole Food-compliant Dijon mustard
1 cup Whole Food-compliant Kalamata olives or other black olives
Fresh tarragon leaves, for serving

1. In a slow cooker, combine the onion, garlic, bacon, carrots, leek, and potatoes. In a small bowl, stir together the lemon juice, broth, and tapioca flour; stir into the slow cooker. In another small bowl, combine the lemon zest, salt, and pepper. Coat the chicken with the olive oil and rub with the salt mixture. Add to the slow cooker. Sprinkle the herbes de Provence over the chicken.
2. Cover and cook on low for 6 to 7 hours or on high for 3 to 3½ hours.
3. Transfer the chicken to shallow serving bowls. Stir the mustard and olives into the cooking liquid. Ladle some of the cooking liquid over the chicken. Sprinkle with fresh tarragon leaves and serve.

Mexican Pork Shoulder Stew

Prep time: 30 minutes | Cook time: 6 hours
Serves 6

1½ teaspoons chipotle powder
1 teaspoon ground cumin
1 teaspoon oregano
1 teaspoon garlic powder
½ teaspoon paprika
1 teaspoon sea salt
½ teaspoon black pepper
2½ to 3 pounds (1.1 to 1.4 kg) pork shoulder or butt roast
1 pound (454 g) baby red potatoes

½ cup chopped onion
4 ounces (113 g) button mushrooms, halved (about 2 cups)
1 (14½-ounce / 411-g) can Whole Food-compliant whole tomatoes, drained
1 large zucchini (about 5 ounces / 142 g), halved and cut into 2-inch chunks
2 cups packed chopped spinach
2 tablespoons tapioca flour

1. In a small bowl, combine the chipotle powder, cumin, oregano, garlic powder, paprika, salt, and pepper. Sprinkle half of the seasoning on the pork. Place the pork in a slow cooker. Add ¼ cup water, the potatoes, onion, and mushrooms.
2. In a large bowl, crush the tomatoes with your hands. Add the remaining seasoning mix to the tomatoes; pour into the slow cooker. Cook for 6 hours on low or 3 hours on high, or until the pork and potatoes are tender. Transfer the pork to a platter and keep warm.
3. Turn the slow cooker to high if using the low setting. Stir the zucchini and spinach into the cooking liquid in the slow cooker.
4. In a small bowl, stir the tapioca flour into 2 tablespoons water. Add to the stew and cook, stirring, for 3 minutes. Using two forks, shred the pork and stir it into the stew.

Slow Cooker Beef Fajita Soup

Prep time: 10 minutes | Cook time: 6 hours
Serves 4

1 pound (454 g) ground beef
1 cup chopped onion
2 cloves garlic, minced
1 medium green bell pepper, coarsely chopped
1 medium red bell pepper, coarsely chopped
1 serrano chile pepper, seeded and chopped
4 cups Whole Food-compliant beef broth
1 (14½-ounce / 411-g) can Whole Food-compliant fire-roasted diced tomatoes, undrained
2 teaspoons chili powder
½ teaspoon salt
Chopped fresh cilantro, for serving
Lime wedges, for serving

1. In a large skillet, cook the beef, onion, and garlic over medium-high heat, breaking up the meat with a wooden spoon, until browned. Drain off any fat and transfer the beef mixture to a slow cooker. Add the bell peppers, serrano pepper, broth, tomatoes, chili powder, and salt. Cover and cook on low for 6 to 7 hours or on high for 3 to 3½ hours.
2. Serve the soup with cilantro and lime wedges.

Italian Chicken Sausage Soup

Prep time: 10 minutes | Cook time: 4 hours
Serves 4

1 pound (454 g) Whole Food-compliant sweet Italian chicken sausage, diagonally sliced ½ inch thick
4 cups Whole Food-compliant chicken broth
1 (14½-ounce / 411-g) can Whole Food-compliant diced tomatoes, undrained
½ cup chopped onion
2 cloves garlic, minced
1½ teaspoons Whole Food-compliant Italian seasoning
¼ teaspoon salt
¼ teaspoon red pepper flakes
1½ cups cauliflower rice or cauliflower crumbles
4 cups baby spinach

1. In a slow cooker, combine the sausage, broth, tomatoes, onion, garlic, Italian seasoning, salt, and red pepper flakes. Cover and cook on low for 4 to 5 hours or on high for 2 to 2½ hours.
2. Turn the slow cooker to high if using the low setting. Stir in the cauliflower. Cover and cook until the cauliflower is tender, 15 to 20 minutes. Stir in the baby spinach. Serve.

Hot and Sour Shrimp Soup

Prep time: 15 minutes | Cook time: 4 hours
Serves 4

6 cups Whole Food-compliant chicken broth
1 pound (454 g) peeled and deveined large shrimp
2 cups quartered cremini mushrooms
2 medium carrots, peeled and grated (½ cup)
2 cups thinly sliced green cabbage
½ cup canned sliced bamboo shoots, rinsed, drained, and cut into strips
½ to 1 serrano chile pepper, seeded, if desired, and minced
2 tablespoons minced fresh ginger
4 cloves garlic, minced
⅛ teaspoon ground white pepper
¼ cup rice wine vinegar
½ teaspoon olive oil
1 large egg, lightly beaten
2 tablespoons sliced green onions

1. In a slow cooker, combine the broth, shrimp, mushrooms, carrots, cabbage, bamboo shoots, serrano chile, ginger, garlic, and white pepper. Cover and cook for 4 hours on low or 2 hours on high, or until the shrimp are pink and opaque and the cabbage is tender.
2. Turn the slow cooker to high if using the low setting. Add the vinegar and olive oil, and then the beaten egg. Stir the soup until the egg is cooked and slightly thickens the soup.
3. Serve, topped with the green onions and additional serrano pepper, if desired.

Italian Chicken Vegetable Soup

Prep time: 15 minutes | Cook time: 6 hours
Serves 4

1¼ pounds (567 g) bone-in chicken thighs, skin removed
1 medium onion, chopped
1 medium zucchini, cut into ½-inch pieces
4 medium carrots, cut into ½-inch pieces (2 cups)
4 cups Whole Food-compliant chicken broth
½ teaspoon salt
¼ teaspoon black pepper
1½ cups sliced button mushrooms
1 (28-ounce / 794-g) can Whole Food-compliant fire-roasted diced tomatoes, undrained
¼ cup chopped fresh basil

1. In a slow cooker, combine the chicken, onion, zucchini, carrots, broth, salt, and pepper. Cover and cook on low for 6 to 7 hours or on high for 3 to 3½ hours.
2. Remove the chicken from the slow cooker. Use two forks to coarsely shred the chicken; discard the bones. Return the chicken to the cooker. Stir in the mushrooms and tomatoes. Cover and cook on high for 30 minutes. Serve topped with basil.

Thyme Chicken Zoodle Soup

Prep time: 25 minutes | Cook time: 6 hours
Serves 6

2 pounds (907 g) boneless, skinless chicken thighs, cut into 1-inch pieces
6 cups Whole Food-compliant chicken broth
3 carrots, peeled and sliced
3 stalks celery with leaves, chopped ¼ inch thick
1 large white onion, coarsely chopped
1 tablespoon fresh lemon juice
1 teaspoon dried thyme
1 teaspoon dried marjoram
1 bay leaf
1 teaspoon salt
½ teaspoon black pepper
1 (10.7-ounce / 303-g) package zucchini noodles or 2 small zucchini, spiralized
Coarse ground black pepper (optional)
Fresh thyme leaves (optional)

1. In a slow cooker, combine the chicken, broth, carrots, celery, onion, lemon juice, dried thyme, marjoram, bay leaf, salt, and pepper. Stir to combine.
2. Cover and cook on low for 6 hours or on high for 3 hours. Remove and discard the bay leaf. Turn the slow cooker to high if using the low setting. Add the zucchini noodles. Cover and cook for 5 minutes or until the noodles are tender.
3. If desired, top servings with coarse ground black pepper and fresh thyme.

Beef and Pepper Soup

Prep time: 25 minutes | Cook time: 5 hours
Serves 4

1 pound (454 g) lean ground beef
1 medium onion, chopped
1 (14½-ounce / 411-g) can Whole Food-compliant diced tomatoes, undrained
1 (15-ounce / 425-g) can Whole Food-compliant tomato sauce
2 medium red or orange bell peppers, chopped
2 cloves garlic, minced
2 teaspoons Whole Food-compliant Italian seasoning
½ teaspoon fennel seeds, crushed
½ teaspoon salt
2½ cups Whole Food-compliant beef broth
Fresh basil leaves (optional)

1. In a large skillet, cook the beef and onion over medium heat, stirring occasionally and breaking up the beef with a wooden spoon, until browned, 8 to 10 minutes. Drain off the fat. Transfer to a slow cooker.
2. Stir in the tomatoes, tomato sauce, bell peppers, garlic, Italian seasoning, fennel seeds, and salt, and then the broth.
3. Cover and cook on low for 5 to 6 hours or on high for 2½ to 3 hours. Top servings with fresh basil, if desired.

Lush Pork Loin Stew

Prep time: 25 minutes | Cook time: 6 hours
Serves 6

1½ pounds (680 g) Whole Food-compliant boneless pork loin, cut into 1-inch pieces
½ small butternut squash, peeled and cut into 1-inch pieces (about 2 cups)
3 medium carrots, peeled and cut into ½-inch pieces
2 medium parsnips, peeled and cut into ½-inch pieces
1 medium yellow onion, chopped
2 teaspoons fresh thyme
½ teaspoon salt
½ teaspoon black pepper
4 cups Whole Food-compliant chicken broth
Chopped fresh parsley, for serving

1. In a slow cooker, combine the pork, squash, carrots, parsnips, onion, thyme, salt, pepper, and broth. Cover and cook on low for 6 to 7 hours or on high 3 to 3½ hours.
2. Serve, topped with parsley.

Kale and Chicken Sausage Stew

Prep time: 20 minutes | Cook time: 6 hours
Serves 4

1 pound (454 g) boneless, skinless chicken breast, cut into 1-inch pieces
4 cups Whole Food-compliant chicken broth
1 (14½-ounce / 411-g) can Whole Food-compliant fire-roasted diced tomatoes, undrained
1 large yellow onion, cut into thin wedges
2 cloves garlic, minced
2 teaspoons grated lemon zest, plus extra for serving
1½ teaspoons fennel seeds, crushed
8 ounces (227 g) Whole Food-compliant smoked kielbasa or chicken-apple sausage, sliced into ½-inch pieces
2 cups packed chopped fresh kale

1. In a slow cooker, combine the chicken, broth, tomatoes, onion, garlic, lemon zest, and fennel seeds.

2. Cover and cook on low for 6 to 7 hours or on high for 3 to 3½ hours. Add the sausage and kale. Cover and let stand for 5 minutes or until the sausage is heated through and the kale is wilted. Serve, topped with additional lemon zest if desired.

Almond Chicken and Sweet Potato Stew

Prep time: 30 minutes | Cook time: 6 hours
Serves 6

1½ pounds (680 g) boneless, skinless chicken thighs, cut into 1½-inch pieces
2 medium sweet potatoes (about 1¼ pounds / 567 g total), peeled and cut into 1½-inch pieces
1 (14½-ounce / 411-g) can Whole Food-compliant stewed tomatoes, undrained
1 medium yellow onion, chopped
3 cloves garlic, minced
1 piece (1 inch) fresh ginger, peeled and finely chopped
¼ teaspoon cayenne pepper
2½ cups Whole Food-compliant chicken broth
1 bunch collard greens, trimmed and coarsely chopped
¼ cup Whole Food-compliant sunflower seed butter
½ cup chopped almonds, toasted
½ cup chopped fresh cilantro or flat-leaf parsley

1. In a slow cooker, combine the chicken, sweet potatoes, tomatoes, onion, garlic, ginger, and cayenne. Add the broth. Cover and cook on low for 6 to 7 hours or on high for 3 to 3½ hours.
2. Turn the slow cooker to high if using the low setting. Use a ladle to remove ½ cup of the cooking liquid from the cooker; set aside. Stir the collard greens into the stew; cover and cook 15 minutes longer. Whisk the sunflower butter into the reserved ½ cup cooking liquid until smooth. Stir into the stew.
3. Serve, sprinkled with almonds and cilantro.

Vegetable Soup with Basil Pesto

Prep time: 30 minutes | Cook time: 15 minutes
Serves 4

Pesto:

1 cup lightly packed fresh basil leaves
¼ cup roasted almonds or toasted pine nuts
1 tablespoon nutritional yeast

(optional)
¼ teaspoon salt
¼ teaspoon black pepper
1 clove garlic, chopped
⅓ cup extra-virgin olive oil

Soup:

1 tablespoon extra-virgin olive oil
1 medium onion, chopped
1 clove garlic, minced
4 cups Whole Food-compliant chicken broth or chicken bone broth
1 (14½-ounce / 411-g) can Whole Food-compliant diced tomatoes, undrained
½ pound (227 g) fresh green beans, trimmed

and cut into 1-inch pieces
½ teaspoon salt
¼ teaspoon black pepper
2 large, thick carrots, spiralized
1 (16-ounce / 454-g) package very small cooked peeled deveined shrimp
1 (10.7-ounce / 303-g) package zucchini noodles; or 2 small zucchini, spiralized

1. Make the pesto: In a food processor, combine the basil leaves, almonds, nutritional yeast (if using), salt, pepper, and garlic. Cover and pulse until finely chopped. With the food processor running, add the oil and process until well combined and nearly smooth.
2. Make the soup: In a large pot, heat the olive oil over medium-high heat. Add the onion and garlic and cook, stirring frequently, until the onions are softened, about 3 minutes. Stir the broth, tomatoes, green beans, salt, and pepper into the pot and bring to a boil. Reduce the heat, cover, and simmer until the beans are crisp-tender, about 5 minutes. Add the carrot noodles and cook for 3 minutes. Add the shrimp and the zucchini noodles and cook until noodles are just tender, about 2 minutes more. Ladle the soup into bowls and top with some of the pesto.

Beef and Vegetable Stew

Prep time: 25 minutes | Cook time: 6 hours
Serves 4

2 tablespoons extra-virgin olive oil
1½ pounds (680 g) beef stew meat, cut into ¾-inch pieces
4 medium carrots, peeled and diagonally sliced 1 inch thick
8 baby red potatoes, quartered
1 medium yellow onion, cut into thin wedges
2 cloves garlic, minced

½ teaspoon salt
½ teaspoon black pepper
1 bay leaf
2 cups Whole Food-compliant beef broth
2 cups Whole Food-compliant vegetable juice
2 tablespoons coconut aminos
2 tablespoons tapioca flour (optional for a thicker stew)

1. In a large skillet, heat the olive oil over medium-high heat. Add the beef and cook in batches if necessary, stirring occasionally, until browned on all sides.
2. Transfer the beef to a slow cooker. Add the carrots, potatoes, onion, garlic, salt, pepper, bay leaf, broth, vegetable juice, and coconut aminos; stir to combine. Cover and cook on low for 6 to 8 hours or on high for 3 to 4 hours, or until the beef and vegetables are tender.
3. If using the tapioca flour, turn the slow cooker to high if using the low setting. In a small bowl, stir together the tapioca flour and 2 tablespoons water. Stir into the stew. Cover and cook for 10 minutes. Remove and discard the bay leaf before serving.

Potato and Green Soup

Prep time: 10 minutes | Cook time: 30 minutes
Serves 4

2 tablespoons extra-virgin olive oil, plus more for serving
2 small to medium leeks, halved lengthwise and sliced (1½ cups)
½ teaspoon salt
½ teaspoon black pepper
3 cloves garlic, minced
6 cups Whole Food-compliant chicken broth or chicken bone

broth
3 medium russet potatoes, peeled and diced
6 cups chopped greens, such as kale, collard greens, or mustard greens
½ cup packed chopped fresh parsley
Grated zest and juice of 1 lemon
8 large eggs

1. Heat the olive oil over medium heat in a large pot. Add the leeks, salt, and pepper and cook, stirring occasionally, until the leeks are softened but not browned, about 4 minutes. Add the garlic and cook, stirring, for 1 minute. Stir in the broth and potatoes and bring to a boil. Reduce the heat, cover, and simmer until the potatoes are tender, about 10 minutes.
2. Add the greens and cook over medium-high heat, stirring occasionally, until the greens are wilted, about 2 minutes. Reduce the heat to low and stir in the parsley and lemon zest. Break an egg into a small bowl and slide it into the soup. Repeat with the remaining eggs. Cover and simmer until the eggs are cooked to desired doneness, 4 to 6 minutes.
3. Drizzle each serving with lemon juice and olive oil. Season with salt and pepper to taste.

Cauliflower Soup with Sausage and Spinach

Prep time: 10 minutes | Cook time: 30 minutes
Serves 4

1 pound (454 g) Whole Food-compliant spicy ground pork sausage
1 tablespoon extra-virgin olive oil
4 cups cauliflower florets
1 medium onion, coarsely chopped
3 stalks celery, coarsely chopped
1 fennel bulb, trimmed, cored, and coarsely

chopped
2 cloves garlic, coarsely chopped
5 cups Whole Food-compliant chicken broth or chicken bone broth
¼ teaspoon paprika
½ teaspoon black pepper
5 ounces (142 g) fresh baby spinach leaves

1. In a large heavy pot, brown the sausage over medium heat. Using a slotted spoon, transfer the sausage to a plate lined with paper towels to drain. Drain off any fat in the skillet.
2. Heat the olive oil in the same pot over medium-high heat. Add the cauliflower, onion, celery, fennel, and garlic and cook, stirring occasionally, for 5 to 6 minutes. Stir in the broth, scraping up any browned bits on the bottom. Bring to a boil, reduce the heat, and simmer for 15 minutes.
3. Carefully transfer the soup to a blender, in batches if necessary, and let cool briefly; blend until the soup is smooth and creamy. (Or use an immersion blender to blend the soup in the pot.) Return the soup to the pot and add the paprika and black pepper. Just before serving, stir the spinach and sausage into the soup.

Spiced Moroccan Meatball Stew

Prep time: 30 minutes | Cook time: 5 hours
Serves 4

1 large shallot, finely chopped
1 large egg, lightly beaten
⅓ cup almond meal
1 teaspoon ground cumin
1 teaspoon ground coriander
1 teaspoon salt
½ teaspoon black pepper
½ teaspoon ground ginger
½ teaspoon ground cinnamon
1½ pounds (680 g) ground beef
1 onion, chopped
2 carrots, peeled and chopped
4 cloves garlic, minced
1 teaspoon ground turmeric
2 (14½-ounce / 411-g) cans Whole Food-compliant beef broth
1 (14½-ounce / 411-g) can Whole Food-compliant diced tomatoes, undrained
8 cups chopped greens, such as kale, mustard greens, chard, and/or spinach
½ cup chopped fresh cilantro

1. Preheat the oven to 400ºF (205ºC).
2. In a medium bowl, combine the shallot, egg, almond meal, cumin, coriander, salt, pepper, ginger, and cinnamon. Add the ground beef and mix just until combined. Form into 1½-inch meatballs. Place the meatballs on a foil-lined shallow baking pan. Bake for 10 minutes.
3. In a slow cooker, combine the onion, carrots, garlic, and turmeric. Add the broth and tomatoes. Arrange the meatballs in an even layer in the slow cooker. Cover and cook on low for 5 hours or on high for 2½ hours.
4. Turn the slow cooker to high if using the low setting. Gently stir in the greens. Cover and cook just until the greens are tender, 5 to 10 minutes. Stir in the cilantro just before serving.

Pork and Green Chile Stew

Prep time: 10 minutes | Cook time: 1 hour |
Serves 6

2 pounds (907 g) boneless pork shoulder, cut into 1-inch pieces
½ teaspoon coarse salt
½ teaspoon black pepper
3 tablespoons clarified butter, ghee, or coconut oil
1 medium onion, chopped
2 cloves garlic, minced
4 cups Whole Food-compliant chicken broth or chicken bone broth
2 (4½-ounce / 128-g) cans chopped green chiles, undrained
1 pound (454 g) small red potatoes, cut into ¾-inch pieces
1 small red bell pepper, cut into matchsticks
Snipped fresh cilantro (optional)

1. Season the pork with the salt and black pepper. Heat 1 tablespoon of the butter in a large pot over medium-high heat. Add half of the pork and cook, stirring occasionally, until browned on all sides, about 5 minutes. Transfer the pork to a plate. Add 1 tablespoon butter to the pot and repeat to cook the remaining pork.
2. Add the remaining 1 tablespoon butter to the pot. Add the onion and cook, stirring, until tender, 2 to 3 minutes. Add the garlic and cook, stirring frequently, until fragrant, about 30 seconds. Add the broth, green chiles, and pork, bring to a boil, then reduce the heat to medium-low. Cook, covered, until the pork is tender, about 30 minutes.
3. Add the potatoes and bell pepper to the pot and bring the stew to a boil. Cook, uncovered, until the potatoes are tender and the stew is slightly thickened, 8 to 10 minutes. Top servings with cilantro.

Mexican Chicken Soup

Prep time: 10 minutes | Cook time: 20 minutes
Serves 4

1 tablespoon extra-virgin olive oil
½ cup chopped onion
1 medium poblano pepper, seeded and chopped
1 medium yellow or red bell pepper, chopped
2 cloves garlic, minced
½ teaspoon salt
4 cups Whole Food-compliant chicken broth or chicken bone broth

1 (14½-ounce / 411-g) can Whole Food-compliant fire-roasted diced tomatoes, undrained
2 teaspoons chili powder
3 cups shredded cooked chicken
Chopped fresh cilantro, for serving
1 avocado, halved, pitted, peeled, and sliced
Lime wedges, for serving

1. Heat the olive oil in a large pot over medium-high heat. Add the onion, poblano, bell pepper, garlic, and salt. Cook, stirring frequently, until the vegetables are crisp-tender, 3 to 5 minutes.
2. Stir the broth, tomatoes, and chili powder into the pot and bring to a boil. Reduce the heat and simmer for 10 minutes. Add the chicken and heat through, about 1 minute.
3. Serve the soup with cilantro, avocado, and lime wedges.

Pork and Napa Cabbage Soup

Prep time: 10 minutes | Cook time: 6 hours
Serves 4

⅓ cup almond meal
1 large egg, lightly beaten
2 green onions, thinly sliced
1 tablespoon sesame seeds
2 cloves garlic, minced
1 teaspoon salt
½ teaspoon black pepper
1½ pounds (680 g) lean ground pork

4 cups Whole Food-compliant chicken broth
2 shallots, chopped
4 cloves garlic, thinly sliced
2 tablespoons coconut aminos
2 tablespoons minced fresh ginger
1 teaspoon olive oil
4 cups thinly sliced Napa cabbage
2 tablespoons sliced fresh basil

1. Preheat the oven to 400ºF (205ºC).
2. In a medium bowl, combine the almond meal, egg, green onions, sesame seeds, garlic, salt, and pepper. Add the pork and mix just until combined. Form into 8 meatballs and place on a foil-lined rimmed baking sheet. Bake for 10 minutes.
3. In a slow cooker, combine the broth, shallots, garlic, coconut aminos, ginger, and olive oil. Place the meatballs in the cooker in a single layer. Cover and cook on low for 6 to 7 hours or on high for 3 to 3½ hours.
4. Turn the slow cooker to high if using the low setting. Transfer the meatballs to serving bowls. Stir the cabbage into the liquid in the slow cooker. Cook on high for 5 minutes. Ladle the soup over the meatballs. Top servings with the basil.

Sweet Potato Pork Stew

Prep time: 30 minutes | Cook time: 6 hours
Serves 6

2 pounds (907 g) lean ground pork
1 quart Whole Food-compliant vegetable broth
3 medium sweet potatoes, peeled and cut into 1-inch pieces
1 Braeburn apple, cored and cut into 1-inch pieces
2 jalapeños, seeded and diced

1 large shallot, minced
1 tablespoon fresh thyme, plus extra for serving
2 teaspoons ground ginger
½ teaspoon salt
½ teaspoon white pepper
Paprika, for serving

1. In an extra-large skillet, cook the pork over medium-high heat, stirring, until no longer pink, about 10 minutes. Using a slotted spoon, transfer the pork to a slow cooker. Add the broth, sweet potatoes, apple, jalapeños, shallot, thyme, ginger, salt, and white pepper.
2. Cover and cook on low for 6 hours or on high for 3 hours. Use a potato masher or fork to gently mash the sweet potatoes to thicken the stew.
3. Serve, sprinkled with paprika and fresh thyme.

Butternut Squash Apple Soup

Prep time: 5 minutes | Cook time: 25 minutes
Serves 4

2 tablespoons clarified butter, ghee, or coconut oil
2 medium yellow onions, coarsely chopped
2 (10-ounce / 283-g) bags frozen diced butternut squash
2 medium apples (such as Braeburn or Fuji), halved, cored, and roughly chopped

2 tablespoons minced fresh ginger
1 teaspoon ground cardamom
1 teaspoon salt
½ teaspoon black pepper
4 cups chicken broth or chicken bone broth
⅔ cup Whole Food-compliant coconut milk
2 tablespoons snipped fresh chives

1. In a large saucepan, heat the butter over medium heat. Add the onion and cook, stirring often, until caramelized, 10 to 12 minutes. Add the squash and apples and cook, stirring, until browned and tender, 8 to 10 minutes. Stir in the ginger, cardamom, salt, and pepper. Add the broth, raise the heat, and bring to a boil. Reduce the heat and stir in the coconut milk.
2. Carefully transfer the soup to a blender, in batches if necessary, and let cool briefly; pulse a few times, then blend until smooth. (Or use an immersion blender to blend the soup in the pot.) Top each serving with snipped chives.

Chicken Avocado Soup

Prep time: 25 minutes | Cook time: 8 hours

Serves 6

2 quarts Whole Food-compliant chicken broth

1 (14½-ounce / 411-g) can Whole Food-compliant diced tomatoes

1 medium white onion, finely diced

1 jalapeño, seeded and finely diced

3 cloves garlic, minced

1 tablespoon chipotle powder or regular chili powder

1 teaspoon ground cumin

1 teaspoon dried oregano

½ teaspoon salt

½ teaspoon black pepper

4 boneless, skinless chicken breasts (2 pounds / 907 g)

½ cup chopped fresh cilantro

½ cup fresh lime juice, plus lime wedges for serving

3 avocados, halved, pitted, peeled, and diced

1. In a slow cooker, stir together the broth, tomatoes, onion, jalapeño, garlic, chipotle powder, cumin, oregano, salt, and pepper. Add the chicken.
2. Cover and cook on low for 8 to 10 hours or on high for 4 to 5 hours.
3. Use tongs to transfer the chicken to a cutting board. Use two forks to shred the chicken. Return the chicken to the cooker and stir in the cilantro and lime juice.
4. Top servings with avocado and serve with lime wedges.

Turnip Leek Soup

Prep time: 10 minutes | Cook time: 35 minutes

Serves 4

4 slices Whole Food-compliant bacon, diced

2 leeks, white parts only, cut into 1-inch pieces

2 turnips, peeled and chopped (about 3½ cups)

1 medium zucchini, ends removed and diced

1 (14½-ounce / 411-g) can Whole Food-compliant coconut milk

1 cup Whole Food-compliant chicken broth or

chicken bone broth

1 teaspoon garlic powder

1 teaspoon onion powder

1 teaspoon dried rosemary

1 teaspoon salt

2 green onions, minced

1. In a large pot, cook the bacon over medium-high heat until crisp, about 3 minutes. Use a slotted spoon to remove the bacon and drain on paper towels. Reserve the drippings in the pot.
2. Reduce the heat to medium. Add the leeks to the pot and cook, stirring, until softened, about 3 minutes. Add the turnips and zucchini and continue to cook, stirring, until tender, about 5 minutes. Stir in the coconut milk, broth, garlic powder, onion powder, rosemary, and salt. Simmer the soup, covered, for 20 minutes.
3. Carefully transfer the soup to a blender, in batches if necessary, and let cool briefly; blend until the soup is smooth and creamy. (Or use an immersion blender to blend the soup in the pot.) Top servings with the bacon and green onions.

Chapter 7: Vegetables and Sides

5-Minute Sugar Snap Peas

Prep time: 5 minutes | Cook time: 5 minutes
Serves 2

1 tablespoon clarified butter or ghee
2 tablespoons finely chopped shallot
1 teaspoon minced fresh ginger
⅛ teaspoon red pepper flakes
1 (8-ounce / 227-g) bag fresh stringless sugar snap peas
2 teaspoons coconut aminos

1. Heat the butter in a medium skillet over medium heat. Add the shallot, ginger, and pepper flakes and cook, stirring, until fragrant, about 1 minute. Add the sugar snap peas and cook until crisp-tender, 3 to 5 minutes longer. Stir in the coconut aminos and serve.

Sweet Potato Cauliflower Mash

Prep time: 5 minutes | Cook time: 15 minutes
Serves 4

1 pound (454 g) sweet potatoes, peeled and chopped
3 cups cauliflower florets
2 cloves garlic, peeled
3 tablespoons clarified butter or ghee
½ teaspoon salt
¼ teaspoon black pepper

1. Place the sweet potatoes, cauliflower, and garlic in a large saucepan, add enough water to cover, and bring to a boil. Reduce the heat, cover, and simmer until the vegetables are tender, 12 to 15 minutes. Drain.
2. Using a potato masher, mash the vegetables until desired consistency. Stir in the butter, salt, and pepper and serve.

Easy Zucchini Noodles

Prep time: 30 minutes | Cook time: 0 minutes
Serves 2

4 zucchini
1 teaspoon kosher salt

1. Trim the ends of the zucchini and pass them through a spiralizer to create noodles. Transfer the zucchini noodles to a colander set over a bowl, sprinkle with the salt, and massage the noodles to coat. Let the zucchini noodles sit until drained of excess moisture, about 30 minutes, or up to 1 hour.
2. Drain the zucchini noodles and serve as desired.

Garlic Kale

Prep time: 8 minutes | Cook time: 5 minutes
Serves 2

2 tablespoons extra-virgin olive oil
5 garlic cloves, chopped or sliced
1 pound (454 g) kale, stemmed, leaves cut crosswise into ½-inch-wide slices
½ teaspoon kosher salt

1. In a medium sauté pan, heat 1 tablespoon of the olive oil over medium heat. Add the garlic and cook, stirring continuously, until it begins to turn brown, making sure not to burn the garlic, about 45 seconds. Immediately remove the garlic and set aside.
2. Increase the heat to medium-high and add the remaining 1 tablespoon olive oil to the pan. Add the greens and ½ teaspoon salt and cook, stirring continuously, until the greens have wilted to your liking, 1½ to 2 minutes. Serve.

Mashed Sweet Potatoes

Prep time: 10 minutes | Cook time: 15 minutes
Serves 4

Kosher salt and freshly ground black pepper, to taste
4 sweet potatoes, peeled and cut into 1-inch cubes
3 tablespoons extra-virgin olive oil, plus

more for finishing
2 garlic cloves, finely chopped
1 tablespoon ghee (optional)
Flaky sea salt, for finishing

1. Bring a large saucepan of water to a boil over high heat. Season the water with 1 tablespoon salt and add the sweet potatoes. Boil until the potatoes are fork-tender, about 15 minutes, then drain them and return them to the pot.
2. Add the olive oil, garlic, and ghee (if using) to the pot with the sweet potatoes. Season with a pinch each of salt and pepper and mash the potatoes with a fork or potato masher until smooth.
3. Transfer the mashed sweet potatoes to a serving bowl, drizzle with a bit more olive oil, and season with a pinch of flaky salt. Serve immediately.

Roasted Cauliflower

Prep time: 5 minutes | Cook time: 50 minutes
Serves 4

1 head cauliflower, preferably with leaves still attached
2 tablespoons plus 1 teaspoon kosher salt
2 tablespoons ghee, at

room temperature
2 tablespoons extra-virgin olive oil
Flaky sea salt, for garnish

1. Preheat the oven to 425ºF (220ºC). Line a baking sheet with parchment paper.
2. Trim the stem of the cauliflower so the cauliflower will stand upright on the board. If the cauliflower has leaves still attached, do not trim them off.

3. Bring a large pot of water to a boil over high heat. Add 2 tablespoons of the salt and submerge the cauliflower in the water, stem-side up. Boil until the florets have slightly softened but are still intact, 10 to 12 minutes. Place the cauliflower stem-side down on a wire rack to drain and let air-dry for 5 minutes.
4. Stand the cauliflower on the prepared baking sheet and, using your hands, spread apart the florets to create some crevices. Rub the florets with the ghee and season with the remaining 1 teaspoon salt. Roast until the florets are golden brown and fork-tender, 40 to 45 minutes.
5. Drizzle the roasted cauliflower with the olive oil and finish with a sprinkle of flaky salt. Serve immediately.

Garlic and Herb Stuffed Portobello Mushrooms

Prep time: 5 minutes | Cook time: 25 minutes
Serves 4

4 large portobello mushroom caps
¼ cup grass-fed butter or ghee, at room temperature
¼ cup finely chopped fresh parsley leaves,

plus more for garnish
1½ teaspoons finely chopped garlic
Kosher salt and freshly ground black pepper, to taste

1. Preheat the oven to 425ºF (220ºC). Line a rimmed baking sheet with parchment paper.
2. Wipe the mushrooms clean with a damp paper towel and place them gill-side up on the prepared baking sheet.
3. In a medium bowl, stir together the butter, parsley, and garlic until well combined. Evenly spread the butter over the gill side of each mushroom and season each with a pinch each of salt and pepper. Bake until the mushrooms are deeply browned and sizzling, 22 to 25 minutes. Garnish with parsley and serve immediately.

Lime-Garlic Zucchini Ribbons

Prep time: 10 minutes | Cook time: 10 minutes
Serves 4

2 medium zucchini, sliced lengthwise into about 6 (¼-inch-thick) planks each
⅛ teaspoon plus ¼ teaspoon kosher salt
¼ teaspoon freshly ground black pepper
2 tablespoons plus 1 teaspoon extra-virgin

olive oil
2 tablespoons fresh lime juice
2 tablespoons chopped scallions
1 tablespoon pressed garlic
Juice from 1 tablespoon grated fresh ginger

1. Season the zucchini planks with ⅛ teaspoon of the salt and the pepper.
2. In a large sauté pan or grill pan, heat 1 teaspoon of the olive oil over high heat. When the oil is hot, reduce the heat to medium and spread the zucchini planks in the pan in a single layer (work in batches if they don't all fit at the same time). Cook until the zucchini is fork-tender but not mushy, about 1½ minutes per side.
3. In a bowl, stir together the remaining 2 tablespoons olive oil, the lime juice, scallions, garlic, ginger juice, and remaining ¼ teaspoon salt.
4. Pour the marinade over the zucchini. Serve.

Garlicky Green Beans with Almonds

Prep time: 5 minutes | Cook time: 8 minutes
Serves 4

1 tablespoon plus ¼ teaspoon kosher salt
1 pound (454 g) French green beans
1 tablespoon extra-virgin olive oil
3 tablespoons slivered

almonds
6 garlic cloves, thinly sliced (about 4 tablespoons)
¼ teaspoon freshly ground black pepper

1. Fill a large pot with water, add 1 tablespoon of the salt, and bring to a boil over high heat. Prepare a large bowl of ice water.

2. Add the green beans to the boiling water and cook for 3 minutes. Drain and plunge into the ice water; let cool for 5 minutes. Drain again and dry the beans. Set aside.
3. In a medium sauté pan, heat the olive oil over medium-high heat. Add the almonds and cook, stirring, until golden, 1 to 2 minutes.
4. Increase the heat to high, add the green beans, garlic, ¼ teaspoon salt, and the pepper, and stir to combine well. Cook, stirring, until the garlic is golden and the green beans are tender, about 2 minutes more.
5. Serve.

Beet and Red Cabbage Salad

Prep time: 10 minutes | Cook time: 0 minutes
Serves 4

1 (8-ounce / 227-g) package refrigerated cooked baby beets; or 1 (15-ounce / 425-g) can whole beets, drained
1 (10-ounce / 283-g) bag shredded red cabbage
⅓ cup finely chopped shallot
½ cup Whole Food-compliant dried dark sweet cherries,

chopped
¼ cup roasted salted sunflower seeds
¼ cup chopped fresh parsley
3 tablespoons red wine vinegar
1 tablespoon balsamic vinegar
¼ cup extra-virgin olive oil
¼ teaspoon salt
¼ teaspoon black pepper

1. Slice the beets and cut into thin strips. Combine the beets, cabbage, shallot, cherries, sunflower seeds, and parsley in a large bowl. Drizzle with both of the vinegars and toss to coat. Drizzle with the olive oil, sprinkle with the salt and black pepper, and toss again.
2. Serve immediately or store in an airtight container in the refrigerator for up to 24 hours.

Roasted Brussels Sprouts with Lemon Tahini

Prep time: 10 minutes | Cook time: 10 minutes
Serves 2

2 cups Brussels sprouts, trimmed and halved (or quartered if large)
2 tablespoons clarified butter or ghee, melted
1 teaspoon paprika
½ to 1 teaspoon red pepper flakes
¼ teaspoon salt
¼ black pepper
2 teaspoons fresh lemon juice
2 tablespoons Whole Food-compliant tahini

1. Preheat the oven to 400°F (205°C). Line a baking sheet with parchment paper.
2. Combine the Brussels sprouts, butter, paprika, pepper flakes, salt, and black pepper in a large bowl. Place the Brussels sprouts in a single layer on the pan.
3. Roast the Brussels sprouts, stirring once halfway through cooking, until the outer leaves are crispy and lightly browned, 8 to 10 minutes. Drizzle the lemon juice over the Brussels sprouts and serve with the tahini for dipping.

Chile Lime Roasted Sweet Potatoes

Prep time: 5 minutes | Cook time: 20 minutes
Serves 4

1 (16-ounce / 454-g) bag frozen cubed sweet potatoes
2 tablespoons coconut oil, melted
½ jalapeño, seeded and finely chopped;
or ¼ to ½ teaspoon chipotle powder
1 teaspoon ground cumin
½ teaspoon salt
Lime wedges, for serving

1. Preheat the oven to 450°F (235°C). Line a large baking sheet with parchment paper.
2. Place the sweet potatoes in a medium bowl, cover with microwave-safe plastic wrap, and pull back a small section of the plastic wrap so the steam can escape. Microwave on high for 2 minutes.
3. Add the coconut oil, jalapeño, cumin, and salt and toss to coat. Place the sweet potatoes on the pan and roast, stirring once halfway through, until golden, about 20 minutes. Serve with the lime wedges.

Balsamic Roasted Root Vegetables

Prep time: 15 minutes | Cook time: 35 minutes
Serves 2

Vegetables:

1 medium red, golden, or Chioggia beet, peeled and cut into 1-inch pieces (8 ounces / 227 g)
1 small turnip, peeled and cut into 1-inch pieces (8 ounces / 227 g)
1 bunch radishes, trimmed and halved lengthwise (8 ounces / 227 g)
1 small onion, cut into 1-inch pieces
3 tablespoons extra-virgin olive oil
½ teaspoon salt
¼ teaspoon black pepper

Vinaigrette:

2 tablespoons extra-virgin olive oil
1 tablespoon balsamic vinegar
1 tablespoon minced shallot
¼ teaspoon salt
⅛ teaspoon black pepper
½ cup roughly chopped fresh parsley

1. Make the vegetables: Preheat the oven to 425°F (220°C). In a large bowl, combine the beet, turnip, radishes, onion, olive oil, salt, and pepper; toss to coat. Transfer the vegetables to a large rimmed baking sheet and spread them into a single layer. Roast for 35 to 45 minutes, stirring once and rotating the baking sheet halfway through the cooking time, until all the vegetables are tender and browned.
2. Make the vinaigrette: In a small bowl, whisk together the olive oil, vinegar, shallot, salt, and pepper.
3. Transfer the roasted vegetables to a large bowl. Drizzle with the vinaigrette and sprinkle with the parsley. Gently toss to coat.

Roasted Parsnips with Lemon and Dill

Prep time: 20 minutes | Cook time: 20 minutes
Serves 4

2 pounds (907 g) parsnips, peeled and cut into 3 × ¼-inch matchsticks
3 tablespoons extra-virgin olive oil
3 cloves garlic, thinly sliced

½ teaspoon salt
⅛ teaspoon black pepper
2 tablespoons fresh lemon juice
2 teaspoons snipped fresh dill or ½ teaspoon dried dill

1. Preheat the oven to 425ºF (220ºC).
2. Combine the parsnips, olive oil, garlic, salt, and pepper in a large bowl and toss to coat. Place the parsnips in an even layer on two baking sheets.
3. Roast, uncovered, stirring twice, until the parsnips are tender and starting to brown, 20 to 30 minutes. Drizzle with the lemon juice and sprinkle with the dill; toss to coat and serve.

Kale and Butternut Squash Salad

Prep time: 20 minutes | Cook time: 0 minutes
Serves 4

1 teaspoon grated lime zest
1 tablespoon fresh lime juice
¾ cup full-fat coconut milk
2 tablespoons fresh orange juice
1 teaspoon white wine vinegar
Salt, to taste
½ butternut squash (8 ounces / 227 g),

peeled and seeded
1 bunch curly leafed or Tuscan kale, stemmed and leaves cut into bite-size pieces (2 cups lightly packed)
¾ cup pomegranate seeds
⅓ cup slivered almonds
⅓ cup roasted unsalted pepitas (pumpkin seeds)

1. In a small bowl, combine lime zest, lime juice, coconut milk, orange juice, vinegar, and salt to taste. Set the dressing aside.
2. Use a vegetable peeler to shave the squash into thin strips (you should have 4 cups lightly packed). In a large bowl, combine the squash, kale, pomegranate seeds, almonds, and pepitas. Drizzle with ½ cup of the dressing and gently toss to coat. Season with salt. Store the remaining dressing in the refrigerator for up to 1 week.

Curried Carrot Sweet Potato Soup

Prep time: 20 minutes | Cook time: 4 to 5 hours
Serves 4

1 tablespoon coconut oil
1 large leek, white and light green parts only, thinly sliced
½ pound (227 g) carrots, sliced
1 tablespoon Madras curry powder
½ teaspoon sea salt
1 teaspoon grated fresh ginger
3 cloves garlic, minced
Pinch of cayenne

pepper
2 Japanese sweet potatoes, peeled and chopped
3 cups chicken bone broth or Whole Food-compliant chicken broth
2 cups full-fat coconut milk
Chopped fresh chives, for serving
Red pepper flakes, for serving

1. Heat the coconut oil in a large skillet over medium heat. Add the leek and carrots and cook, stirring frequently, until the leek is soft, 5 to 7 minutes.
2. Add the curry powder, salt, ginger, garlic, and cayenne to the skillet. Cook, stirring, until the garlic is fragrant, about 1 minute. Transfer the leek mixture to a slow cooker. Add the sweet potatoes, broth, and coconut milk to the slow cooker. Cover and cook on low for 4 to 5 hours.
3. Turn off the slow cooker and remove the lid; let the soup cool slightly. Using an immersion blender, purée the soup until smooth. Ladle the soup into bowls and top with chives and red pepper flakes.

Mustard Brussels Sprout Slaw

Prep time: 30 minutes | Cook time: 0 minutes

Serves 2

2 pounds (907 g) Brussels sprouts, trimmed
1 small apple, cored and chopped
¼ cup chopped walnuts, toasted
¼ cup thinly sliced green onions
2 tablespoons extra-virgin olive oil
1 tablespoon white wine vinegar
2 teaspoons snipped fresh thyme
1 teaspoon Whole Food-compliant coarse-grain mustard
¼ teaspoon coarse salt

1. Cut the Brussels sprouts in half lengthwise. Place the halves, cut sides down, on a cutting board and thinly slice the halves. (You should have about 10 cups sliced sprouts.) Transfer 1½ cups of the sliced sprouts to a medium bowl. Place the remaining sprouts in an airtight container or plastic bag; seal and store in the refrigerator for up to 3 days.
2. Add the apple, walnuts, and green onions to the bowl with the Brussels sprouts and toss to combine. In a small bowl, whisk together the oil, vinegar, thyme, mustard, and salt. Drizzle the dressing over the slaw and toss to coat. Let stand for 5 to 10 minutes before serving; toss again before serving.

Greek Lemon Potatoes

Prep time: 15 minutes | Cook time: 1½ hours

Serves 6

½ cup chicken bone broth or Whole Food-compliant chicken broth
½ cup fresh lemon juice
⅓ cup extra-virgin olive oil
1 tablespoon dried thyme, crushed
1 tablespoon dried oregano, crushed
3 cloves garlic, minced
½ teaspoon sea salt
6 medium russet potatoes, peeled, if desired, and cut into ½-inch-thick wedges

1. Preheat the oven to 400ºF (205ºC).
2. Combine the broth, lemon juice, olive oil, thyme, oregano, garlic, and salt in a large bowl. Mix well.
3. Arrange the potato wedges in a single layer in a large baking dish. Pour the broth mixture over the potatoes. Cover with aluminum foil and bake, stirring once, for 1 hour 30 minutes.

Pistachio Kale Salad

Prep time: 10 minutes | Cook time: 30 minutes

Serves 2 or 3

Dressing:

3 tablespoons extra-virgin olive oil
2 anchovy fillets
2 teaspoons fresh lemon juice
2 cloves garlic
1 teaspoon Whole Food-compliant Dijon mustard
⅛ teaspoon cayenne pepper
1 hard-cooked egg, yolk and white separated
Salt and black pepper, to taste

Salad:

1 bunch curly leafed or Tuscan kale, stemmed and leaves sliced
⅓ cup roasted salted pistachios, chopped

1. Make the dressing: In a blender, combine the olive oil, anchovy fillets, lemon juice, garlic, mustard, cayenne, and the hard-cooked egg yolk (reserve the egg white for another use or chop it and add it to the finished salad). Cover and blend until smooth. (Alternatively, place the ingredients in a bowl and use an immersion blender.) Season with salt and black pepper.
2. Make the salad: Place the kale in a large bowl; add the dressing. Using your hands, work the dressing into the kale for 15 seconds. Chill for 30 minutes or up to 2 hours. Sprinkle the pistachios over the salad just before serving.

Thai Red Curry Cauliflower

Prep time: 5 minutes | Cook time: 35 minutes
Serves 4

6 cups cauliflower florets	½ teaspoon salt
3 tablespoons clarified butter or ghee, melted	¼ teaspoon black pepper
2 teaspoons Whole Food-compliant red curry powder	2 tablespoons chopped fresh cilantro
	Lime wedges, for serving

1. Preheat the oven to 400°F (205°C). Line a large rimmed baking sheet with parchment paper.
2. Place the cauliflower in a large bowl and drizzle it with the melted butter; mix well. Add the curry powder, salt, and pepper and toss to evenly coat the cauliflower. Spread the cauliflower evenly on the prepared baking sheet.
3. Roast for 20 minutes, then stir. Roast for 15 to 20 minutes more, until the cauliflower is tender and browned. Transfer to a serving bowl. Sprinkle with the cilantro and serve with lime wedges.

Red Cabbage with Bacon and Apple

Prep time: 5 minutes | Cook time: 15 minutes
Serves 4

8 ounces (227 g) sliced bacon	thinly sliced apple
5 cups thinly sliced red cabbage (about ⅔ of a small head)	1 tablespoon white vinegar
1 cup peeled and	1 teaspoon kosher salt
	¼ teaspoon freshly ground black pepper

1. Bring a large pot of water (about 4 quarts) to a boil over high heat.
2. Meanwhile, in a large skillet over medium-high heat, fry the bacon until done, 6 to 8 minutes. Transfer the bacon to a cutting board, leaving as much bacon fat in the pan as possible, and slice into ½-inch pieces. Set aside.

3. Pour the bacon fat into a bowl. Measure 2 tablespoons of the bacon fat, return it to the pan, and discard the remaining fat. Set the pan aside.
4. Add the red cabbage to the boiling water and cook until tender but still a bit crunchy, about 3 minutes. Drain the cabbage and set aside.
5. Heat the reserved bacon fat over medium-high heat. Add the apple and cook, stirring, until just soft, about 1 minute. Add the cabbage, bacon, vinegar, salt, and pepper and stir to combine thoroughly. Serve.

Grilled Romaine with Lemon Tahini Dressing

Prep time: 10 minutes | Cook time: 6 minutes
Serves 2

1 tablespoon fresh lemon juice	4 teaspoons avocado oil
1 teaspoon tahini	1 romaine heart, halved lengthwise
½ to 1 teaspoon coconut aminos	Fresh cilantro leaves (optional)
¼ teaspoon olive oil	Chopped toasted almonds (optional)
1 clove garlic, minced	
Pinch of salt	

1. Preheat a grill to medium heat.
2. In a small bowl, whisk together the lemon juice, tahini, coconut aminos, olive oil, garlic, and salt. Slowly whisk in 3 teaspoons of the avocado oil.
3. Brush the romaine halves with the remaining 1 teaspoon avocado oil.
4. Grill the romaine, cut sides down, over direct heat for 4 to 6 minutes, until slightly charred. Place the romaine on salad plates, cut sides up. Drizzle with the dressing. Sprinkle with cilantro and almonds, if desired.

Hasselback Zucchini with Basil

Prep time: 10 minutes | Cook time: 25 minutes
Serves 4

4 small zucchini
2 tablespoons extra-virgin olive oil
2 cloves garlic, minced

1 teaspoon grated lemon zest
2 tablespoons finely chopped fresh basil
½ teaspoon salt

1. Preheat the oven to 425ºF (220ºC). Line a baking sheet with foil.
2. Arrange two chopsticks or wooden spoons lengthwise on opposite sides of one zucchini. Cut the zucchini crosswise into ¼-inch-thick slices, stopping when the knife reaches the chopsticks to prevent slicing all the way through. Carefully fan the slices slightly. Repeat with the remaining zucchini. Place the zucchini on the pan.
3. In a small bowl, combine the olive oil, garlic, lemon zest, basil, and salt. Carefully spoon the gremolata between the zucchini slices and over the tops.
4. Roast the zucchini just until tender, 25 to 30 minutes.

Dukkah Brussels Sprouts

Prep time: 5 minutes | Cook time: 20 minutes
Serves 4

Dukkah:
½ cup shelled pistachios
¼ cup sesame seeds
3 tablespoons coriander seeds

2 tablespoons cumin seeds
1 teaspoon kosher salt
½ teaspoon cracked black pepper

Brussels Sprouts:
1½ pounds (680 g) Brussels sprouts

3 tablespoons extra-virgin olive oil

1. Make the dukkah: Preheat the oven to 350ºF (180ºC). Place the pistachios on a rimmed baking sheet and toast for 5 minutes; add the sesame seeds, coriander, and cumin and toast for 5 minutes more, until the nuts are golden and the spices are fragrant. Remove from the oven and let cool (keep the oven on). Place the pistachio mixture in a food processor and add the salt and pepper. Pulse just until roughly chopped (do not overprocess). Let cool completely. Store the dukkah in an airtight container at room temperature for up to 1 week. (Makes about 1 cup.)
2. Make the Brussels sprouts: Increase the oven temperature to 400ºF (205ºC). Trim the ends from the Brussels sprouts and remove any yellow outer leaves. Cut each sprout in half lengthwise and place them in a 10 × 15-inch baking pan. Drizzle with the olive oil and toss to coat. Sprinkle with 3 tablespoons of the dukkah and stir to coat. Roast for 20 minutes, stirring after 15 minutes, until the Brussels sprouts are golden brown and crisp on the outside and tender inside.

Carrots with Fennel and Shallots

Prep time: 10 minutes | Cook time: 20 minutes
Serves 4

3 tablespoons clarified butter
1 cup thinly sliced fennel
½ cup chopped shallots

4 large carrots, cut on the bias into ¼-inch-thick slices (4 cups)
1 teaspoon kosher salt

1. In a large sauté pan, melt 2 tablespoons of the clarified butter over medium heat. Add the fennel and shallots and cook, stirring continuously, until soft and lightly golden, about 8 minutes. Using a slotted spoon, transfer the shallots and fennel to a bowl and set aside.
2. Add the remaining 1 tablespoon clarified butter to butter remaining in the pan and melt over medium heat. Add the carrots and cook, stirring, until the soft, about 9 minutes. Add the salt and stir to combine. Return the fennel and shallots to the pan and stir together. Serve.

Creamy Broccoli Soup

Prep time: 15 minutes | Cook time: 25 minutes
Serves 4

2 tablespoons extra-virgin olive oil
1 yellow onion, diced
1 carrot, diced
Kosher salt and freshly ground black pepper, to taste
2 garlic cloves, coarsely chopped
1 teaspoon sweet paprika

½ teaspoon cayenne pepper (optional)
4 cups chicken stock
3 small sweet potatoes, peeled and cut into 2-inch cubes (about 3½ cups)
2 heads broccoli (about 1½ pounds / 680 g), finely chopped, including stems
¼ cup nutritional yeast powder or flakes

1. In a large Dutch oven or heavy-bottomed pot, heat the olive oil over medium-high heat. Add the onion and carrot and season with ¼ teaspoon each salt and black pepper. Cook, stirring, until the vegetables are slightly softened, 5 to 6 minutes. Add the garlic and cook, stirring, for an additional minute, followed by the paprika and cayenne (if using), and cook, stirring, for 1 minute more so everything is evenly coated with the spices.
2. Add the stock, sweet potatoes, and all but 1½ cups of the broccoli. Add 4 cups water and bring to a boil. Cook at a boil until the sweet potatoes are fork-tender, about 12 minutes. Stir in the nutritional yeast. Remove from the heat and use an immersion blender to blend the soup until smooth and creamy. (Alternatively, let the soup cool slightly, carefully transfer it to a blender, and blend until smooth and creamy, then return the soup to the pot.) Taste and adjust the salt and pepper, as desired.
3. Stir in the remaining florets and cook over medium heat until the broccoli is just tender, 2 to 3 minutes. Let the soup cool for 5 to 10 minutes, then ladle it into individual bowls and serve.

Sautéed Greens with Pine Nuts

Prep time: 5 minutes | Cook time: 15 minutes
Serves 3 or 4

1 pound (454 g) Tuscan kale
Kosher salt, to taste
¼ cup pine nuts
3 tablespoons extra-virgin olive oil, plus more for

finishing
2 garlic cloves, thinly sliced
1 teaspoon red pepper flakes
½ lemon, cut into wedges, for serving

1. Trim the lower parts of the kale stems and use your hands to strip the leaves from the stems. Finely chop the stems and set aside. Stack the leaves on top of one another, cut them crosswise into 1-inch ribbons, and set aside.
2. Fill a large bowl with ice and water and set it nearby.
3. Bring a large pot of water to a boil over high heat. Season the water with 2 tablespoons salt, add the kale leaves, and cook until tender and bright green, about 3 minutes. Transfer the kale to the ice water and let stand for 3 minutes to stop the cooking and set the vivid green color. Drain the kale very well before cooking.
4. In a large sauté pan, toast the pine nuts over medium heat until lightly browned and fragrant, 3 to 4 minutes. Transfer the nuts to a bowl or plate and set aside.
5. In the same pan, heat the olive oil over medium heat. Add the chopped kale stems and the garlic and season with a pinch of salt. Cook, stirring, until the kale stems soften, about 3 minutes. Add the red pepper flakes and cook for 1 minute. Add the kale leaves and season with another small pinch of salt. Toss the kale to coat in the oil. Add 2 tablespoons water and quickly cover the pan to trap the steam. Cook until wilted and tender, 3 minutes, stirring once about halfway through. Taste and adjust the seasoning.
6. Transfer the cooked kale to a serving platter, garnish with the toasted pine nuts, drizzle with a bit more olive oil, and serve with the lemon wedges alongside for squeezing over the top.

Almond Green Beans

Prep time: 5 minutes | Cook time: 8 minutes
Serves 4

1 tablespoon coconut oil
1 pound (454 g) fresh green beans, trimmed
1 teaspoon grated lemon zest
1 to 2 teaspoons fresh lemon juice

¼ teaspoon salt
¼ teaspoon black pepper
¼ cup sliced almonds, toasted

1. Heat the coconut oil in a large skillet over medium-high heat. Add the green beans and cook, without stirring, until the beans begin to blister, about 2 minutes. Stir and continue to cook, stirring occasionally, until crisp-tender and blistered in spots, 5 to 6 minutes.
2. Remove the skillet from the heat and stir in the lemon zest and juice, salt, and black pepper. Sprinkle with the almonds and serve.

Chapter 8: Red Meat

Russian Beef Stew

Prep time: 25 minutes | Cook time: 3 hours
Serves 4

2 tablespoons avocado oil
2 pounds (907 g) beef stew meat, such as chuck, cut into 2-inch pieces
3 yellow onions (about 1 pound / 454 g), diced
4 small carrots (about 10 ounces / 283 g total), cut into rounds

2 teaspoons kosher salt, plus more as needed
1 tablespoon freshly ground black pepper, plus more as needed
3 garlic cloves, coarsely chopped
1 pound (454 g) yellow potatoes (about 4), peeled and cut into 3-inch-long wedges

1. In a Dutch oven or heavy-bottomed pot, heat the avocado oil over medium-high heat. Add the beef and cook, stirring regularly, until browned on all sides and all the moisture has evaporated, about 15 minutes. Add the onions, carrots, salt, and pepper and cook, stirring and scraping up any browned bits from the bottom of the pan, until the vegetables have started to caramelize, 8 to 10 minutes. Add the garlic and cook, stirring, for 1 minute.
2. Add enough water to barely cover the meat and bring the liquid to a simmer. Reduce the heat to medium-low, cover, and cook, stirring occasionally, until the beef is soft, 1½ to 2 hours. If at any point the liquid evaporates enough that the meat is exposed, add water as needed to just barely cover the beef.
3. Add the potatoes and enough water to cover the contents of the pot. Cook until the potatoes are soft, 25 to 30 minutes. Taste and adjust the seasoning. Let cool for 5 minutes before serving.

Asian Beef Zoodle Soup

Prep time: 15 minutes | Cook time: 10 minutes
Serves 4

2 tablespoons coconut oil
1 small onion, halved and thinly sliced
6 ounces (170 g) fresh shiitake mushrooms, stemmed and sliced
2 cloves garlic, minced
2 teaspoons minced fresh ginger
5 cups beef bone broth or Whole Food-

compliant beef broth
2 tablespoons coconut aminos
2 teaspoons Red Boat fish sauce
1 teaspoon salt
2 medium zucchini
12 ounces (340 g) boneless beef sirloin steak, thinly sliced across the grain

Toppings:
Fresh Thai basil leaves
Fresh cilantro leaves

Sliced green onion
Sliced jalapeño
Lime wedges

1. In a large pot, heat the coconut oil over medium heat. Add the onion and cook, stirring, until softened, about 2 minutes. Add the mushrooms and cook, stirring, for about 3 minutes. Add the garlic and ginger and cook, stirring, until fragrant, about 30 seconds. Add the broth, coconut aminos, fish sauce, and salt. Bring to a boil; reduce the heat to medium-low and simmer, uncovered, for 5 minutes.
2. Meanwhile, use a spiral slicer or julienne peeler to cut the zucchini lengthwise into long, thin strands (or use a regular vegetable peeler to cut the zucchini lengthwise into thin ribbons). Add the zucchini noodles to the simmering soup and cook until just tender, about 2 minutes. Add the sliced steak and simmer until just cooked, 30 to 60 seconds. Ladle the soup into bowls and serve with the toppings of your choice.

Pineapple Beef Kabobs

Prep time: 25 minutes | Cook time: 10 minutes

Serves 4

2 pounds (907 g) lean beef steak (sirloin, flank, strip), cut into 1-inch pieces
¼ cup unsweetened pineapple juice
3 tablespoons coconut aminos
2 tablespoons fresh lemon juice
1 serrano chile pepper, seeded and thinly sliced
2 teaspoons grated

fresh ginger
1 clove garlic, minced
¼ teaspoon salt
¼ teaspoon black pepper
1 small pineapple, peeled, cored, and cut into 1½-inch chunks
2 bell peppers, seeded and cut into 1½-inch pieces
1 onion, cut into 8 wedges

1. Place the steak in a resealable plastic bag or nonreactive bowl with a lid and add the pineapple juice, coconut aminos, lemon juice, serrano chile, ginger, garlic, salt, and black pepper. Toss the steak to coat thoroughly with the marinade. Seal the bag or cover the bowl and marinate the steak in the refrigerator for 1 to 24 hours.
2. If using wooden skewers, soak them in water for 30 minutes to 1 hour to prevent them from burning.
3. Remove the steak from the refrigerator 30 minutes before cooking. Preheat a grill to medium heat.
4. Drain the steak, reserving the marinade. Prepare the kabobs by threading the steak, pineapple, bell peppers, and onion onto the skewers, leaving a ¼-inch space between each piece. Brush the kabobs with the marinade.
5. Grill the kabobs over direct heat, brushing them with the marinade and turning them once or twice, for 8 to 12 minutes, until the vegetables are tender and steak is cooked to the desired doneness. Discard any remaining marinade.

Beef Stuffed Bell Peppers

Prep time: 20 minutes | Cook time: 30 minutes

Serves 2

4 red, yellow, or orange bell peppers (preferably round in shape)
3 tablespoons cooking fat
¼ cup finely chopped onion
2 cloves garlic, minced (or 1 teaspoon garlic powder)
4 kale leaves, stems removed, leaves finely chopped

1 pound (454 g) ground meat (beef, lamb, bison)
2 tablespoons tomato paste
¼ teaspoon cumin
¼ teaspoon chili powder
½ teaspoon salt
¼ teaspoon black pepper
1 cup finely chopped peeled winter squash (butternut, acorn, etc.)

1. Preheat the oven to 350ºF (180ºC). Line a deep baking dish with parchment paper.
2. With a paring knife, slice around the top of each bell pepper and gently pull up on the stem. Discard the seeded core. Place the peppers in the prepared dish. Bake for 10 minutes, until softened. Set aside.
3. Meanwhile, melt the cooking fat in a large skillet over medium heat and swirl to coat the bottom. When the fat is hot, add the onion and cook, stirring with a wooden spoon, until translucent, 2 to 3 minutes. Add the garlic and continue to cook until aromatic, about 1 minute. Add the kale and cook for 1 minute, stirring. Add the ground meat and cook, breaking up the meat with a spatula or wooden spoon and stirring it into the vegetables, for 2 to 3 minutes. Stir in the tomato paste, cumin, chili powder, salt, and pepper. Cook until the meat is mostly browned, 7 to 9 minutes. Stir in the squash and cook until the squash is slightly softened, 2 to 3 minutes.
4. Divide the meat and squash mixture evenly among the softened bell peppers. Return to the oven and bake for 10 minutes, until the peppers look wrinkly and the beef is slightly browned on top.

Basil Sirloin Medallions with Carrots

Prep time: 20 minutes | Cook time: 15 minutes
Serves 2

¼ cup coconut aminos
2 garlic cloves, finely chopped
1 teaspoon grated fresh ginger
1 teaspoon arrowroot starch
½ teaspoon fish sauce
1 to 2 tablespoons coconut oil
2 top sirloin medallions (8 ounces / 227 g total), thinly sliced against the grain
2 carrots, thinly sliced on an angle
2 celery stalks, thinly

sliced on an angle
2 scallions, white and green parts separated and thinly sliced on an angle
½ cup raw unsalted cashews
1 fresh Thai bird's-eye chile, finely chopped
1 cup loosely packed fresh basil leaves, coarsely chopped if large
Cauliflower rice or steamed jasmine rice, for serving

1. In a mason jar, combine the coconut aminos, garlic, ginger, arrowroot starch, and fish sauce. Seal the jar tightly and shake vigorously until the sauce is completely smooth. Set aside.
2. In a large wok or cast-iron skillet, melt the coconut oil over high heat. Add the beef and cook, undisturbed, until browned on the bottom, 2 to 3 minutes. Add the carrots, celery, scallion whites, cashews, and Thai chile and cook, stirring frequently, until the vegetables have softened slightly but retain some crunch, 4 to 5 minutes. Pour in the coconut aminos sauce and toss to coat. Cook until the sauce has reduced by one-quarter, about 4 minutes. If you find that the sauce is drying out too quickly, add 1 to 2 tablespoons water as needed.
3. Remove the pan from the heat and sprinkle in the basil and the scallion greens. Toss to combine and serve immediately over cauliflower rice.

Beef, Zucchini, and Mushroom Stir-Fry

Prep time: 20 minutes | Cook time: 15 minutes
Serves 2 to 4

2 top sirloin medallions (about 8 ounces / 227 g total), sliced very thinly against the grain
2 tablespoons avocado oil
1 cup thinly sliced cremini or white button mushrooms
½ yellow onion, sliced
Kosher salt, to taste
1 zucchini, sliced into half-moons
1 jalapeño, seeded

and thinly sliced (optional)
2 garlic cloves, thinly sliced
1 cup bean sprouts
¼ cup coconut aminos
½ teaspoon fish sauce
2 scallions, white and light green parts only, sliced into 2-inch pieces
1 tablespoon olive oil
1 tablespoon sesame seeds, for garnish

1. Pat the beef very dry with paper towels and set aside on a plate.
2. Heat a large stainless-steel sauté pan over medium heat for 5 minutes. Increase the heat to high, pour in the avocado oil, and heat until shimmering. Working in batches, add the beef and cook until browned, about 4 minutes, being careful not to overcrowd the pan. Transfer the cooked beef to a bowl and repeat to brown the remaining beef. You may notice that the beef bubbles and releases excess moisture as it browns; simply cook until it evaporates.
3. Reduce the heat to medium and add the mushrooms and onion. Season with salt and cook, stirring regularly to avoid burning, until softened, 3 to 4 minutes. Add the zucchini and jalapeño (if using) and cook, stirring, for 2 minutes. Add the garlic and cook, stirring, for 1 minute. Add the bean sprouts, coconut aminos, and fish sauce and cook, stirring occasionally, until the sauce has reduced by half, about 5 minutes.
4. Remove the pan from the heat. Return the beef to the pan and add the scallions and olive oil. Toss everything to coat. Garnish with the sesame seeds and serve immediately.

Onion-Braised Beef Brisket

Prep time: 15 minutes | Cook time: 4 hours

Serves 2

1 tablespoon salt
1 teaspoon black pepper
1½ pounds (680 g) beef brisket, trimmed
3 tablespoons cooking fat

½ medium onion, peeled and quartered
4 cloves garlic, peeled
2 sprigs fresh thyme
5 cups beef bone broth or water

1. Preheat the oven to 350°F (180°C).
2. Mix the salt and pepper in a small bowl and use to season the brisket evenly on both sides.
3. In a Dutch oven or deep flameproof roasting pan, melt the cooking fat over medium-high heat, coating the bottom of the pan. When the fat is hot, add the brisket and sear until golden brown, about 2 minutes on each side. Remove the brisket from the pan.
4. Reduce the heat to medium under the same pan and add the onion. Cook, scraping the bottom of the pot with a wooden spoon to prevent burning, until the onion is softened, 2 to 3 minutes. Add the garlic and cook until aromatic, about 1 minute. Add the thyme, broth or water, and brisket, increase the heat to medium-high, and bring to a boil.
5. Cover the pot, transfer to the oven, and bake, turning the meat after each hour, for 3½ to 4 hours, until the brisket is fork tender.
6. Transfer the brisket to a bowl and shred or slice thin, discarding the excess fat. Discard the thyme stems.
7. Ladle the cooking liquid, onions, and garlic from the pan into a food processor or blender. Blend the sauce completely. Place the pan back on the stovetop, return the sauce to the pan, and bring to a simmer over medium-high heat. Simmer until the sauce coats the back of a wooden spoon, about 5 minutes.
8. Serve the brisket warm with the sauce.

Tunisian Lamb and Squash Stew

Prep time: 30 minutes | Cook time: 7 hours

Serves 6

1½ pounds (680 g) ground lamb or ground beef
1 to 2 tablespoons harissa
1 teaspoon ground cumin
1 teaspoon ground coriander
½ teaspoon ground ginger
½ teaspoon ground turmeric
¼ teaspoon cayenne pepper
¼ teaspoon ground cinnamon
1 medium butternut squash (about 1½ pounds / 680 g), peeled, seeded, and cut into 1-inch cubes

1 medium green bell pepper, coarsely chopped
1 medium yellow onion, chopped
3 cloves garlic, minced
3 cups Whole Food-compliant beef broth
1 (14½-ounce / 411-g) can Whole Food-compliant fire-roasted diced tomatoes, undrained
⅓ cup unsulfured golden raisins
⅓ cup chopped fresh parsley
⅓ cup pine nuts, toasted
Lemon wedges, for serving

1. In a large skillet over medium heat, cook the lamb, breaking it up with a wooden spoon, until browned, about 5 minutes. Drain off the fat. Add the harissa, cumin, coriander, ginger, turmeric, cayenne, and cinnamon and stir until combined. Transfer the meat to a slow cooker. Stir in the squash, bell pepper, onion, and garlic. Pour the broth over all.
2. Cover and cook on low for 7 to 8 hours or on high for 3½ to 4 hours. Turn the slow cooker to high if using the low setting. Stir the tomatoes and raisins into the stew. Cover and cook for 10 minutes.
3. Serve, topped with the parsley and pine nuts and accompanied by lemon wedges.

Beef Short Ribs Braised with Mushrooms

Prep time: 30 minutes | Cook time: 2 hours
Serves 2

3 tablespoons extra-virgin olive oil
1 cup chopped carrots
½ cup thinly sliced celery
½ cup chopped onion
4 to 6 bone-in beef short ribs (1 to 1¼ pounds / 454 to 567 g total)
1 cup beef bone broth or Whole Food-compliant beef broth

¾ teaspoon salt
Black pepper, to taste
¼ cup dried porcini mushrooms
Boiling water
1 cup sliced cremini mushrooms
1 clove garlic, minced
2 teaspoons coconut aminos
1 teaspoon Whole Food-compliant coarse-grain mustard

1. Preheat the oven to 325°F (163°C).
2. Heat 1 tablespoon of the olive oil in a 3- to 4-quart brazier or oven-safe skillet over medium heat. Add the carrots, celery, and onion to the hot oil and cook, stirring occasionally, for 5 minutes. Use a slotted spoon to transfer the vegetables to a bowl. Add the short ribs to the pan. Brown the ribs, turning to brown all sides evenly. Spoon the vegetables around the ribs in the pan. Add ½ cup of the broth. Sprinkle the meat and vegetables with ½ teaspoon of the salt and pepper to taste. Bring to a boil. Cover the pan with the lid, transfer to the oven, and cook for 2 to 2½ hours, until the meat is very tender.
3. Place the dried mushrooms in a small bowl and add just enough boiling water to cover them. Let stand for 10 minutes. Drain the mushrooms in a fine-mesh sieve set over a bowl to catch the soaking liquid; set the liquid aside. Rinse the mushrooms well and chop them.
4. In a medium saucepan, heat the remaining 2 tablespoons oil over medium heat. Add the porcini and cremini mushrooms and cook, stirring occasionally, until tender and lightly browned, 6 to 8 minutes. Add the garlic and cook, stirring, for 1 minute more.
5. In a small bowl, whisk together the coconut aminos and mustard. Add the mustard mixture to the pan with the mushrooms. Stir in the remaining ½ cup broth and the mushroom soaking liquid. Bring to a boil. Reduce the heat to medium-low and simmer, uncovered, until the liquid has reduced slightly, 3 to 5 minutes. Add the remaining ¼ teaspoon salt and pepper to taste.
6. Transfer the ribs to a serving platter. Use a slotted spoon to transfer the vegetables to the pan with the mushrooms. Skim the fat off the top of the cooking juices in the brazier. Add the cooking juices to the mushroom mixture and bring just to a boil. Spoon the vegetables and sauce over the ribs to serve.

Black Pepper Beef and Cabbage Stir-Fry

Prep time: 10 minutes | Cook time: 6 hours
Serves 4

1½ pounds (680 g) beef stir-fry strips
2 cups thinly sliced onions
5 cloves garlic, minced
1 tablespoon minced fresh ginger
½ cup Whole Food-compliant beef broth or beef bone broth
2 teaspoons Red Boat fish sauce

1 teaspoon black pepper
1 (14-ounce / 397-g) bag packaged coleslaw mix (shredded cabbage and carrots)
½ teaspoon grated lime zest
1 tablespoon lime juice
Chopped fresh cilantro and/or basil (optional)

1. Combine the beef, onions, garlic, ginger, broth, fish sauce, and ½ teaspoon of the black pepper in a slow cooker. Cover and cook on low for 6 to 7 hours or on high for 3 to 4 hours.
2. Just before serving, stir in the remaining ½ teaspoon black pepper, the coleslaw mix, and the lime zest and juice. Top each serving with cilantro and/or basil, if desired.

Hearty Hamburger Soup

Prep time: 20 minutes | Cook time: 1 hour | Serves 6 to 8

1 tablespoon extra-virgin olive oil
1 pound (454 g) lean ground beef
3 celery stalks, diced (about 1½ cups)
3 carrots, diced (about 1½ cups)
1 red onion, diced
1 red bell pepper, diced
Kosher salt, to taste
4 garlic cloves, finely chopped
4 cups beef stock

1 (28-ounce / 794-g) can crushed tomatoes
3 yellow potatoes, peeled, if desired, and cubed
2 bay leaves
1 tablespoon fresh thyme leaves
½ teaspoon freshly ground black pepper, plus more as needed
2 cups frozen chopped green beans
½ cup thinly sliced dill pickles, for garnish

1. In a large Dutch oven or heavy-bottomed stockpot, heat the olive oil over medium-high heat. Working in batches, add the ground beef and cook, breaking up the meat with a wooden spoon as it cooks, until browned, 10 to 12 minutes. Using a slotted spoon, transfer the beef to a bowl and repeat to brown the remaining beef.
2. Discard all but 2 tablespoons of the rendered fat from the pot. Return the pot to medium heat and add the celery, carrots, onion, and bell pepper. Season with salt. Cook the vegetables for 2 to 3 minutes, using a wooden spoon to scrape up any browned bits from the bottom of the pot. Add the garlic and cook, stirring, for 1 minute.
3. Return the browned beef back to the pot and add the stock, crushed tomatoes, potatoes, bay leaves, thyme, pepper, and 2 cups water. Bring to a boil over high heat, then reduce the heat to medium-low, cover, and cook at a steady simmer, stirring occasionally to prevent burning, for 30 minutes. Add the green beans and cook until they are warmed through, 2 to 3 minutes. Taste and adjust the seasoning.
4. For best results, let the soup cool in the pot for about 30 minutes before serving. Ladle into individual bowls, top with slices of dill pickle, and serve.

Grilled Steaks with Garlic-Shallot Purée

Prep time: 15 minutes | Cook time: 25 minutes Serves 2

2 steaks (5 ounces / 142 g each) for grilling (sirloin, strip, rib eye, tenderloin)
1 teaspoon salt
1 teaspoon black pepper

2 cloves garlic, peeled
1 shallot, peeled
2 tablespoons extra-virgin olive oil
1 avocado, split lengthwise, pitted, and peeled

1. Remove the steaks from the refrigerator 30 minutes before cooking. Preheat a grill to high heat and the oven to 350ºF (180ºC). Line a baking sheet with foil.
2. Mix the salt and pepper in a small bowl and use two-thirds of the mixture to season the steaks.
3. Toss the garlic and shallot in 1 tablespoon of the olive oil and arrange on the prepared baking sheet. Season evenly with the remaining salt and pepper. Roast in the oven for 25 minutes, until the cloves are soft throughout. Transfer the garlic and shallots to a food processor, add the remaining 1 tablespoon olive oil, and purée. Transfer the purée to a dish, cover with foil to keep warm, and set aside.
4. Lay the steaks on the hot grill and sear for 2 to 3 minutes. The steaks should pull off easily when they are seared. Turn the steaks over and sear the other side, 1 to 2 minutes, or to desired doneness. Let the steaks rest for 5 to 10 minutes.
5. Meanwhile, sear the avocado halves pitted side down on the grill until lightly browned, 3 to 4 minutes.
6. Arrange the avocado and steaks on plates and top the steaks with the warm garlic and shallot purée.

Steak Fajita Bowls with Vegetables

Prep time: 20 minutes | Cook time: 10 minutes
Serves 4

Beef:

1 pound (454 g) flank steak or skirt steak, thinly sliced
1 teaspoon paprika
½ teaspoon salt
½ teaspoon dried oregano
½ teaspoon garlic powder

½ teaspoon ground cumin
¼ teaspoon black pepper
⅛ teaspoon cayenne pepper
1 tablespoon extra-virgin olive oil

Vegetables:

1 tablespoon extra-virgin olive oil
2 small red, green, and/or yellow bell peppers, cut into ½-inch strips
1 small red onion, halved and cut into ¼-inch slices
1 clove garlic, minced
1 (12-ounce / 340-g) package frozen riced cauliflower or 4 cups

raw riced cauliflower
¼ teaspoon salt
⅛ teaspoon black pepper
1 cup Whole Food-compliant guacamole
½ cup Whole Food-compliant salsa
¼ cup chopped fresh cilantro (optional)
Lime wedges (optional)

1. Make the beef: Place the beef in a medium bowl. In a small bowl, combine the paprika, salt, oregano, garlic powder, cumin, black pepper, and cayenne. Sprinkle the spice mixture over the beef and toss to coat. Let stand while cooking the vegetables.
2. Make the vegetables: In a large skillet, heat 1 table-spoon olive oil over medium heat. Add the bell peppers and onion. Cook, stirring frequently, until the vegetables are crisp-tender, 7 to 8 minutes. Stir in the garlic. Transfer the vegetables to a serving dish; cover to keep warm.
3. Meanwhile, prepare the cauliflower rice according to the package directions. Add the salt and pepper; stir to combine. Cover to keep warm.
4. In the same large skillet, heat 1 tablespoon olive oil over medium heat; add the beef. Cook, stirring frequently, 3 to 4 minutes or to desired doneness.
5. Spoon the cauliflower into four shallow serving bowls. Top with the vegetables, beef, guacamole, and salsa. If desired, sprinkle with cilantro and serve with lime wedges.

Sweet Potato Beef Chili

Prep time: 20 minutes | Cook time: 25 minutes
Serves 4

1 tablespoon olive oil
1 pound (454 g) ground beef, bison, or lamb
2 cups chopped onion
1 medium serrano chile, seeded and finely chopped
3 cloves garlic, minced
1 (28-ounce / 794-g) can Whole Food-compliant fire-roasted diced tomatoes, undrained
1 cup beef bone broth or Whole Food-compliant beef broth

1 large sweet potato, peeled and cut into ¾-inch chunks (about 2 cups)
1 cup chopped red bell pepper
2 tablespoons chili powder
½ teaspoon ground chipotle chile pepper
½ teaspoon salt, plus more as needed
Chopped fresh cilantro (optional)
Sliced green onions (optional)

1. Heat the olive oil in a large pot over medium-high heat. Add the ground beef, onion, serrano chile, and garlic and cook, stirring frequently and breaking up the meat with a wooden spoon, until the meat is browned, about 5 minutes.
2. Stir in the tomatoes with their juices, broth, sweet potato, bell pepper, chili powder, chipotle, and salt and bring to a boil. Reduce the heat to low, cover, and simmer, stirring occasionally, until the sweet potato is tender, 20 to 25 minutes. If desired, season with additional salt. Serve the chili topped with cilantro and green onions, if desired.

Beef and Broccoli Stir-Fry

Prep time: 15 minutes | Cook time: 15 minutes
Serves 4

2 tablespoons coconut aminos
1 tablespoon minced fresh ginger
4 cloves garlic, minced
¼ teaspoon salt
1 pound (454 g) boneless top sirloin steak, trimmed and cut against the grain into ⅛-inch slices
4 tablespoons olive oil
3 cups small broccoli florets
1 medium red onion, quartered and thinly sliced

1 cup packaged shredded carrots, or 2 medium carrots, shredded
1 cup low-sodium Whole Food-compliant beef broth or beef bone broth
2 teaspoons arrowroot
¼ to ½ teaspoon red pepper flakes
6 cups packaged shredded green cabbage
1 tablespoon sesame seeds, toasted

1. In a medium bowl, combine the coconut aminos, ginger, garlic, and salt. Add the beef and mix well. Let the beef stand at room temperature while cooking the vegetables.
2. In a large skillet, heat 1 tablespoon of the olive oil over medium-high heat. Add the broccoli, onion, and carrots. Cook, stirring, until the vegetables are crisp-tender, about 3 minutes. Transfer the vegetables to a bowl and set aside.
3. Add 1 tablespoon olive oil to the skillet. Add half the beef and cook, stirring, until slightly pink in the center, 2 to 3 minutes. Add to the bowl with the vegetables. Add 1 tablespoon olive oil to the skillet and cook the remaining beef, stirring, until slightly pink in center, 2 to 3 minutes. Return the vegetables and cooked beef to the skillet.
4. In a small bowl, whisk together the broth, arrowroot, and pepper flakes until smooth. Push the meat and vegetables to the edges of the skillet. Pour the broth mixture into the center. Cook over medium-high heat, stirring, until thickened, 1 to 2 minutes. Stir the meat and vegetables into the sauce. Transfer the stir-fry to a large serving bowl and cover to keep warm. Carefully wipe out the skillet with paper towels.
5. Add the remaining 1 tablespoon olive oil to the skillet and heat over medium-high heat. Add the cabbage and cook, stirring, until bright green and wilted, 1 to 2 minutes. Spoon the stir-fry over the cabbage, sprinkle with the sesame seeds, and serve.

Tender Pot Roast

Prep time: 15 minutes | Cook time: 6 to 8 hours
Serves 2

1½ pounds (680 g) beef roast (chuck, boneless short ribs, brisket, top round, rump)
1 teaspoon salt
½ teaspoon black pepper
1 onion, sliced
3 carrots, unpeeled and cut into 2-inch

pieces
3 stalks celery, cut into 1-inch pieces
1 small butternut squash, peeled and large-diced
2 cloves garlic
2 sprigs thyme
2 cups beef broth or water

1. Set your slow cooker to low heat, and season your roast with the salt and pepper.
2. Add the beef roast, onions, carrots, celery, butternut squash, garlic, and thyme sprigs to the slow cooker. Top with the broth or water (or enough to cover the roast halfway) and leave the roast to cook for 6 to 8 hours. The roast should be fork-tender when done.
3. Remove the roast, transfer to a large plate or serving dish, and cover with foil. Allow the meat to rest for 15 minutes before serving.
4. Remove the thyme springs from the broth and discard. Slice the roast against the grain. Divide the meat and vegetables on individual plates, and ladle broth over the top.

Classic Borscht

Prep time: 25 minutes | Cook time: 3 hours
Serves 8 to 10

2 pounds (907 g) cross-cut beef short ribs, cut into pieces between the bones
3 bay leaves
Kosher salt, to taste
1 teaspoon whole black peppercorns
2 tablespoons avocado oil
1½ pounds (680 g) beets, grated
3 carrots, grated
1 yellow onion, coarsely chopped
1 (6-ounce / 170-g) can tomato paste

2 pounds (907 g) white potatoes, peeled and cut into 2-inch cubes
1 large parsnip, peeled and diced
1 small green cabbage, thinly sliced
Juice of 1 lemon, plus more if needed
Freshly ground black pepper, to taste
¼ cup loosely packed fresh dill leaves, coarsely chopped
¼ cup loosely packed fresh parsley leaves, coarsely chopped

1. In a very large stockpot or Dutch oven, combine the ribs, bay leaves, 2 tablespoons salt, and the peppercorns. Add enough water to cover the ribs and bring to a boil over high heat. Reduce the heat to maintain a steady simmer, cover, and cook, skimming off any foam that rises to the surface, until the meat is falling off the bone, 1½ to 2 hours.
2. While the ribs cook, in a 4-quart stockpot, heat the avocado oil over medium heat. Add the beets, carrots, and onion and season with a pinch of salt. Cook, stirring often, until the vegetables are tender, about 12 minutes. Add the tomato paste and cook, stirring to coat the vegetables, until thickened, about 3 minutes. Remove from the heat and set aside.
3. When the ribs are tender and the meat is falling off the bone, add the potatoes and parsnip to the pot and cook until fork-tender, about 25 minutes. Reduce the heat to low, stir in the beet-carrot mixture, and cook until the broth has turned red, about 10 minutes. Add the cabbage and lemon juice and cook until the cabbage is slightly softened, about 10 minutes.
4. Taste the borscht and season with salt, pepper, or lemon juice as desired (it should taste sweet and sour). Remove from the heat and stir in the dill and parsley. Let the soup stand for 10 minutes before serving.

Mici

Prep time: 5 minutes | Cook time: 8 minutes
Serves 4 or 5

2 pounds (907 g) lean ground beef
1 pound (454 g) ground pork
½ cup carbonated mineral water
4 garlic cloves, minced
1 tablespoon kosher salt, plus more for seasoning
2 teaspoons baking soda
1 teaspoon dried oregano
1 teaspoon freshly ground black pepper
¼ cup Dijon mustard, for serving

1. In a large bowl, combine the ground beef, ground pork, carbonated water, garlic, salt, baking soda, oregano, and pepper. Use your hands to thoroughly mix until the mixture is tacky and well combined. Test the seasoning by frying a tablespoon of the mixture in a dry nonstick skillet over medium-high heat. Taste the cooked portion and season the raw mixture with salt as needed. Cover the bowl with plastic wrap and refrigerate for at least 6 hours or up to overnight.
2. Line a baking sheet with parchment paper. Using your hands, form small, log-shaped kebabs approximately 3½ inches long and 1 inch thick, placing them on the baking sheet as you form them.
3. Heat a grill to medium-high (a charcoal grill is ideal, though gas is fine, too) or heat a cast-iron grill pan over medium-high heat. Grill the mici until browned and cooked through, 3 to 4 minutes per side.
4. Serve immediately, with toothpicks for picking up the mici and mustard for dipping.

Catalina Beef Tacos

Prep time: 10 minutes | Cook time: 1½ hours
Serves 4 to 6

1⅔ cups chicken stock
1 dried ancho chile
1 dried New Mexico chile
1 tablespoon avocado oil
2 pounds (907 g) ground beef (80 to 85% lean ground beef is preferred but leaner ground beef will work as well)
1 yellow onion, diced

¾ teaspoon kosher salt, plus more as needed
5 garlic cloves, finely chopped
1 tablespoon granulated onion
1 teaspoon hot paprika
1 teaspoon ground cumin
1 teaspoon dried oregano, preferably Mexican

1. In a small saucepan, combine the stock, ancho chile, and New Mexico chile. Bring to a boil over high heat, remove from the heat, and cover with a lid. Let the chiles soak until soft, about 15 minutes. Stem and seed the chiles and transfer the flesh to a high-speed blender. Add the stock and blend on high until very smooth. Set aside.
2. In a large sauté pan or Dutch oven, heat the avocado oil over medium-high heat. Working in batches, add the ground beef and cook, breaking up the meat with a wooden spoon as it cooks, until browned, about 12 minutes. Use a slotted spoon to transfer the browned meat to a bowl and repeat to brown the remaining meat.
3. Discard all but 2 tablespoons of the fat from the pan. Return the pan to medium heat and add the onion and ¼ teaspoon of the salt. Cook, scraping up any browned bits from the bottom of the pan, until the onion is soft and translucent, 3 to 4 minutes. Add the garlic and cook, stirring, for 1 minute. Add the granulated onion, paprika, cumin, oregano, and remaining ½ teaspoon salt and cook, stirring, for 1 minute more.
4. Add the beef and the puréed chile mixture to the pan and toss to coat. Bring the mixture to a simmer, reduce the heat to low, cover, and cook, stirring occasionally, for at least 30 minutes or up to 1½ hours for a more concentrated flavor. Taste and adjust the salt before serving.

Mongolian Beef and Mixed Greens

Prep time: 12 minutes | Cook time: 8 minutes
Serves 4

2 tablespoons coconut aminos
1 tablespoon Red Boat fish sauce
2 teaspoons olive oil
1 pound (454 g) beef sirloin tips, skirt steak, or boneless short ribs, thinly sliced
1 piece (3 inches) fresh ginger, peeled and cut into matchsticks
2 fresh red chile

peppers, seeded and cut into matchsticks or thinly sliced (optional)
3 cloves garlic, minced
3 green onions, cut into 3-inch lengths, white and green parts separated
4 tablespoons clarified butter, ghee, or coconut oil
1 (5-ounce / 142-g) container mixed greens

1. Combine the coconut aminos, fish sauce, and olive oil in a large bowl. Add the beef and turn to coat. Cover the bowl and marinate in the refrigerator for 15 to 20 minutes.
2. Meanwhile, in a small bowl, combine the ginger, chile peppers, garlic, and white parts of the green onions.
3. In a large skillet, melt 1 tablespoon of the butter over medium heat. Add the beef and marinade to the skillet and cook, tossing with tongs occasionally, until no longer pink, 4 to 5 minutes. Transfer the meat and sauce to a bowl.
4. In the same skillet, heat the remaining 3 tablespoons butter. Add the ginger mixture and cook over medium heat, stirring, until fragrant, 1 to 2 minutes. Add the meat and green parts of green onions to the skillet; toss to combine.
5. Serve the beef and sauce over the mixed greens.

Indian Pepper Steak Stir-Fry

Prep time: 15 minutes | Cook time: 10 minutes

Serves 4

1 tablespoon Whole Food-compliant garam masala
½ teaspoon garlic salt
2 tablespoons coconut oil
1 medium onion, cut into thin wedges
2 large yellow and/or red bell peppers, cut into strips
1½ pounds (680 g) strip steak, flank steak, or skirt steak, cut into strips
2 teaspoons minced fresh ginger
Fresh cilantro, for serving

1. In a small bowl, stir together 3 tablespoons water, the garam masala, and garlic salt; set aside.
2. Heat 1 tablespoon of the oil in a large skillet over medium-high heat. Add the onion and cook, stirring, for 1 minute. Add the bell pepper and cook, stirring, until beginning to soften but still crisp, about 3 minutes. Transfer the onion and pepper to a plate and cover to keep warm.
3. In the same skillet, heat the remaining 1 tablespoon oil over medium-high heat. Add the meat and ginger and cook, stirring, until meat is desired doneness 1 to 2 minutes. Stir in the onion and pepper and heat through, about 1 minute. Garnish with the cilantro and serve.

Grilled Skirt Steak

Prep time: 10 minutes | Cook time: 10 minutes

Serves 2

2 tablespoons fresh lime juice
2 tablespoons finely chopped onion
1 tablespoon plus 2 teaspoons extra-virgin olive oil
2 teaspoons finely chopped fresh ginger
3 cloves garlic, minced
½ teaspoon coarse salt
¼ teaspoon black pepper
1 (12-ounce / 340-g) beef skirt or scored flank steak
16 cherry tomatoes
1 cup fresh cilantro leaves
½ cup fresh parsley leaves
2 tablespoons fresh oregano leaves
¼ cup avocado oil or extra-virgin olive oil
2 teaspoons red wine vinegar
¼ teaspoon red pepper flakes
Lettuce leaves, for serving (optional)

1. In a shallow dish, combine the lime juice, onion, 1 tablespoon of the olive oil, the ginger, one-third of the garlic, ⅛ teaspoon of the salt, and ⅛ teaspoon of the black pepper. Add the steak and turn to coat. Cover and marinate in the refrigerator for 1 to 4 hours, turning the meat occasionally.
2. If using wooden skewers, soak them in water to cover for 30 minutes to 1 hour to prevent them from burning.
3. In a medium bowl, combine the tomatoes, remaining 2 teaspoons olive oil, ⅛ teaspoon of the salt, and remaining ⅛ teaspoon black pepper. Toss to coat. Thread the tomatoes evenly on two 10- to 12-inch skewers, leaving ¼ inch of space between the tomatoes.
4. Preheat a grill to medium heat. Remove the steak from the marinade and discard the marinade. Grill the steak over direct heat until the internal temperature reaches 145 to 150°F (63 to 66°C), 10 to 12 minutes for skirt steak or 15 to 17 minutes for flank steak. Grill the tomatoes for 4 to 6 minutes, or until softened and browned. Remove the steak and tomatoes from the grill. Cover the steak with aluminum foil and let rest for 5 minutes.
5. Meanwhile, in a food processor or blender, combine the cilantro, parsley, avocado oil, oregano, vinegar, remaining ⅛ teaspoon salt, the red pepper flakes, and remaining garlic. Process or blend until the mixture is well combined and finely chopped, but not completely smooth.
6. Thinly slice the steak across the grain. Serve on plates with the tomatoes. Spoon the cilantro sauce evenly over all. If desired, serve with lettuce leaves to make lettuce wraps. (Use any leftover cilantro sauce on your morning eggs.)

Thyme Lamb Chops and Fingerlings

Prep time: 10 minutes | Cook time: 25 minutes
Serves 2

Chops:

4 lamb loin or rib chops (about 1 pound / 454 g)	2 teaspoons snipped fresh thyme
1 clove garlic, halved	Coarse salt and black pepper, to taste

Potatoes:

6 fingerling potatoes	virgin olive oil
Coarse salt, to taste	Black pepper, to taste
1 tablespoon extra-	

Pesto:

2 cups packed arugula	1 tablespoon fresh lemon juice
½ cup almonds, toasted	1 clove garlic, minced
½ cup walnut oil or extra-virgin olive oil	¼ teaspoon coarse salt
1 teaspoon grated lemon zest	⅛ teaspoon cayenne pepper

1. Preheat a grill to medium heat.
2. Make the chops: Trim the fat from the chops. Rub both sides of the chops with the garlic. Lightly season the chops with the thyme and salt and black pepper to taste, rubbing in the seasoning with your fingers. Let stand at room temperature while you prepare the potatoes and pesto.
3. Make the potatoes: Put the potatoes in a large saucepan with enough water to cover. Lightly salt the water. Bring to a boil and cook until the potatoes can be pierced with the tip of a knife but are not completely tender, 9 to 10 minutes. Drain. When cool enough to handle, cut the potatoes in half lengthwise and toss with the olive oil and salt and black pepper to taste.
4. Make the pesto: In a food processor, combine the arugula, almonds, walnut oil, lemon zest and juice, garlic, salt, and cayenne. Process until smooth.
5. Grease the grill rack. Place the chops and potatoes on the greased rack over direct heat. Cover and grill the chops, turning once, for 12 to 14 minutes for medium-rare (145ºF / 63ºC) or 15 to 17 minutes for medium (160ºF / 71ºC). Grill the potatoes, turning once, for 10 minutes, or until they are tender and have grill marks.
6. Serve the lamb chops with the pesto and grilled potatoes.

Asian Beef with Mushrooms and Snow Peas

Prep time: 25 minutes | Cook time: 7 hours
Serves 4

1 large sweet onion, halved and cut lengthwise into thin wedges	aminos
	4 cloves garlic, minced
	2 tablespoons grated fresh ginger
1 green bell pepper, thinly sliced lengthwise	1 teaspoon olive oil
1 boneless beef arm roast (2½ to 3 pounds / 1.1 to 1.4 kg), trimmed	2 cups snow peas, trimmed
	8 ounces (227 g) shiitake mushrooms, stemmed and sliced
Salt and black pepper, to taste	1 bunch green onions, white and green parts, cut into 1-inch pieces
3 tablespoons coconut	

1. In a slow cooker, combine the onion and bell pepper. Season the beef with salt and pepper and add to the slow cooker. In a small bowl, combine the coconut aminos, garlic, ginger, and olive oil. Drizzle over the beef.
2. Cover and cook on low for 7 to 8 hours or on high for 3½ to 4 hours, or until tender. Remove the roast from the cooker. Cover with foil to keep warm.
3. Turn the slow cooker to high if using the low setting. Stir the snow peas, mushrooms, and green onions into the slow cooker. Cover and cook until the snow peas are crisp-tender and mushrooms are softened, 10 to 20 minutes. Slice or shred the beef and serve with the vegetables and mushrooms.

Authentic Picadillo

Prep time: 20 minutes | Cook time: 1 hour | Serves 6 to 8

1 tablespoon avocado oil
2 pounds (907 g) lean ground beef
1 large yellow onion, thinly sliced
1 red bell pepper, diced
5 garlic cloves, finely chopped
2 teaspoons smoked Spanish paprika
2 teaspoons ancho chile powder
1 teaspoon ground cumin
1 teaspoon dried oregano
1 teaspoon kosher salt, plus more as needed
1 teaspoon freshly ground black pepper, plus more as needed
1½ cups chicken stock
1½ cups sliced pitted green olives, such as Manzanilla
¼ cup no-sugar-added dark raisins (optional)
2 bay leaves

1. In a large Dutch oven or heavy-bottomed pot, heat the avocado oil over medium-high heat. Working in batches, add the ground beef and cook, breaking it up with your spoon as it cooks, until browned, about 12 minutes. Transfer the beef to a bowl and repeat to cook the remaining meat.
2. Discard all but 2 tablespoons of the rendered fat from the pot and set it over medium heat. Add the onion and bell pepper and cook, stirring, until the onion is slightly caramelized, 8 to 10 minutes. Add the garlic and cook, stirring, until fragrant, about 1 minute. Add the paprika, ancho chile powder, cumin, oregano, salt, and black pepper. Stir, letting the spices warm and toast, for 1 minute. Add the stock and stir, using your spoon to scrape up any browned bits from the bottom of the pot.
3. Return the beef to the pot and add the olives, raisins (if using), and bay leaves. Increase the heat to medium-high and bring the sauce to a simmer. Reduce the heat to low, cover, and cook, stirring occasionally to prevent burning, until the beef is tender, at least 30 minutes or up to 1 hour for a more intensely flavored finished product.

Taste and season with additional salt and pepper as desired. Discard the bay leaves. Let stand 10 minutes before serving.

Lamb Loaves with Apricots and Cauliflower

Prep time: 15 minutes | Cook time: 45 minutes Serves 4

12 unsulphured dried apricots, finely chopped
6 cups bite-sized cauliflower florets
2 tablespoons olive oil
2 teaspoons salt
1 large egg, lightly beaten
⅓ cup chopped green onion
2 tablespoons chopped fresh cilantro
2 ¼ teaspoons chili powder
1½ pounds (680 g) lean ground lamb or lean ground beef
1 tablespoon balsamic vinegar

1. Preheat the oven to 375ºF (190ºC). Line a rimmed baking pan with parchment paper.
2. Place the apricots in a small saucepan and add enough water to cover. Bring to a boil. Remove from the heat and let stand while preparing the cauliflower.
3. In a large bowl, toss together the cauliflower, olive oil, and ½ teaspoon of the salt. Arrange on one end of the pan and bake for 10 minutes. Remove from the oven and stir.
4. Meanwhile, using the same bowl, stir together the egg, green onion, cilantro, chili powder, and remaining 1½ teaspoons salt. Drain the apricots well. Add the drained apricots and lamb to the egg mixture and gently mix well. Divide the lamb mixture into four equal portions. Shape each portion into a 4 × 2-inch loaf. Place the loaves on the other end of the pan. Bake, stirring the cauliflower once, until the cauliflower is tender and the internal temperature of the meat loaves is 160ºF (71ºC), 30 to 35 minutes.
5. Drizzle the lamb loaves with the balsamic vinegar and serve with the cauliflower.

Rosemary Beef Eye of Round Roast

Prep time: 5 minutes | Cook time: 3 hours
Serves 6

1 (2½-pound / 1.1-kg) beef eye of round roast	1 teaspoon chopped fresh rosemary
3 tablespoons extra-virgin olive oil	½ teaspoon dried oregano
2 teaspoons kosher salt	5 garlic cloves, smashed and unpeeled
1 teaspoon freshly ground black pepper	1 cup chicken stock

1. Preheat the oven to 500°F (260°C).
2. Put the beef in a roasting pan. Thoroughly coat with the olive oil, rolling it around to completely cover. Season the beef with the salt, pepper, rosemary, and oregano. Remove the beef from the pan and set aside.
3. Set a roasting rack securely in the pan and spread the unpeeled garlic cloves over the bottom of the pan. Pour ½ cup of the stock into the pan, then put the beef on the rack.
4. Transfer to the oven and reduce the oven temperature to 475°F (245°C). Roast for 12½ minutes if you prefer medium-rare, or about 16 minutes for medium. (In case your roast is not exactly 2½ pounds (1.1 kg), the calculation is 5 minutes per pound for medium-rare and closer to 6½ minutes per pound for medium.) Turn off the oven and leave the beef in the (turned-off) oven to slowly cook for 2½ hours more.
5. Remove the beef from the oven and transfer it to a cutting board to rest for 30 minutes.
6. Set the roasting pan on the stovetop over low heat. Add the remaining ½ cup stock and stir, scraping up all the caramelized bits from the bottom of the pan. Transfer the liquid to a small saucepan and set aside.
7. Slice as much of the beef as needed for serving. Pour any juices from the cutting board into the saucepan, stir, and warm the jus over medium heat.
8. Pour the jus over the sliced meat and serve. To keep it juicy, store the leftover piece of beef whole, not sliced.

Hot Roast Beef

Prep time: 30 minutes | Cook time: 8 hours
Serves 6

1 beef arm roast (2½ to 3 pounds / 1.1 to 1.4 kg)	2-inch chunks
6 cloves garlic, peeled	1 (8-ounce / 227-g) package button mushrooms, halved
½ teaspoon dried rosemary	1 medium yellow onion, sliced
1 teaspoon salt	2 tablespoons tapioca flour
¼ teaspoon black pepper	¼ teaspoon garlic powder
2 pounds (907 g) russet potatoes, peeled and cut into	2 tablespoons clarified butter or ghee

1. Cut three slits each into the top and bottom of the roast. Insert a garlic clove into each slit. In a small bowl, combine the rosemary, salt, and pepper. Sprinkle on both sides of roast. Place the roast in a slow cooker with ¼ cup water. Add the potatoes, mushrooms, and onion.
2. Cover and cook on low for 8 to 10 hours or on high for 4 to 5 hours. Transfer the beef to a cutting board or platter. Cover and keep warm. Transfer the potatoes to a large bowl.
3. Turn the slow cooker to high if using the low setting. In a small bowl, stir together the tapioca flour and 2 tablespoons water. Pour into the slow cooker. Cook, stirring occasionally, until the gravy has thickened, about 5 minutes.
4. Meanwhile, sprinkle the potatoes with the garlic powder; add the butter. Use a potato masher or fork to mash the potatoes to your desired consistency.
5. Serve the roast over the mashed potatoes, with gravy ladled over the top.

Thai Coconut Beef Curry with Green Beans

Prep time: 25 minutes | Cook time: 7 hours
Serves 4

1 tablespoon coconut oil, plus more as needed
2 pounds (907 g) charcoal steak, cut into 1-inch cubes
1 teaspoon coarse salt
½ teaspoon black pepper
1 yellow onion, sliced

3 cloves garlic, minced
1 (14-ounce / 397-g) can full-fat coconut milk
3 tablespoons Whole Food-compliant Thai red curry paste
2 teaspoons Red Boat fish sauce
1 pound (454 g) fresh green beans, trimmed

1. Heat the coconut oil in a heavy skillet over medium-high heat. Season the steak with the salt and pepper. Add the beef to the skillet and cook, stirring occasionally, until browned on all sides, about 5 minutes. Place the meat in a slow cooker.
2. Cook the onion in the same skillet, adding additional coconut oil if needed. Cook, stirring, until the onion is soft, 4 to 5 minutes. Add the garlic and cook, stirring, until fragrant, about 30 seconds. Add the coconut milk and curry paste, stirring to scrape up any brown bits from the bottom of the skillet. Stir in the fish sauce. Transfer to the slow cooker.
3. Cover and cook on low for 7 to 8 hours or on high for 3½ to 4 hours. Add the green beans and cook on high for 30 minutes more, until the beans are crisp-tender.

Balsamic Roast Beef and Veggies

Prep time: 30 minutes | Cook time: 5½ hours
Serves 4

1 tablespoon coconut oil
1½ to 2 pounds (680 to 907 g) boneless chuck roast or bottom round, cut into 1½-inch cubes
Salt and black pepper, to taste
1 pound (454 g) large carrots, peeled and cut into 1-inch pieces
1 pound (454 g) parsnips, peeled and cut into ½-inch pieces
1 pound (454 g) small red potatoes, halved

1 medium onion, chopped
1 clove garlic, minced
2 cups Whole Food-compliant beef broth or beef bone broth
¼ cup balsamic vinegar
2 teaspoons Whole Food-compliant dried Italian seasoning
Chopped fresh parsley (optional)

1. Heat the coconut oil in a large heavy skillet over medium-high heat. Season the beef lightly with salt and pepper. Add the beef to the skillet and cook, stirring occasionally, until browned on all sides, about 5 minutes. Place the beef in a slow cooker with the carrots, parsnips, and potatoes.
2. Add the onion to the same skillet and add additional coconut oil if needed. Cook, stirring frequently, until the onion is soft, 4 to 5 minutes. Add the garlic and cook, stirring, until fragrant, about 30 seconds. Add the broth, vinegar, and Italian seasoning and stir to scrape up any brown bits on the bottom of the skillet. Transfer to the slow cooker.
3. Cover and cook on low for 5½ to 6 hours or on high for 3 hours. Top servings with parsley, if desired.

Cuban-Style Beef and Peppers

Prep time: 10 minutes | Cook time: 8 hours
Serves 4

3 cloves garlic, minced
2 teaspoons dried oregano
1 teaspoon ground cumin
1 teaspoon salt
½ teaspoon black pepper
1 boneless beef chuck roast (2 pounds / 907 g)

2 large red bell peppers, seeded, cored, and sliced
2 medium yellow onions, cut into 6 wedges each
¼ cup orange juice
¼ cup lime juice
1 avocado, halved, pitted, peeled, and sliced

1. In a small bowl, combine the garlic, oregano, cumin, salt, and black pepper. Rub the spice mixture onto both sides of the roast.
2. In a slow cooker, layer the peppers and onions. Pour the juices over the vegetables. Place the roast on the vegetables. Cover and cook on low for 8 to 10 hours or on high for 4 to 5 hours.
3. Using a slotted spoon, transfer the meat to a cutting board. Using a slotted spoon, remove the peppers and onions and set aside. Strain the cooking liquid and set aside. Use two forks to shred the meat; return to the slow cooker. Stir in the onions, peppers, and ½ cup of the cooking liquid. Serve the meat and vegetables with the avocado.

Beef Brisket Braised with Potatoes

Prep time: 20 minutes | Cook time: 10 hours
Serves 6

1 tablespoon Whole Food-compliant coarse-grain mustard
3 cloves garlic, minced
1 teaspoon caraway seeds, crushed
½ teaspoon coarse salt
¼ teaspoon black pepper
2 to 2½ pounds (907 g to 1.1 kg) beef brisket, trimmed

1 to 1¼ pounds (454 to 567 g) 2- to 3-inch Yukon gold potatoes, scrubbed and halved
1 medium onion, cut into thin wedges
1 small head cabbage, cored and cut into 8 wedges
2 tablespoons cider vinegar
1 tablespoon clarified butter or ghee
1½ teaspoons snipped fresh dill

1. In a small bowl, combine the mustard, garlic, caraway seeds, salt, and pepper. Spread all over brisket. Place the potatoes, onion, and ½ cup water in a slow cooker. Lay the brisket on top of the vegetables. Cover and cook on low for 10 to 11 hours or on high for 5 to 5½ hours.
2. Turn the slow cooker to high if using the low setting. Add the cabbage to the slow cooker. Cover and cook until tender, about 30 minutes.
3. Transfer the brisket and vegetables to a serving platter. Skim the fat from the cooking juices; add the vinegar, butter, and dill. Whisk until well combined. Drizzle the liquid over the beef and vegetables and serve.

Beef Stroganoff with Coconut Cream

Prep time: 15 minutes | Cook time: 15 minutes
Serves 2

Coconut Sour Cream:

1 (13½-ounce / 383-g) can full-fat coconut milk, unshaken and refrigerated overnight

Juice of 1 lemon, plus more if needed

Stroganoff:

2 tablespoons avocado oil

½ pound (227 g) beef steak (such as top sirloin medallions, top sirloin, flank, flat iron, or even tenderloin), cut into thin strips

1 tablespoon ghee

1 cup thinly sliced cremini or white button mushrooms

Kosher salt, to taste

1 shallot, thinly sliced

3 garlic cloves, thinly sliced

½ cup chicken stock

1 tablespoon whole-grain or Dijon mustard

Freshly ground black pepper, to taste

2 tablespoons finely chopped fresh dill, plus more for garnish

1. Make the coconut sour cream: Without shaking the can, carefully open it and spoon the solidified white cream into a medium bowl (save the coconut water left in the can, if you'd like). Add the lemon juice to the coconut cream and whisk until smooth and creamy. Taste and add more lemon juice, if desired. Cover the bowl with plastic wrap and refrigerate until ready to use. (The coconut sour cream will keep in the refrigerator for up to 5 days.)
2. Make the stroganoff: In a large stainless-steel or cast-iron skillet, heat the avocado oil over high heat. Add the steak and cook, undisturbed, until browned on the first side, 2 to 3 minutes. Flip the steak slices and cook for 1 minute, until lightly browned. Transfer the browned steak to a bowl.
3. Reduce the heat to medium and add the ghee to the pan. When it has melted, add the mushrooms and season with salt. Cook, stirring, until the mushrooms have browned and any moisture they release has evaporated, 4 to 5 minutes. Add the shallot and garlic and cook, scraping up any browned bits from the bottom of the pan, for 2 to 3 minutes. Pour in the stock and stir, scraping up any stubborn browned bits, and cook until the stock has reduced by one-quarter, about 1 minute.
4. Add 1 cup of the coconut sour cream (reserve the rest for another use), the mustard, and a pinch of pepper and stir to combine. Gently simmer the sauce for 2 to 3 minutes, reducing the heat if needed to maintain a simmer. Taste and adjust the seasoning as desired. Return the beef to the pan and toss to coat with the sauce. Remove the pan from the heat, sprinkle in the dill, and toss once more to combine. Garnish with more dill and serve immediately.

Mushroom Stuffed Beef Roulade

Prep time: 25 minutes | Cook time: 25 minutes

Serves 4

5 tablespoons extra-virgin olive oil

8 ounces (227 g) cremini mushrooms, finely chopped

1 cup finely chopped red onion

½ cup finely chopped red bell pepper

4 cloves garlic, minced

1 tablespoon chopped fresh oregano

¾ cup chopped fresh basil

1 tablespoon almond flour

1 teaspoon grated lemon zest

1 teaspoon salt

1 pound (454 g) green beans, trimmed

½ teaspoon red pepper flakes

1 beef sirloin or round steak (1¼ to 1½ pounds / 567 to 680 g)

2 tablespoons Whole Food-compliant tomato paste

1 cup beef bone broth or Whole Food-compliant beef broth

1. Preheat the oven to 400ºF (205ºC).
2. Heat 1 tablespoon of the olive oil in a large skillet over medium-high heat. Add the mushrooms and cook, stirring occasionally, until lightly browned, about 3 minutes. Add ½ cup of the onion and the bell pepper. Cook, stirring occasionally, until the onion is tender, 3 minutes. Add half the garlic and the oregano. Cook, stirring, for 1 minute more. Remove from the heat and stir in ½ cup of the basil, the almond flour, lemon zest, and ½ teaspoon of the salt. Transfer the mushroom mixture to a bowl and set aside to cool slightly. Rinse and dry the skillet.
3. Trim away any excess fat from the edges of the steak. Place the steak on a work surface. With the notched edge of a meat mallet, pound the steak to about ¼ inch thick. Spread the mushroom mixture over the steak to within ½ inch of the edges. Starting on a long side, roll up the meat and tie it with 100% cotton kitchen string.
4. In a medium bowl, combine the green beans, 2 tablespoons of the oil, the remaining garlic, and the remaining ½ teaspoon salt and toss. Spread the beans evenly on a large baking sheet. Roast for 18 to 20 minutes, until the beans are lightly browned and crisp-tender.
5. In the same skillet, heat the remaining 2 tablespoons olive oil over medium-high heat. Sear the meat in the hot oil and cook, turning occasionally, to sear evenly on all sides. Remove the meat from the skillet. Add the remaining ½ cup onion to the skillet. Cook, stirring, until softened, about 5 minutes. Stir in the tomato paste, then whisk in the broth. Bring the broth to a boil. Return the meat to the skillet and spoon some of the sauce over the meat. Cover and reduce the heat to medium-low. Simmer gently, turning once, until the internal temperature of the roulade is 160ºF (71ºC), 8 to 10 minutes. Sprinkle with the remaining ¼ cup basil.
6. Transfer the roulade to a cutting board and let rest for 5 to 10 minutes. Remove the string and cut into ½-inch-thick slices. Serve the meat and sauce with the green beans.

Seared Sirloin Steak

Prep time: 10 minutes | Cook time: 40 minutes
Serves 4

1 pound (454 g) asparagus
1 pound (454 g) sirloin steak
2 teaspoons kosher salt
½ teaspoon freshly ground black pepper
5 tablespoons plus 2 teaspoons extra-virgin

olive oil
1 pound (454 g) brown mushrooms, trimmed
and quartered lengthwise
2 teaspoons coconut aminos

1. Preheat the oven to 400ºF (205ºC).
2. Cut off the woody stems of the asparagus. Peel the rough ends and, with your knife at a 45-degree angle to the cutting board, cut each stalk into thirds. Set aside.
3. Thoroughly season the steak with 1 teaspoon of the salt and the pepper.
4. Heat a large oven-safe skillet (I use heavy-duty cast iron) over high heat. Add 2 tablespoons of the olive oil, being sure to coat the bottom of the pan. Reduce the heat to medium-high and add the steak to the skillet. Cook until well browned on the first side, about 3 minutes. Flip and brown the other side for 1 minute. Transfer the skillet to the oven and cook the steak until medium-rare, about 4 minutes (or 3 to 4 minutes longer, if you prefer medium). Remove the skillet from the oven and transfer the steak to a wooden board, reserving the juice from the skillet. Partially tent the steak with aluminum foil and let rest for 15 minutes.
5. Return the skillet to medium-high heat. Add half the mushrooms, season with ⅛ teaspoon of the salt, and add 1 tablespoon of the olive oil, if needed. Cook, stirring, for 2 minutes, then cover and cook until they have released liquid and look shiny, about 2 minutes more. Transfer the mushrooms, along with all the juices from the skillet, to a bowl and set aside. Add 1 tablespoon of the olive oil, the remaining mushrooms, and ⅛ teaspoon of the salt to the pan and cook the same way as the first batch.
6. In the same skillet, heat 1 tablespoon plus 2 teaspoons of the olive oil over medium heat. Add the asparagus and ½ teaspoon of the salt and cook for 4 minutes, stirring once halfway through. Stir again, cover, and cook for 2 minutes more. Stir again and cook, uncovered, until the asparagus is soft and cooked through, about 4 minutes more.
7. Turn off the heat and add the steak jus, mushrooms and all their juices, and the coconut aminos to the skillet with the asparagus. Stir to combine well.
8. Cut the steak into ¼-inch-thick slices and serve on top of the mushrooms and asparagus.

Chapter 9: Pork

Pork Carnitas

Prep time: 15 minutes | Cook time: 2½ hours
Serves 2

1½ tablespoons salt
1 teaspoon black pepper
2 pounds (907 g) pork butt, cut into 4-inch cubes
2 tablespoons cooking fat
½ medium onion, roughly chopped
3 cloves garlic, minced
½ teaspoon chili powder
¼ teaspoon ground cinnamon
¼ cup sliced (½-inch pieces) green onions
Juice of ½ lime

1. Preheat the oven to 350ºF (180ºC).
2. Mix 1 tablespoon of the salt and all of the pepper in a bowl. Use to season the pork butt evenly.
3. In a heavy pot or Dutch oven over medium heat, melt the cooking fat, swirling to coat the bottom of the pan. When the fat is hot, add the pork (be sure not to overcrowd) and brown all sides, 3 to 4 minutes per side. Remove the pork from the pot and set aside.
4. In the same pot, reduce the heat to medium-low, add the onion, and cook, stirring, until translucent, 4 to 5 minutes. Add the garlic and cook, stirring vigorously to prevent burning, until aromatic, about 1 minute. Add 1 cup of water, the chili powder, and cinnamon. Increase the heat to medium high, return the pork to the pot, and bring to a boil.
5. Cover the pot with a lid or tightly wrapped foil. Transfer to the oven and bake for 2 ½ hours, turning the meat after each hour. The pork should be fork-tender when done.
6. Transfer the pork to a bowl and shred with a fork or two, discarding any excess fat. Incorporate the cooking liquid from the pot, then add the green onions and lime juice. Season with the remaining ½ tablespoon salt.

Applesauce Pork Chops

Prep time: 5 minutes | Cook time: 20 minutes
Serves 2

1 teaspoon salt
1 teaspoon black pepper
2 bone-in pork chops (about 1 pound / 454 g total)
3 tablespoons cooking fat
1 onion, sliced
2 apples, peeled, cored and diced
½ cup apple cider
½ teaspoon ground ginger
½ teaspoon allspice
1 pinch nutmeg
2 generous handfuls frisée

1. Preheat the oven to 350ºF (180ºC).
2. Mix the salt and pepper in a small bowl and use to season both sides of the pork chops.
3. Melt 2 tablespoons of the cooking fat in a large skillet over medium-high heat. When the fat is hot, add the pork chops and sear until you see a golden brown crust, 2 to 3 minutes. Turn and sear the other side for 2 minutes.
4. Transfer the pork chops to a baking dish and roast in the oven until the internal temperature reaches 140ºF (60ºC), 10 to 15 minutes, depending on thickness.
5. While the pork is roasting, combine the remaining 1 tablespoon fat and the onion in the same skillet. Cook over medium heat until the onion is translucent, 2 to 3 minutes. Add the apple, apple cider, ginger, allspice, and nutmeg. Cook (while scraping all the tasty bits off the bottom with a wooden spoon), until the apples soften, about 5 minutes.
6. Transfer the applesauce to a food processor or blender and blend until smooth.
7. Place the frisée on plates. Top with the pork and serve with the applesauce.

Pork Lettuce Wraps with Peach Salsa

Prep time: 30 minutes | Cook time: 8 hours
Serves 4

Pork:

1 large sweet onion, cut into thin wedges
1 tablespoon chili powder
2 teaspoons ground cumin
2 teaspoons salt
1 teaspoon garlic powder
Pinch of cayenne pepper
2 pounds (907 g) boneless pork shoulder
1 tablespoon extra-virgin olive oil
1 cup chicken bone broth or Whole Food-compliant chicken broth

Salsa:

1 ripe medium peach, peeled, pitted, and chopped
¼ cup roughly chopped fresh cilantro
2 tablespoons finely chopped shallot
½ to 1 small jalapeño, seeded and finely chopped
1 tablespoon fresh lime juice
Pinch of salt
8 to 12 large butterhead or Bibb lettuce leaves

1. Make the pork: Place the onion wedges in a slow cooker. In a large bowl, combine the chili powder, cumin, salt, garlic powder, and cayenne. Trim the fat from the pork shoulder. Cut the pork into 2-inch pieces and add to the spice mixture. Toss gently to coat.
2. Heat the olive oil in a large skillet over medium-high heat. Cook the pork, in two batches, in the hot oil until browned on all sides. Using a slotted spoon, transfer the pork to the slow cooker. Pour the broth over the pork. Cover and cook on low for 8 to 10 hours or on high for 4 to 5 hours.
3. Make the salsa: Meanwhile, in a medium bowl, combine the peach, cilantro, shallot, jalapeño, lime juice, and salt. Cover and chill for up to 2 hours.
4. To serve: Use a slotted spoon to transfer the pork to a cutting board and use two forks to shred the pork. Place the shredded pork in a bowl. Remove the onion from the cooking liquid and add to the pork. Skim off the fat from the cooking liquid. Add enough cooking liquid to the pork mixture to moisten. Spoon the shredded pork into the center of the lettuce leaves. Top with the salsa.

Apricot Stuffed Pork Chops

Prep time: 25 minutes | Cook time: 15 minutes
Serves 2

2 teaspoons clarified butter or ghee
½ cup finely chopped celery
1 shallot, minced
6 unsulfured dried apricots, chopped
1 tablespoon chicken bone broth or Whole Food-compliant chicken broth
⅛ teaspoon salt, plus more as needed
⅛ teaspoon red pepper flakes
2 teaspoons finely chopped fresh parsley
2 boneless pork chops, ¾ inch thick
Black pepper, to taste
1 tablespoon extra-virgin olive oil

1. Preheat the oven to 350°F (180°C).
2. Melt the butter over medium heat in a small skillet. Add the celery and shallot and cook, stirring until the celery is crisp-tender, 3 minutes. Add the apricots and broth and cook, until the apricots are softened, about 1 minute. Season with the salt and red pepper flakes. Stir in the parsley. Remove the skillet from the heat.
3. Make a pocket in each chop with a small sharp knife, cutting almost through to the opposite side. Spoon the apricot mixture into the pockets, pressing lightly to close the opening as much as possible. Season the chops lightly with additional salt and black pepper.
4. Heat the olive oil over high heat in an oven-safe skillet. Sear the chops in the hot oil until browned, about 2 minutes per side. Transfer the skillet to the oven and bake for about 15 minutes or until the chops are cooked through and their internal temperature is 145°F (63°C). Let the chops rest for 5 minutes. Serve.

Green Chile Pork

Prep time: 20 minutes | Cook time: 2½ hours
Serves 6

2 tablespoons coconut oil or extra-virgin olive oil
3 to 3½ pounds (1.4 to 1.6 kg) boneless pork shoulder, trimmed
1 teaspoon salt
½ teaspoon black pepper
1 medium yellow onion, chopped
1 (16-ounce / 454-g) jar Whole Food-compliant salsa verde
2 poblano chile peppers, seeded and chopped
1 jalapeño, seeded and chopped (optional)
2 cloves garlic, minced
1 tablespoon Whole Food-compliant chili powder
2 teaspoons ground cumin
1 teaspoon dried oregano, crushed
1 teaspoon ground coriander

1. Preheat the oven to 325ºF (163ºC).
2. In a large Dutch oven over medium-high heat, heat the oil. Rub the pork with salt and pepper on all sides. Add the pork and cook until all sides are browned, about 3 minutes per side. Remove the pork. Add the onion and bring to a simmer, scraping the browned bits with a wooden spoon. Add the salsa verde, poblanos, jalapeño (if using), garlic, chili powder, cumin, oregano, and coriander. Mix together.
3. Return the pork to the Dutch oven; cover and place in the oven. Bake until the meat is very tender and the internal temperature is 145ºF (63ºC), 2½ to 3 hours. Transfer the meat to a cutting board. Use two forks to pull the meat apart into large shreds and place the shreds in a serving bowl. Skim the fat from the cooking liquid. Drizzle about 2 cups cooking liquid over the meat to moisten. Discard the remaining cooking liquid.

Cider Pulled Pork

Prep time: 10 minutes | Cook time: 6 hours
Serves 6 to 8

Rub:
1 tablespoon salt
1½ teaspoons smoked paprika
1½ teaspoons garlic powder
½ teaspoon chili powder
½ teaspoon ground ginger
½ teaspoon black pepper

Pork:
4 pounds (1.8 kg) boneless pork butt
1 large sweet onion, sliced
1½ cups unsweetened, unfiltered apple cider

1. Make the rub: Combine all the seasonings in a small bowl. Sprinkle the rub over the pork and rub it in with your fingers.
2. Arrange the onion slices on the bottom of a slow cooker. If necessary, cut the pork to fit in the cooker then place on top of the onions. Add the apple cider. Cover and cook on low for 8 to 10 hours or on high for 6 to 7 hours.
3. Carefully transfer the meat to a large platter and allow it to rest for a few minutes. Strain the cooking liquid through a fine-mesh strainer into a large bowl. Place 1 cup of the liquid back into the slow cooker; discard the remaining liquid and the onion.
4. Using two forks, shred the meat. Return the meat to the slow cooker and toss with the cooking liquid. Season to taste with additional salt and pepper, if desired.

Pork Chops with Parsnip Purée

Prep time: 10 minutes | Cook time: 25 minutes
Serves 4

Parsnip Purée:

4 cups chicken stock
2 pounds (907 g)
parsnips, peeled and
cut into ¼-inch-thick
rounds

2 tablespoons clarified
butter
1 teaspoon granulated
garlic

Pork and Greens:

8 thin-cut boneless
pork chops (about 1½
pounds / 680 g)
1 teaspoon kosher salt
½ teaspoon freshly
ground black pepper
3 tablespoons extra-
virgin olive oil

6 cups greens of
your choice (such as
spinach, Swiss chard,
or kale), rinsed and
dried
Chopped fresh parsley,
for garnish

1. For the parsnip purée: In a medium pot,
   bring the stock to a boil over high heat. Add
   the parsnips, partially cover the pot, and
   cook until tender, about 20 minutes. Drain
   the parsnips, reserving ½ cup of the stock,
   and return both to the pot.
2. Using an immersion blender, purée the
   parsnips with the reserved broth until
   smooth. Add the clarified butter and
   the granulated garlic and stir until well
   combined.
3. For the pork and greens: Season the pork
   chops on both sides with the salt and
   pepper.
4. In a large sauté pan, heat the olive oil over
   medium-high heat. Working in batches if
   necessary, add the pork chops and cook
   until well browned on the edges, 3½ to 4½
   minutes on the first side. Then flip and cook
   until done, about 1 minute more. If needed
   to brown evenly, use a bacon presser to
   flatten the pork chops in the pan. Transfer
   the pork chops to a large plate and set
   aside. Repeat with the remaining pork
   chops.
5. Add the greens to the pan and cook over
   medium heat, stirring, until just wilted, 1 to
   2 minutes, depending on the greens you've
   chosen.
6. Serve the pork chops on top of the parsnip
   purée with the greens alongside, and top
   with any pork drippings from the plate, if
   you're lucky enough to have them.

Green Pork Curry with Asparagus

Prep time: 15 minutes | Cook time: 7 hours
Serves 4 to 6

1½ to 2 pounds (680
to 907 g) boneless
pork shoulder, cut into
2-inch cubes
3 medium red, yellow,
and/or green bell
peppers, sliced, or
3 cups frozen sliced
bell peppers, thawed
slightly
1 medium onion, cut
into ½-inch wedges
1 cup Whole Food-
compliant chicken
broth or chicken bone
broth
¼ cup Whole Food-
compliant green curry
paste

1 pound (454 g)
asparagus, cut into 1-
to 2-inch pieces
1 (14-ounce / 397-
g) can full-fat Whole
Food-compliant
coconut milk
1 cup sliced fresh basil
leaves
1 (12-ounce / 340-
g) bag frozen riced
cauliflower, cooked
according to package
directions; or 3 cups
cauliflower rice,
cooked (optional)
Lime wedges
(optional)

1. Combine the pork, bell peppers, onion,
   broth, and curry paste in a slow cooker.
   Cover and cook on low for 7 to 8 hours or
   on high for 3½ to 4 hours.
2. Turn the slow cooker to high if using the low
   setting. Stir in the asparagus. Cover and
   cook until the asparagus is crisp-tender, 15
   to 20 minutes. Stir in the coconut milk and
   basil. Serve the stew over the cauliflower
   rice and with lime wedges, if desired.

Pork Scaloppini with Mushrooms

Prep time: 10 minutes | Cook time: 15 minutes
Serves 2

2 thick, boneless center-cut pork chops (4 to 6 ounces / 113 to 170 g each)
Salt and black pepper, to taste
2 tablespoons clarified butter or ghee
1 tablespoon extra-virgin olive oil
8 ounces (227 g) cremini mushrooms, sliced
1 clove garlic, minced
⅔ cup Whole Food-compliant coconut milk
1 tablespoon chopped fresh tarragon

1. Cut each pork chop in half horizontally to make a total of four thin pieces. Place each between two sheets of plastic wrap and use the flat side of a meat mallet to flatten to an ⅛-inch thickness. (Your butcher can do this for you.) Season both sides of the chops with ¼ teaspoon salt and ¼ teaspoon pepper.
2. Heat the butter in a heavy large skillet over medium-high heat. As soon as the butter begins to smoke, carefully add the chops to the pan. Cook, turning once, until browned, 2 to 4 minutes. Transfer the chops to a serving platter and cover with foil to keep warm.
3. Add the olive oil to the same skillet and reduce the heat to medium. Add the mushrooms, ⅛ teaspoon salt, and ⅛ teaspoon pepper and cook, stirring frequently, until the mushrooms are tender and browned, 4 to 5 minutes longer. Add the garlic and cook for 1 minute. Add the coconut milk and scrape up any browned bits on the bottom of the skillet. Bring to a boil, reduce the heat, and simmer, 3 minutes longer. Stir in the tarragon. Spoon the sauce over the chops and serve.

Rosemary Pork Chops with Red Potatoes

Prep time: 20 minutes | Cook time: 10 minutes
Serves 2

3 tablespoons extra-virgin olive oil
1 tablespoon Whole Food-compliant whole-grain mustard
2 cloves garlic, minced
1 teaspoon chopped fresh rosemary
¼ teaspoon salt
¼ teaspoon black pepper
8 small red potatoes, quartered
1 small red onion, cut into 8 wedges
2 bone-in pork chops, cut ½ to ¾ inch thick

1. Preheat the oven to 425°F (220°C).
2. In a small bowl, stir together 1 tablespoon of the olive oil, the mustard, garlic, rosemary, salt, and pepper. In a medium bowl, toss the potatoes and onion with half of the mustard mixture. Brush the remaining mustard mixture on both sides of the chops.
3. Heat 1 tablespoon of the olive oil in a large cast-iron or heavy ovenproof skillet over medium-high heat. Add the chops to the skillet and cook, turning once, until browned, about 2 minutes. Transfer the chops to a plate and cover to keep warm.
4. Heat the remaining 1 tablespoon olive oil in the same skillet over medium heat. Add the potatoes and onion and cook, stirring occasionally, until browned, about 5 minutes.
5. Arrange the chops in with the potatoes and onions. Transfer the skillet to the oven and bake until the internal temperature of the chops is 145°F (63°C) and the potatoes are tender, 10 to 15 minutes.

Basil Pork and Cauliflower Curry

Prep time: 10 minutes | Cook time: 25 minutes
Serves 4

2 teaspoons coconut oil
2 tablespoons Whole Food-compliant green curry paste
1 pound (454 g) pork tenderloin, sliced into bite-size strips
1 small onion, chopped
1 Thai chile, seeded and finely chopped (optional)
3 cups bite-size cauliflower florets
¾ cup diced orange bell pepper

1 cup full-fat coconut milk
¾ cup chicken bone broth or Whole Food-compliant chicken broth
1½ teaspoons Red Boat fish sauce or coconut aminos
4 fresh basil leaves (preferably Thai basil), rolled and sliced crosswise into thin ribbons
Lime wedges, for serving

1. Heat the coconut oil in a large nonstick skillet over medium-high heat. Add the curry paste and cook, stirring, for 1 minute. Add the pork and cook, stirring occasionally, until no longer pink, 3 to 5 minutes. Transfer the pork to a bowl and cover to keep warm.
2. Add the onion and the chile (if using) to the same skillet and cook over medium-high heat, stirring occasionally, until tender, 3 to 4 minutes. Add the cauliflower and bell pepper and cook, stirring occasionally, for 2 minutes more. Stir in the coconut milk and broth. Bring to a simmer. Cover and simmer for 8 minutes. Stir in the pork and fish sauce and cook, uncovered, until the pork is heated through, about 2 minutes. Garnish with the sliced basil and serve with lime wedges.

Sausage Potato Hash

Prep time: 20 minutes | Cook time: 20 minutes
Serves 4

¼ cup fresh blood orange juice or orange juice
1 tablespoon sweet paprika
1 tablespoon chopped fresh parsley
2 teaspoons fennel seeds, lightly crushed
1 teaspoon dried oregano, crushed
1 teaspoon kosher salt
½ teaspoon black pepper

1 pound (454 g) ground pork
1½ cups chopped onion
1 cup chopped red or yellow bell pepper
1 pound (454 g) Yukon Gold potatoes, peeled, if desired, and diced
⅓ cup beef bone broth or Whole Food-compliant beef broth
4 cups fresh baby spinach

1. In a large bowl, combine the orange juice, paprika, parsley, fennel seeds, oregano, salt, and black pepper. Add the pork and mix with your hands until thoroughly combined.
2. Cook the meat mixture in a large skillet over medium-high heat until browned, breaking it up into small pieces with a wooden spoon as it cooks. Add the onion and bell pepper and cook, stirring frequently, until the vegetables are just tender, about 5 minutes.
3. Stir in the potatoes. Cook, stirring, for 2 minutes. Add the broth and bring to a boil. Reduce the heat to medium-low, cover, and simmer, stirring occasionally, until the potatoes are very tender, 15 to 20 minutes. Gently stir in the spinach. Remove the skillet from the heat and let stand until the spinach is wilted, 4 to 5 minutes.

Apple Pork Chops and Spinach

Prep time: 20 minutes | Cook time: 15 minutes

Serves 2

2 tart red apples, cored and sliced
3 tablespoons extra-virgin olive oil
2 bone-in pork chops (about 8 ounces / 227 g each)
¼ teaspoon salt
¼ teaspoon black pepper
2 tablespoons finely chopped shallot
½ cup chicken bone broth or Whole Food-compliant chicken broth
¼ cup apple cider
1 teaspoon Whole Food-compliant whole-grain mustard
4 cups packed fresh spinach

1. Preheat the oven to 425°F (220°C).
2. Toss the apple slices with 1 tablespoon of the olive oil in a bowl. Spread the apple slices in a single layer on a rimmed baking sheet. Bake for 10 minutes.
3. Meanwhile, heat 1 tablespoon of the oil in a medium skillet over medium heat. Pat the pork chops dry with paper towels and sprinkle both sides with the salt and pepper. Add the pork chops to the hot skillet. Cook until browned, about 2 minutes per side. Transfer the chops to the baking sheet with the apples and roast for 10 to 15 minutes, until the internal temperature of the chops is at least 145°F (63°C) and the apples are tender.
4. Combine the remaining 1 tablespoon oil and the shallot in the same skillet used to brown the pork chops. Cook over medium heat until the shallot is translucent, 2 to 3 minutes. Add the broth, apple cider, and mustard. Bring to a boil, stirring to scrape up any brown bits from the bottom of the skillet. Reduce the heat and simmer, uncovered, until reduced by half, 3 to 4 minutes. Stir in the spinach and cook, stirring, until wilted, about 30 seconds.
5. Using a slotted spoon, divide the wilted spinach between two plates. Top with the pork chops and apples. Serve with the remaining pan sauce, if desired.

Lemon-Tarragon Grilled Pork Rib Chops

Prep time: 20 minutes | Cook time: 10 minutes

Serves 2

2 tablespoons extra-virgin olive oil
2 tablespoons Whole Food-compliant coarse-grain mustard
¼ teaspoon black pepper
1 tablespoon chopped fresh tarragon
2 bone-in pork rib chops, cut ¾ inch thick
1 large zucchini
12 to 14 cherry tomatoes
1 tablespoon fresh lemon juice
Pinch of salt

1. In a small bowl, stir together the olive oil, mustard, tarragon, and pepper. Spoon half the marinade into a second small bowl.
2. Brush half the marinade over both sides of the chops. Place the chops on a plate and cover with plastic wrap. Marinate in the refrigerator for 30 minutes to 1 hour.
3. If using wooden skewers, soak them in water for 30 minutes to 1 hour to prevent them from burning.
4. Preheat a grill to high.
5. Use a vegetable peeler or mandoline to slice the zucchini lengthwise into long, thin strips (you should have 12 strips). Thread the zucchini strips accordion-style on the skewers, placing the tomatoes between the zucchini. Stir the lemon juice and salt into the reserved marinade. Drizzle or brush the marinade over the kabobs.
6. Grill the chops over direct heat until they are seared on both sides and easily come off the grill, 4 to 6 minutes. Reduce the grill temperature to medium (or move the chops to indirect heat). Grill until the internal temperature is 145°F (63°C), 3 to 5 minutes. Let the chops rest for 3 to 5 minutes.
7. Grill the kabobs over direct heat, turning occasionally, until the zucchini is just tender and starting to brown, 3 to 4 minutes.
8. Serve the chops with the kabobs.

Grilled Pork Chops with Watermelon Salad

Prep time: 15 minutes | Cook time: 10 minutes
Serves 4

Pork Chops:

2 teaspoons chili powder
½ teaspoon salt
¼ teaspoon black pepper
2 tablespoons extra-virgin olive oil

2 teaspoons fresh lime juice
4 boneless pork loin chops (6 ounces / 170 g each), cut 1 inch thick

Salad:

4 cups chopped seedless watermelon, chilled
¼ cup thinly sliced red onion
2 tablespoons chopped fresh cilantro
1 tablespoon extra-virgin olive oil

1 tablespoon fresh lime juice
¼ teaspoon salt
⅛ teaspoon black pepper
Lime wedges and chopped fresh cilantro, for serving (optional)

1. Make the pork chops: Preheat a grill to medium heat.
2. In a small bowl, combine the chili powder, salt, and pepper. Whisk in the olive oil and lime juice. Brush both sides of the pork chops with the oil mixture. Grill the chops, turning once, until the internal temperature is 145°F (63°C), 7 to 9 minutes. Let the chops rest for 3 to 5 minutes.
3. Make the salad: In a medium bowl, combine the watermelon, onion, and cilantro. Drizzle with the olive oil and lime juice. Sprinkle with the salt and pepper; toss gently to coat.
4. Serve the grilled pork chops with the watermelon salad. If desired, serve with lime wedges and sprinkle with additional cilantro.

Potato, Sausage, and Kale Soup

Prep time: 10 minutes | Cook time: 30 minutes
Serves 4

1 pound (454 g) ground pork
2 teaspoons Italian seasoning, crushed
½ teaspoon salt, plus more as needed
½ teaspoon smoked paprika
¼ teaspoon fennel seeds
¼ teaspoon black pepper, plus more as needed
⅛ teaspoon red pepper flakes
1 tablespoon extra-virgin olive oil

½ cup chopped onion
3 cloves garlic, minced
4 cups chicken bone broth or Whole Food-compliant chicken broth
1 (14½-ounce / 411-g) can diced tomatoes, undrained
1 pound (454 g) red potatoes, cut into ¾-inch chunks
4 cups chopped fresh kale or Swiss chard leaves
2 teaspoons chopped fresh thyme leaves

1. In a large bowl, combine the ground pork, Italian seasoning, salt, paprika, fennel seeds, black pepper, and red pepper flakes; mix well.
2. Heat the olive oil in a large pot over medium heat. Add the pork mixture, the onion, and the garlic. Cook, stirring frequently, until the meat is browned.
3. Stir in the broth, tomatoes with their juices, and potatoes. Bring to a boil. Reduce the heat to low, cover, and simmer, stirring occasionally, until the potatoes are just tender, 15 to 20 minutes. Add the kale and thyme and cook, uncovered, until the kale is tender, 5 minutes more. Season with additional salt and black pepper and serve.

Coriander Crusted Pork Tenderloin

Prep time: 15 minutes | Cook time: 25 minutes
Serves 2

3 tablespoons plus 1 teaspoon Whole Food-compliant Dijon mustard
1 Whole Food-compliant pork tenderloin (1 to 1½ pounds / 454 to 680 g), trimmed
3 tablespoons coriander seeds, lightly crushed
1 tablespoon black peppercorns, lightly crushed
¾ teaspoon coarse salt
2 tablespoons extra-virgin olive oil
1 large shallot, thinly sliced
1 tart-sweet apple (such as Pink Lady), cored and thinly sliced
½ teaspoon dried thyme leaves, crushed
½ cup unfiltered apple cider
1 tablespoon cider vinegar
⅛ teaspoon black pepper

1. Preheat the oven to 400°F (205°C).
2. Spread 3 tablespoons of the mustard over the tenderloin. Evenly press the coriander seeds and peppercorns onto the tenderloin. Season with ½ teaspoon salt.
3. In an extra-large ovenproof skillet, heat 1 tablespoon olive oil over medium-high heat. Add the tenderloin, top side down, and brown on all sides, 8 to 10 minutes. (If the mustard-and-seed crust falls off in places, use a spoon to press it onto the top of the tenderloin after you turn it.)
4. Transfer the skillet to the oven. Roast for 10 to 15 minutes, until the tenderloin is 145°F (63°C). Carefully remove the skillet from the oven; transfer the tenderloin to a cutting board. Tent with foil and let rest for 5 minutes.
5. Meanwhile, in a medium skillet, heat the remaining 1 tablespoon olive oil over medium heat. Add the shallot, apple, and thyme. Cook, stirring frequently, until the shallot and apple are crisp-tender, 4 to 5 minutes. Add the cider and simmer until reduced by half, about 3 minutes. Whisk in the vinegar and remaining 1 teaspoon mustard. Season with the remaining ¼ teaspoon salt and the pepper.
6. To serve, slice the tenderloin into medallions. Arrange 3 medallions on each of two plates. Top with a generous ⅓ cup of the apple compote. (You will probably have some leftover pork and compote.)

Roasted Pork with Butternut Squash

Prep time: 10 minutes | Cook time: 3 hours
Serves 2

2 teaspoons paprika
1 teaspoon chili powder
1 teaspoon garlic powder
1 teaspoon onion powder
1 teaspoon salt
½ teaspoon black pepper
½ lime, juiced
1½ pounds (680 g) pork shoulder (boneless)
1 butternut squash, 1-inch diced
1 bunch kale, stems removed, leaves chopped
1 cup diced tomatoes

1. Preheat the oven to 300°F (150°C).
2. Mix the paprika, chili powder, garlic powder, onion powder, salt, and pepper in a small bowl. Add the lime juice and stir. Place the pork in a Dutch oven or deep roasting pan and coat all sides of the pork with the spice mixture. Add 1 cup of water and cover tightly with a lid or aluminum foil. Cook in the oven, turning the pork shoulder in the pan every 45 minutes.
3. After 2 hours and 15 minutes, add the butternut squash and ½ cup of water to the Dutch oven or pan. Cook for 30 more minutes, then add the kale and tomatoes. Place back in the oven for 15 minutes more.
4. Remove the pan from the oven and leave covered until you are ready to serve. With tongs or a slotted spoon, arrange the vegetables on plates, then break the pork apart into generous chunks and place over the vegetables. Spoon the braising liquid from the pan over the pork.

Pork with Sweet Potato Colcannon

Prep time: 15 minutes | Cook time: 25 minutes
Serves 4

1 large sweet potato, peeled and roughly chopped
2 tablespoons clarified butter or ghee
1 bunch Swiss chard, stalks removed, roughly chopped

1 leek, finely sliced
½ teaspoon salt
½ teaspoon black pepper
4 (1-inch-thick) boneless pork loin chops

1. Fill a large saucepan with salted water and bring to a boil. Add the sweet potato, reduce the heat to a simmer, and cook until softened, 6 to 8 minutes. Drain the water and heat the potato in the saucepan for 1 minute to remove excess moisture. Transfer to a bowl and cover to keep warm.
2. In the same saucepan, heat 1 tablespoons of the butter over low heat. Add the chard, leek, ¼ teaspoon of the salt, and ¼ teaspoon of the black pepper. Cook, stirring, until the leek and chard are softened, 6 to 8 minutes. Remove from the heat and keep warm.
3. Meanwhile, in a large skillet, heat the remaining 1 tablespoon butter over high heat. Lightly season the pork chops with the remaining ¼ teaspoon salt and ¼ teaspoon black pepper. Add the chops to the skillet and cook until the internal temperature is 145°F (63°C), 3 to 4 minutes on each side.
4. Combine the leeks, Swiss chard, and sweet potato. Serve with the pork chops.

Pork and Bell Pepper Stir-Fry

Prep time: 15 minutes | Cook time: 10 minutes
Serves 2

2 tablespoons coconut aminos
2 tablespoons apple cider
1 tablespoon rice vinegar
2 cloves garlic, minced
2 teaspoons minced fresh ginger
⅛ teaspoon red pepper flakes
2 tablespoons coconut oil

12 ounces (340 g) pork tenderloin, cut into thin, bite-size strips
1 small red bell pepper, cut into bite-size strips
1 (8-ounce / 227-g) bag fresh sugar snap peas
2 green onions, sliced on the bias, white and green parts separated
2 teaspoons sesame seeds, toasted

1. In a small bowl, mix the coconut aminos, cider, vinegar, garlic, ginger, and pepper flakes; set aside.
2. Heat 1 tablespoon of the coconut oil in a large skillet or wok over medium-high heat. Add the pork and cook, stirring, until no longer pink, 2 to 3 minutes. Remove the pork from the skillet.
3. In the same skillet, heat the remaining 1 tablespoon coconut oil over medium-high heat. Add the bell pepper, snap peas, and white parts of the green onions. Cook, stirring, until the vegetables are crisp-tender, 3 to 5 minutes. Stir in the coconut aminos mixture. Cook, stirring, for 1 minute more. Return the pork to the skillet and heat through.
4. Serve the stir-fry topped with the remaining green onions and the sesame seeds.

Pork Chops with Mashers and Pepita Pesto

Prep time: 25 minutes | Cook time: 20 minutes
Serves 4

Pesto:

½ cup extra-virgin olive oil
1 bunch curly kale, stemmed
½ cup unsalted roasted pepitas (pumpkin seeds)
1 tablespoon lemon juice

1 tablespoon Whole Food-compliant prepared horseradish
1 teaspoon grated lemon zest
½ teaspoon coarse salt

Mashers:

2 pounds (907 g) Yukon Gold potatoes, peeled, if desired, and quartered
1 pound (454 g) parsnips, peeled and cut into 2-inch pieces
¼ cup clarified butter or ghee

½ cup chicken bone broth or Whole Food-compliant chicken broth
½ teaspoon coarse salt
½ teaspoon black pepper

Chops:

4 bone-in pork loin chops (6 to 8 ounces / 170 to 227 g each), cut ½ to 1 inch thick

Coarse salt and black pepper, to taste
Finely chopped fresh chives

1. Make the pesto: In a food processor, combine the olive oil, kale, pepitas, lemon juice, horseradish, lemon zest, and salt. Process until smooth. Refrigerate until ready to serve.
2. Make the mashers: Place the potatoes and parsnips in a large saucepan or Dutch oven. Add cold water to cover and bring to a boil. Reduce the heat to low and simmer until tender, 20 to 25 minutes. Drain and return the vegetables to the hot saucepan. In a small saucepan, heat the butter and broth over medium-low heat until hot. Add the hot broth mixture to the vegetables. Add the salt and pepper. Mash with a potato masher until smooth.
3. Make the chops: While the potatoes are cooking, preheat a grill to high. Lightly season the chops with salt and pepper. Sear the chops on the grill over direct heat until a crust forms, 1 to 2 minutes per side. Reduce the grill temperature to medium or move the chops to indirect heat. Close the grill lid and cook until the internal temperature of the chops is 145°F (63°C), about 5 minutes. Let the chops rest for 3 to 5 minutes.
4. Sprinkle the potato-parsnip mashers with chives and serve alongside the pork chops, topped with the pesto.

Cider-Brined Roasted Pork

Prep time: 30 minutes | Cook time: 15 minutes
Serves 3

Pork:

2 cups apple cider
3 tablespoons salt
2 bay leaves
2 cloves garlic, crushed

2 teaspoons caraway seeds
1 teaspoon black peppercorns
1 pork tenderloin (1¼ to 1½ pounds / 567 to 680 g)

Slaw:

¼ cup apple cider
2 tablespoons extra-virgin olive oil
1 tablespoon apple cider vinegar
1 teaspoon caraway seeds
1 teaspoon Whole Food-compliant coarse-grain mustard
¼ teaspoon salt
1 (16-ounce / 454-g) jar Whole Food-compliant

sauerkraut, drained well
1 red or green bell pepper, seeded and finely chopped
1 large carrot, coarsely shredded
½ small sweet onion, finely chopped
1 stalk celery, finely chopped
1 tablespoon extra-virgin olive oil
Black pepper, to taste

1. Make the pork: In a small saucepan, combine the apple cider, salt, bay leaves, garlic, caraway, and peppercorns. Bring to a boil, stirring to dissolve the salt. Remove from the heat and let stand for 15 minutes. Stir in ½ cup ice cubes. Let stand until completely cool.
2. Trim the pork tenderloin, removing any tough silver skin. Place in a resealable plastic bag and pour in the cooled brine. Squeeze any air from the bag and seal. Place the bag in a dish and refrigerate for 6 to 8 hours.
3. Make the slaw: In a medium bowl, whisk together the apple cider, olive oil, vinegar, caraway, mustard, and salt. Add the sauerkraut, bell pepper, carrot, onion, and celery; toss to coat. Cover and chill for at least 2 hours before serving.
4. Preheat the oven to 425ºF (220ºC). Remove the pork from the brine and pat it dry with paper towels (discard the brine). Rub the pork with the olive oil and sprinkle with black pepper. Heat a large oven-safe skillet over medium-high heat. Sear the pork on all sides until lightly browned. Transfer the skillet to the oven and roast the tenderloin for 15 to 20 minutes or until the internal temperature is 145ºF (63ºC). Let rest for 10 minutes.
5. Thinly slice the pork and serve it over or alongside the slaw.

Spice-Crusted Roast Pork Tenderloin

Prep time: 15 minutes | Cook time: 25 minutes
Serves 2 or 3

Vinaigrette:

¼ cup extra-virgin olive oil
2 tablespoons apple cider vinegar
1 tablespoon fresh orange juice

1 teaspoon fresh lime juice
1 clove garlic, minced
Salt and black pepper, to taste

Pork:

1 cup fresh orange juice
¼ cup fresh lime juice
1¾ teaspoons ground cumin
1 teaspoon salt
1 teaspoon smoked paprika
½ teaspoon dried oregano, crushed

2 cloves garlic, minced
1 pork tenderloin (1 to 1¼ pounds / 454 to 567 g)
2 teaspoons orange zest
½ teaspoon black pepper
1 tablespoon extra-virgin olive oil

Salad:

1 tablespoon extra-virgin olive oil
3 rings fresh pineapple (1 inch thick)
2 bunches watercress, thick stems removed, or

3 cups baby arugula
½ ripe avocado, peeled and cubed
Red onion slivers

1. Make the vinaigrette: In a small bowl, whisk together the olive oil, vinegar, orange juice, lime juice, and garlic. Season with salt and pepper. Cover and refrigerate until ready to serve.
2. Make the pork: In a resealable plastic bag or nonreactive bowl with a lid, combine the orange juice, lime juice, ¾ teaspoon of the cumin, ½ teaspoon of the salt, the paprika, oregano, and garlic. Add the pork to the bag or bowl and turn the meat to coat it with the marinade. Seal the bag or cover the bowl and marinate in the refrigerator, turning occasionally, for 2 hours.
3. Preheat the oven to 425ºF (220ºC). Remove the pork from the marinade and pat it dry with paper towels (discard the marinade).
4. In a small bowl, combine the orange zest, the remaining ½ teaspoon salt, remaining 1 teaspoon cumin, and the pepper. Rub the mixture over the pork with your fingers.
5. Heat the olive oil in a large oven-safe skillet over medium-high heat. Add the pork and sear on both sides, about 10 minutes. Transfer the skillet to the oven and roast for 15 minutes, until the internal temperature is 145ºF (63ºC). Transfer the pork to a cutting board and let rest for 5 minutes before slicing.
6. Make the salad: In a ceramic nonstick skillet, heat the olive oil over medium heat. Add the pineapple rings and cook, turning once, until caramelized, 5 to 8 minutes. Let the pineapple cool slightly and then cut it into bite-size pieces. Place the watercress in a medium bowl and toss with half the vinaigrette. Arrange the watercress on a platter and top with the pineapple and avocado. Drizzle with the remaining vinaigrette and sprinkle with red onion.
7. Serve the pork with the salad.

Banger Sausage Patties with Sweet Potatoes

Prep time: 25 minutes | Cook time: 25 minutes
Serves 2

Sausage:

1 pound (454 g) ground pork
¼ teaspoon ground sage
¼ teaspoon garlic powder
¼ teaspoon dried thyme
¼ teaspoon onion powder

⅛ teaspoon cayenne pepper
⅛ teaspoon nutmeg
1 teaspoon salt
⅛ teaspoon black pepper
Grated zest of 1 lemon

Sweet Potatoes:

2 medium sweet potatoes, peeled and cut into large dice
4 tablespoon ghee or clarified butter
½ cup full-fat coconut milk

1 onion, thinly sliced
¼ teaspoon salt
¼ teaspoon black pepper

1. Preheat the oven to 350°F (180°C). Bring 4 cups of water to a boil in a medium pot over medium-high heat. Line a baking sheet with parchment paper.
2. Prepare the sausage: In a large mixing bowl, mix all the sausage ingredients. Form into 8 equal patties. Place on a plate and chill in the freezer for 10 to 15 minutes while starting the sweet potato mash.
3. Cook the sweet potatoes in the boiling water until fork tender, 10 to 15 minutes. Drain and return the potatoes to the pot. Add 1 tablespoon of the ghee and coconut milk. Using a potato masher, immersion blender, or large kitchen fork, mash and mix the sweet potatoes with the ghee and the coconut milk. Cover the pot to keep warm and set aside.
4. Remove the sausage from the freezer and place on the parchment paper-lined baking sheet. Bake the sausage patties in the oven for 12 to 15 minutes, until the internal temperature reaches 145°F (63°C), and no pink remains in the middle of the patty.
5. Meanwhile, heat the remaining 3 tablespoons of ghee in a large skillet over medium heat, swirling to coat the bottom of the pan. When the ghee is hot, add the onion and cook for 15 minutes, turning them periodically as they begin to brown and caramelize. (Do not rush this step, the browner the color, the more concentrated the flavor will be.)
6. Transfer the mashed sweet potatoes to a bowl or serving dish and top with the caramelized onions. Season with salt and pepper and stir to combine. Serve with the sausage patties.

Chili Verde Pork

Prep time: 25 minutes | Cook time: 50 minutes
Serves 10

Verde Sauce:

2 jalapeños
6 tomatillos, husks removed and chopped (about 2 cups)

1 (16-ounce / 454-g) can roasted green chilies
¼ cup fresh cilantro leaves, plus more for garnish

Chili Base:

1 tablespoon extra-virgin olive oil or avocado oil
2 pounds (907 g) Whole Food-compliant pork tenderloin, cut into ½-inch cubes
4 cloves garlic, minced
1 medium yellow onion, chopped
1 pound (454 g) Yukon Gold potatoes, chopped
1 green bell pepper, chopped
1 tablespoon ground cumin

½ teaspoon salt
1½ teaspoons Whole Food-compliant chili powder
1 teaspoon black pepper
1 teaspoon dried oregano
6 cups Whole Food-compliant chicken broth
¾ cup Whole Food-compliant coconut milk

1. Adjust the oven racks so one is about 6 inches from the broiler heat. Preheat the broiler. Line a small baking pan with foil.
2. Make the verde sauce: Cut the jalapeños in half; remove the seeds, if desired. Place the jalapeños, cut sides down, on the baking pan. Broil until charred, about 4 minutes.
3. Place the jalapeños, tomatillos, green chilies, and cilantro in a blender. Cover and pulse until combined yet chunky.
4. Make the chili base: In a large pot over medium-high heat, heat the olive oil. Add the pork and cook until opaque, 5 to 7 minutes. Add the garlic, onion, potatoes, bell pepper, cumin, salt (if desired), chili powder, black pepper, and oregano. Cook, stirring, until the vegetables begin to soften, 6 to 7 minutes.

5. Add the verde sauce and chicken broth to the pork mixture. Turn the heat to medium-high and bring to a gentle boil for 5 minutes. Turn the heat to low and simmer until the pork is cooked through and the potatoes are tender, about 30 minutes. Stir in the coconut milk.
6. Top servings with cilantro.

Chapter 10: Poultry

Asian Chicken Curry

Prep time: 15 minutes | Cook time: 40 minutes

Serves 4

2 pounds (907 g) ground chicken (half dark meat and half white meat, if you can find it)
½ cup chopped fresh basil, plus ½ cup sliced into ribbons for garnish, if desired
2 tablespoons minced garlic (about 8 cloves)
3 scallions, thinly sliced
4 tablespoons coconut aminos
¼ cup plus 1 tablespoon red curry paste
2½ teaspoons kosher salt
2 tablespoons coconut oil
1¼ cups chicken stock, warmed

3 tablespoons extra-virgin olive oil
¾ cup finely diced yellow onion
1 (14-ounce / 397-g) can full-fat unsweetened coconut milk, blended
3 tablespoons fresh lime juice
1 tablespoon arrowroot starch
1 tablespoon very cold water
2 teaspoons red pepper flakes
½ teaspoon cayenne pepper
4 heads baby bok choy, coarsely chopped
½ cup chopped fresh cilantro, for garnish (optional)

1. In a large bowl, mix the chicken, the chopped basil, 1 tablespoon of the garlic, the scallions, 3 tablespoons of the coconut aminos, 1 tablespoon of the red curry paste, and the salt until combined well.

2. In a large skillet with high sides, melt the coconut oil over medium-high heat. Using a large spoon, transfer the chicken mixture, spoonful by spoonful (rather than dumping it in), to the skillet. Using a wooden spoon, cook, stirring continuously and breaking up the chicken as it cooks, until cooked through, about 5 minutes. Remove the chicken from the pan and set aside.

3. Return the skillet to the heat and add ¼ cup of the warm stock, stirring and scraping up all the bits of goodness from the bottom of the pan. Pour everything from the skillet over the cooked chicken.

4. In a bowl, stir together the remaining ¼ cup curry paste and 1 cup stock until the curry paste has dissolved. Set aside.

5. In the same skillet, heat 2 tablespoons of the olive oil over medium heat. Add the onion and cook, stirring continuously, until soft, about 2 minutes. Add the remaining 1 tablespoon garlic and cook, stirring, until fragrant, about 1 minute more. Add a bit of the curry-stock mixture and stir, scraping up any bits of loveliness from the bottom of the pan. Add the remainder of the curry-stock mixture and stir to combine well.

6. Add the coconut milk to the skillet and whisk until everything is dissolved and smooth. Add the lime juice and the remaining 1 tablespoon coconut aminos, then stir to combine.

7. Make a slurry by mixing together the arrowroot and cold water in a small bowl, then add to the skillet and stir to combine well.

8. Return the chicken with the juices to the skillet and add the red pepper flakes and cayenne. Stir to combine, and bring to a simmer, stirring occasionally, for 20 minutes.

9. In a medium sauté pan, heat the remaining 1 tablespoon olive oil over medium-high heat. Add the bok choy and cook, stirring continuously, until the leaves are bright green and the bok choy has released some of its liquid, about 2 minutes.

10. Plate the bok choy and spoon the chicken curry over the top. Garnish with the basil ribbons and cilantro, if desired, and serve.

Creamy Spinach Artichoke Chicken

Prep time: 5 minutes | Cook time: 20 minutes
Serves 4

4 (6-ounce / 170-g) boneless, skinless chicken breasts
Kosher salt and freshly ground black pepper, to taste
2 tablespoons extra-virgin olive oil
2 garlic cloves, finely chopped
½ cup chicken stock
1 cup full-fat coconut milk
1 tablespoon Dijon mustard
⅓ cup loosely packed baby spinach
1 (14-ounce / 397-g) can artichoke hearts packed in water, drained and sliced in half

1. Set the chicken breasts on a cutting board. Place one hand flat on one chicken breast and extend your fingers away from the board for safety. With your knife blade held parallel to the cutting board, slice the chicken breast in half horizontally. Repeat with the remaining chicken breasts. Pat the chicken slices dry with paper towels and season both sides with salt and pepper.
2. In a large skillet, heat the olive oil over medium-high heat. Add the chicken and cook until golden brown on both sides and cooked through, 4 to 5 minutes per side. Transfer the chicken to a plate and set aside.
3. Add the garlic to the skillet and cook, stirring continuously, for 30 seconds. Add the stock and cook, scraping up any browned bits from the bottom of the pan with your spoon, for 1 to 2 minutes. Add the coconut milk, ¼ teaspoon salt, and ¼ teaspoon pepper and cook until the sauce has reduced by half, 3 to 4 minutes. Stir in the mustard.
4. Add the spinach and artichokes and cook until the spinach has wilted, about 2 minutes. Taste and season with salt and pepper as desired. Return the chicken to the pan and serve immediately.

Mojo Roast Chicken

Prep time: 5 minutes | Cook time: 30 minutes
Serves 4

½ cup fresh orange juice
¼ cup fresh lime juice
¼ cup extra-virgin olive oil
4 garlic cloves, peeled
1 jalapeño
1 teaspoon dried oregano
1 tablespoon ground coriander
3½ to 4 pounds (1.6 to 1.8 kg) chicken wings
Kosher salt and freshly ground black pepper, to taste
¼ cup loosely packed fresh cilantro leaves
8 fresh mint leaves

1. In a blender, combine the orange juice, lime juice, olive oil, garlic, jalapeño, oregano, and coriander. Blend on high speed until smooth.
2. Season both sides of the chicken wings with 3 teaspoons salt and ½ teaspoon pepper. Place the wings in a large zip-top plastic bag and pour in half the marinade. Massage the wings to coat with the marinade, then squeeze out as much air from the bag as possible and seal the bag. Set it on a rimmed baking sheet and refrigerate for at least 4 hours or up to overnight.
3. Add the cilantro and mint to the remaining marinade and blend until smooth. Taste and season with salt and pepper as desired. Transfer the mojo sauce to a jar, cover, and refrigerate until needed.
4. Position an oven rack in the lower third of the oven and preheat the oven to 425°F (220°C). Line a rimmed baking sheet with parchment paper.
5. Arrange the wings in a single layer on the prepared baking sheet (discard the marinade left in the bag) and roast for 30 to 35 minutes, until the wings are golden brown and register 165°F (74°C) on an instant-read thermometer.
6. Serve the wings with the mojo sauce alongside for dipping.

Chicken and Artichoke Stew

Prep time: 10 minutes | Cook time: 55 minutes

Serves 4 to 6

10 bone-in, skin-on chicken thighs
2 teaspoons kosher salt
1 teaspoon freshly ground black pepper
1½ tablespoons duck fat
1¼ cups chicken stock
1 (14½-ounce / 411-g) can whole tomatoes, with juices
2 tablespoons balsamic vinegar
5 garlic cloves, pressed
1 teaspoon dried oregano
¾ cup green Cerignola olives, pitted and halved lengthwise
1 cup drained canned artichoke hearts, halved

1. Preheat the oven to 375ºF (190ºC).
2. Thoroughly season the chicken thighs with the salt and pepper.
3. In a large Dutch oven, melt the duck fat over medium heat. Add the chicken thighs, skin-side down, and fry until golden, 4 to 6 minutes. Flip the chicken and fry until golden on the second side, about 4 minutes more. When done, transfer the chicken thighs to a large plate and set aside.
4. Add the stock to the pan and stir to scrape up any browned bits from the bottom of the pot. Bring the stock to a simmer and cook for 2 minutes. Add the tomatoes, crushing them with your hands, then add the juices from the can. Bring to a simmer and cook for 2 minutes more. Add the vinegar, garlic, and oregano and bring to a boil. Reduce the heat and simmer for 1 minute.
5. Return the chicken to the Dutch oven and cover. Transfer the pot to the oven and bake for 15 minutes. Then remove the lid and bake for 20 minutes more. Return the pot to the stovetop.
6. Remove the chicken from the pot and set aside. Add the olives and artichokes to the pot and stir to combine. Bring the stew to a boil, then reduce the heat and simmer for 1 minute. Return the chicken to the pot. Serve.

Comforting Chicken Fricassée

Prep time: 5 minutes | Cook time: 20 minutes

Serves 4

4 boneless, skinless chicken breasts (about 2½ pounds / 1.1 kg total)
2¼ teaspoons kosher salt
1 teaspoon freshly ground black pepper
4 tablespoons clarified butter
4 cups finely julienned carrots (3 or 4 medium carrots)
1 cup chicken stock
1 teaspoon arrowroot starch
4 teaspoons apple cider vinegar
2 tablespoons full-fat unsweetened coconut milk, blended
1½ tablespoons chopped fresh tarragon leaves

1. Remove the tender from each chicken breast and set them aside for another use (such as a stir-fry or chicken salad). Season the chicken liberally with 2 teaspoons of the salt and the pepper.
2. In a large sauté pan, melt 3 tablespoons of the clarified butter over medium-high heat. Add the chicken and cook until browned, 4 minutes per side. Reduce the heat to medium, cover the pan, and cook until the chicken is cooked through, 3 to 5 minutes more. Transfer the chicken to a bowl and set aside.
3. In the same pan, melt the remaining 1 tablespoon clarified butter over medium heat. Add the carrots and the remaining ¼ teaspoon salt and cook, stirring, until tender, 3 to 4 minutes. Remove the carrots from the pan and set aside with the chicken.
4. Stir together the stock and arrowroot, then add the mixture to the pan and stir to scrape up any browned bits from the bottom. Add the vinegar and coconut milk and stir to combine. Return the chicken and the carrots to the pan, along with any juices that have collected in the bowl. Bring to a boil. Reduce the heat to medium and simmer for 2 minutes more. Top with the tarragon leaves and serve.

Thai Lemon Curry Chicken Bowls

Prep time: 30 minutes | Cook time: 4½ hours
Serves 6

3 tablespoons Whole Food-compliant red curry paste
4 tablespoons olive oil
1 tablespoon grated fresh ginger
1 teaspoon grated lemon zest
12 small bone-in chicken thighs, skin removed
6 medium carrots, peeled and cut into 1½-inch pieces
1 small red onion, cut into thin wedges
⅔ cup Whole Food-compliant chicken broth
2 (10.7-ounce / 303-g) packages zucchini noodles or 3 medium zucchini, spiralized, long noodles snipped if desired
1 tablespoon sesame seeds, toasted
⅓ cup chopped fresh cilantro
¼ cup slivered almonds, toasted
Lemon wedges, for serving

1. In a small bowl, combine the curry paste, 2 tablespoons of the olive oil, the ginger, and lemon zest. Place half the chicken in a large bowl. Spoon half the curry mixture on the chicken and rub all over. Repeat with remaining chicken and curry mixture. (If desired, cover and marinate the chicken in the refrigerator for up to 2 hours.)
2. Transfer the chicken to a slow cooker. Top with the carrots and onion. Pour the broth over all. Cover and cook on low for 4½ to 5 hours or on high for 2¼ to 2½ hours.
3. Meanwhile, in a large skillet, cook the zucchini noodles in the remaining 2 tablespoons olive oil over medium heat, stirring frequently, until the noodles are crisp, 3 to 4 minutes. Remove from the heat. Stir in 2 teaspoons of the sesame seeds.
4. In a small bowl, combine the cilantro, almonds, and remaining 1 teaspoon sesame seeds. Serve the chicken and vegetables over the zucchini noodles; spoon some of the cooking juices on top. Sprinkle with the cilantro-almond-sesame mixture and serve with lemon wedges.

Chicken with Mushrooms and Sweet Potatoes

Prep time: 30 minutes | Cook time: 6 hours
Serves 6

1 cup Whole Food-compliant chicken broth
3 cloves garlic, minced
4 small sweet potatoes, scrubbed and halved lengthwise (about 1 pound / 454 g total)
1 teaspoon dried thyme
¾ teaspoon salt
¾ teaspoon black pepper
12 small bone-in chicken thighs, skin removed
3 cups thinly sliced cremini mushrooms
½ cup chopped red onion
1 tablespoon coconut oil, melted
3 strips Whole Food-compliant bacon, crisp-cooked and crumbled
Fresh thyme leaves (optional)

1. In a slow cooker, combine the chicken broth and garlic. Place the potatoes, cut sides down, in the cooker. In a small bowl, combine the dried thyme, ½ teaspoon of the salt, and ½ teaspoon of the pepper. Place half the chicken thighs, meaty sides up, on the potatoes. Sprinkle with half the thyme mixture. Repeat with remaining chicken and thyme mixture. Add the mushrooms and red onion to the cooker in an even layer.
2. Cover and cook on low for 6 to 7 hours or on high for 3 to 3½ hours. Remove the chicken and potatoes from the cooker. When cool enough to handle, remove the potato skins. Place the potato flesh in a medium bowl; add the coconut oil and the remaining ¼ teaspoon salt and ¼ teaspoon pepper. Using a potato masher, mash potatoes until smooth.
3. Serve the chicken and vegetables with the mashed potatoes and drizzle with the cooking liquid. Top the servings with bacon and, if desired, fresh thyme.

Roasted Pepper Chicken

Prep time: 10 minutes | Cook time: 4 hours
Serves 4

1 (12-ounce / 340-g) jar Whole Food-compliant roasted red peppers, drained and sliced
1 cup thinly sliced onion
½ cup Whole Food-compliant chicken broth
2 cloves garlic, minced
½ teaspoon salt
1½ pounds (680 g) boneless, skinless chicken breasts
2 teaspoons Whole Food-compliant garlic and herb seasoning
¼ cup pitted Whole Food-compliant Kalamata olives, quartered
1 tablespoon chopped flat-leaf parsley
1 teaspoon grated lemon zest
1 tablespoon extra-virgin olive oil

1. In a slow cooker, combine the red peppers, onion, broth, garlic, and salt. Top with the chicken; sprinkle with the garlic and herb seasoning. Cover and cook on low for 4 hours or on high for 2 hours.
2. Transfer the chicken and vegetables to a serving platter. Discard the cooking liquid. Top the chicken with the olives, parsley, and lemon zest. Drizzle with the olive oil.

Garlic Herb Chicken and Veggies

Prep time: 15 minutes | Cook time: 6 hours
Serves 4

1 pound (454 g) new red potatoes, halved
4 medium carrots, peeled, halved lengthwise, and cut into 1-inch pieces
1 medium onion, cut into thin wedges
½ cup Whole Food-compliant chicken broth
1 teaspoon salt
½ teaspoon black pepper
8 bone-in chicken thighs, skin removed
1½ teaspoons Whole Food-compliant Italian seasoning
½ teaspoon garlic powder
Chopped fresh flat-leaf parsley, for serving

1. In a slow cooker, combine the potatoes, carrots, onion, broth, ½ teaspoon of the salt, and ¼ teaspoon of the pepper. Top with the chicken. Sprinkle with the Italian seasoning, garlic powder, and remaining salt and pepper.
2. Cover and cook on low for 6 to 8 hours or on high for 3 to 4 hours.
3. Strain the cooking liquid. Serve the chicken and vegetables drizzled with some of the cooking liquid. Top with parsley.

Sticky Apricot Drumsticks

Prep time: 15 minutes | Cook time: 5 hours
Serves 4

½ cup water
2 tablespoons coconut aminos
2 tablespoons Whole Food-compliant Dijon mustard
1 clove garlic, minced
½ teaspoon salt
¼ teaspoon red pepper flakes
8 chicken drumsticks (1½ to 2 pounds / 680 to 907 g total), skin removed
6 ounces (170 g) dried apricots, chopped
1 shallot, thinly sliced (about ⅓ cup)
2 packages (12 ounces / 340 g each) frozen riced cauliflower, prepared according to package directions, or 3 cups raw cauliflower rice
Chopped fresh parsley (optional)

1. In a slow cooker, combine the water, coconut aminos, mustard, garlic, salt, and red pepper flakes. Add the chicken, apricots, and shallot and toss to coat.
2. Cover and cook on low for 5 to 6 hours or on high for 2½ to 3 hours. Transfer the chicken to a plate and cover to keep warm. Use an immersion blender to blend the mixture in the cooker until smooth. Add water, 1 tablespoon at a time, if needed for desired consistency. Return the chicken to the slow cooker and toss gently with tongs to coat.
3. Serve the drumsticks over the cauliflower rice. Top with the sauce and chopped parsley, if desired.

Greek Lemon Chicken and Potatoes

Prep time: 15 minutes | Cook time: 50 minutes

Serves 4

Lemon and Garlic Sauce:

½ cup fresh lemon juice

½ cup extra-virgin olive oil

2½ tablespoons red wine vinegar

1 garlic clove, pressed

1 teaspoon dried oregano

¾ teaspoon kosher salt

½ teaspoon Dijon mustard

¼ teaspoon freshly ground black pepper

Chicken:

1 (4-pound / 1.8-kg) whole chicken, cut in half

1 teaspoon kosher salt

½ teaspoon freshly ground black pepper

1½ teaspoons extra-virgin olive oil

4 Yukon Gold potatoes, sliced into ¼-inch-thick rounds

1 lemon, sliced into ¼-inch-thick rounds

Chopped fresh parsley, for garnish

1. Adjust the oven rack to 6 inches below the broiler. Preheat the oven to broil. Line a large baking sheet with parchment paper.
2. For the sauce: In a large bowl, add the lemon juice and using a whisk, slowly add the olive oil. Then add the vinegar, garlic, oregano, salt, mustard, and black pepper, stirring well. Set aside.
3. For the chicken: Thoroughly season each chicken half with the salt and black pepper, then generously rub every crevice with the olive oil. Put the chicken skin-side down on the lined baking sheet and put the pan on the adjusted rack in the oven. Broil for 15 minutes, until beginning to turn golden.
4. Remove the baking sheet from the oven and flip the chicken over to the other side. Return to the oven and broil for 20 minutes more, or until cooked through, golden brown, and bubbling. Remove the pan from the oven and set the chicken aside. Once cool enough to handle, cut each half into 3 pieces: legs, thighs, and breasts with wings attached.
5. Arrange the sliced potatoes and lemons on the baking sheet. Return to the oven and cook for 10 to 12 minutes, or until the potatoes and lemons begin to brown. Remove the baking sheet from the oven, put the chicken on top of the potatoes and lemons, and pour ½ cup of the lemon and garlic sauce evenly over the top.
6. Return to the oven and broil until the chicken is further browned and crispy, about 5 minutes. Remove the chicken from the pan and drain off any excess liquid from the pan (so that the potatoes can cook to a crisp). Return the potatoes to the oven and broil until crisped and cooked through, 10 to 15 minutes more.
7. Serve the potatoes and lemons with the chicken and the remaining lemon and garlic sauce, either poured over the top or as a dipping sauce.

Chipotle Chicken Thighs with Tomatoes

Prep time: 15 minutes | Cook time: 5 hours

Serves 4

1 (14½-ounce / 411-g) can Whole Food-compliant fire-roasted crushed tomatoes

1 medium yellow bell pepper, coarsely chopped

2 cloves garlic, minced

2 teaspoons chili powder

1 teaspoon chipotle powder

½ teaspoon salt

8 boneless, skinless chicken thighs (1½ to 2 pounds / 680 to 907 g total)

1 (12-ounce / 340-g) package frozen cauliflower rice, prepared according to package directions or 3 cups raw cauliflower rice

Sliced green onions, for serving

Lime wedges, for serving

1. In a slow cooker, stir together the tomatoes, bell pepper, garlic, chili powder, chipotle powder, and salt. Add the chicken and turn to coat. Cover and cook on low for 5 to 6 hours or on high for 2½ to 3 hours.
2. Serve the chicken on cauliflower rice and top with green onions. Serve with lime wedges.

Piri Piri Chicken

Prep time: 10 minutes | Cook time: 45 minutes
Serves 4

1 small yellow onion, halved
¼ cup extra-virgin olive oil
¼ cup red wine vinegar
Juice of ½ lemon
4 garlic cloves, peeled
2 fresh red finger chiles (or Anaheim chiles, if not available)
1 (1-inch) piece fresh ginger, peeled
1 tablespoon kosher

salt
1 teaspoon smoked paprika
1 teaspoon sweet paprika
1 teaspoon dried oregano
½ teaspoon cayenne pepper, plus more if desired
1 (2½- to 3-pound / 1.1- to 1.4-kg) whole chicken

1. In a blender, combine the onion, olive oil, vinegar, lemon juice, garlic, chiles, ginger, salt, smoked paprika, sweet paprika, oregano, cayenne, and ¼ cup water. Blend on high speed until smooth.
2. Dry the chicken with paper towels. Using sharp kitchen shears or a sharp knife, cut along one side of the backbone, leaving the other side attached. Lay the chicken breast-side up on a cutting board and press down on the breastbone with your hands to flatten the chicken. Put the chicken in a large zip-top plastic bag and pour in the marinade. Massage the marinade all over the chicken, then squeeze as much air out of the bag as possible and seal. Place it on a baking sheet with the chicken breast-side down and refrigerate for at least 4 hours or up to overnight.
3. Preheat the oven to 425ºF (220ºC). Line a 4-inch-deep roasting pan with parchment paper.
4. Remove the chicken from the marinade, letting any excess drip off (discard the bag). Place the chicken in the prepared roasting pan and roast on the bottom rack for 40 to 45 minutes, until the thickest part of the thigh registers 165ºF (74ºC) on an instant-read thermometer. Use a turkey baster or large spoon to baste the chicken with the rendered juices in the pan.
5. Set the oven to broil, but keep the chicken on the bottom rack (putting the parchment paper closer to the broiler could cause it to catch fire). Broil for 4 to 5 minutes, until the skin is golden brown and crispy.
6. Transfer the chicken to a grooved cutting board to catch any juices and let it rest for 5 to 10 minutes before carving and serving.

Spanish Chicken Cauliflower Skillet

Prep time: 20 minutes | Cook time: 20 minutes
Serves 4

4 slices Whole Food-compliant bacon, chopped
1 pound (454 g) boneless, skinless chicken breasts or thighs, diced
1 medium onion, chopped
1 red bell pepper, chopped
4 cloves garlic, minced
1 (28-ounce / 794-

g) can Whole Food-compliant diced tomatoes
½ teaspoon black pepper
¼ teaspoon cayenne pepper
¼ teaspoon salt
4 cups cauliflower florets
½ cup pimento-stuffed Spanish olives, halved

1. In a large skillet, cook the bacon over medium-high heat until crisp, about 5 minutes. Transfer with a slotted spoon to paper towels to drain, leaving the bacon fat in the skillet.
2. Add the chicken to the skillet and cook, stirring, until opaque, 2 to 3 minutes. Stir in the onion, bell pepper, and garlic. Cook, stirring until the onions are softened, about 4 minutes. Add the tomatoes, black pepper, cayenne pepper, and salt. Bring to a boil and add the cauliflower. Cover and simmer until the cauliflower is just tender, about 5 minutes. Top with the bacon and olives and serve.

Green Chile Chicken Stew

Prep time: 25 minutes | Cook time: 6 hours
Serves 4

1½ pounds (680 g) baby red or gold potatoes
8 bone-in chicken thighs (about 2 pounds / 907 g total), skin removed
1 (4-ounce / 113-g) can Whole Food-compliant diced green chiles
½ cup Whole Food-compliant chicken broth
2 medium tomatillos, husks removed and diced
3 cloves garlic, minced
2 teaspoons ground cumin
1 teaspoon ground coriander
1 teaspoon salt
½ teaspoon black pepper
Grated zest and juice of 1 lime
½ cup chopped fresh cilantro

1. Place the potatoes in a slow cooker. Arrange the chicken over the potatoes. In a medium bowl, combine the green chiles, broth, tomatillos, garlic, cumin, coriander, salt, and pepper. Pour over the chicken and potatoes in the cooker. Cover and cook on low for 6 hours or on high for 3 hours.
2. Drizzle the chicken and potatoes with the lime juice and sprinkle with the lime zest and cilantro.

Sweet Potato and Chicken Hash

Prep time: 15 minutes | Cook time: 5 to 10 minutes
Serves 2

2 tablespoons cooking fat
1 pound (454 g) boneless, skinless chicken thighs, cut into 1-inch dice
½ teaspoon salt
½ teaspoon black pepper
¼ cup chopped walnuts
1 sweet potato, peeled and grated
1 Granny Smith apple, cored, peeled, and diced
½ teaspoon red pepper flakes
¼ cup apple cider
2 generous handfuls arugula or baby spinach

1. In a large skillet, heat the cooking fat over medium-high heat, swirling to coat the bottom of the pan. When the fat is hot, add the chicken, being sure not to crowd the pieces. Season the chicken with the salt and pepper. Cook until browned, 2 to 3 minutes. Turn the chicken to brown the other sides, add the walnuts, and cook until the chicken is browned and the walnuts are toasted, 2 to 3 minutes. (Shake the pan occasionally so the walnuts don't burn.) Add the sweet potato, apple, and red pepper flakes and cook, stirring often, until the chicken is fully cooked, 3 to 4 minutes.
2. Add the apple cider and mix all the ingredients together, scraping the bottom of the pan with a wooden spoon to bring up any tasty bits. Add the arugula and cook for another 30 seconds, gently stirring to the wilt leaves. Serve immediately.

Lemony Chicken with Green Beans

Prep time: 15 minutes | Cook time: 8 hours
Serves 4

1 cup Whole Food-compliant chicken broth
¾ pound (340 g) green beans, trimmed and halved crosswise
1 small white onion, diced
3 Roma (plum) tomatoes, cored and quartered
8 bone-in chicken thighs (2 to 2½ pounds / 907 g to 1.1 kg total), skin removed
¾ teaspoon salt
½ teaspoon black pepper
½ teaspoon dried thyme
2 lemons, cut into ¼-inch-thick slices, seeds removed

1. In a slow cooker, combine the broth, green beans, onion, and tomatoes. Place the chicken on the vegetables and sprinkle with the salt, pepper, and thyme. Top the chicken with the lemon slices.
2. Cover and cook on low for 8 hours or on high for 4 hours. Serve the chicken with the vegetables.

Crispy Chicken Schnitzel

Prep time: 5 minutes | Cook time: 10 minutes
Serves 2

2 (6-ounce / 170-g) boneless, skinless chicken breasts
¼ cup arrowroot starch
¼ cup cassava flour
2 large eggs
¼ teaspoon kosher salt
⅛ teaspoon freshly ground black pepper
3 tablespoons avocado oil
1 teaspoon sesame seeds, for serving
Flaky sea salt, for serving

1. Line a baking sheet with a wire rack.
2. Set the chicken breasts on a cutting board. Place one hand flat on one chicken breast and extend your fingers away from the board for safety. With your knife blade held parallel to the cutting board, slice the chicken breast in half horizontally. Repeat with the second chicken breast. Lay the chicken slices flat on the cutting board, cover them with plastic wrap, and pound them with a meat mallet or rolling pin until they are approximately ¼ inch thick.
3. Place the arrowroot starch, cassava flour, and eggs into three separate bowls. Season the cassava flour with the salt and pepper. Add 2 tablespoons water to the eggs and whisk vigorously until frothy.
4. Dredge each piece of chicken in the arrowroot starch to coat both sides, then dip into the egg wash, letting any excess drip off. Dredge in the seasoned cassava flour to coat and set aside on a large plate.
5. In a large nonstick skillet, heat the avocado oil over medium-high heat for 1 to 2 minutes, until it shimmers. Carefully add the breaded chicken to the hot oil and cook until golden brown, about 4 minutes. Flip and cook for 2 minutes more, until browned on the second side. Transfer the cooked schnitzel to the wire rack. Sprinkle them evenly with the sesame seeds and season each with a tiny pinch of flaky sea salt. Serve immediately.

Chicken Cacciatore

Prep time: 15 minutes | Cook time: 40 minutes
Serves 2

4 tablespoons cooking fat
1 pound (454 g) chicken legs (bone-in, skin-on)
½ pound (227 g) chicken thighs (boneless)
½ teaspoon salt
½ teaspoon black pepper
½ onion, minced
½ red bell pepper, finely diced
1 cup mushrooms, sliced
2 cloves garlic, minced
1 tablespoon Whole Food-compliant capers, drained
1 (14½-ounce / 411-g) can diced tomatoes
1 cup chicken broth or water
1 tablespoon fresh basil leaves, rough chopped

1. In a large skillet with high edges, heat 2 tablespoons of the cooking fat over medium-high heat, swirling to coat the bottom of the pan. Season the chicken with the salt and pepper and place in the pan. Sear the chicken until golden brown, about 3 minutes on each side. Remove the chicken from the pan and set aside.
2. With the same pan still on medium-high heat, add the remaining 2 tablespoons of cooking fat, onions, and peppers and sauté for 2 to 3 minutes, until the onion becomes translucent. Add the mushrooms and continue to cook, stirring for 2 minutes. Add the garlic and stir until aromatic, about 1 minute. Add the capers and diced tomatoes.
3. Return the chicken to the pan and cover everything with the chicken broth or water. Reduce the heat to medium and bring everything to a simmer. Turn the heat down to low and continue to simmer (not boil) until the chicken reaches an internal temperature of 160°F (71°C), about 30 minutes.
4. Garnish with the chopped basil and serve.

Chicken Meatballs with Creamy Tomato Sauce

Prep time: 10 minutes | Cook time: 30 minutes

Serves 3 or 4

Meatballs:

2 pounds (907 g) ground chicken

1 large egg

¼ cup finely chopped fresh parsley leaves

2 tablespoons finely chopped sun-dried tomatoes packed in olive oil, drained

1 shallot, finely chopped

2 garlic cloves, finely chopped

2 teaspoons kosher salt

1 teaspoon dried basil

½ teaspoon freshly ground black pepper

2 tablespoons extra-virgin olive oil, plus more as needed

Sun-Dried Tomato Cream Sauce:

1 tablespoon extra-virgin olive oil

1 red bell pepper, diced

1 shallot, finely chopped

2 garlic cloves, finely chopped

1¼ cups full-fat coconut milk

2 tablespoons coarsely chopped sun-dried tomatoes packed in olive oil, drained

1 tablespoon Dijon mustard

Kosher salt and freshly ground black pepper, to taste

1. Make the meatballs: In a large bowl, combine the ground chicken, egg, parsley, sun-dried tomatoes, shallot, garlic, salt, basil, and pepper. Mix with your hands until well combined. Rub a small amount of olive oil on your hands and form the mixture into meatballs slightly larger than golf balls, setting them on a baking sheet as you roll them.
2. In a large sauté pan, heat the olive oil over medium-high heat. Add the meatballs to the pan and cook until browned on all sides and cooked through, about 15 minutes. Transfer the meatballs to a platter and set aside.
3. Make the sun-dried tomato cream sauce: Wipe the sauté pan clean with a paper towel, return the pan to medium-high heat, and pour in the olive oil. Add the bell pepper and shallot and cook, stirring, until slightly softened, 3 to 4 minutes. Add the garlic and cook, stirring, for 30 seconds. Add the coconut milk, sun-dried tomatoes, and mustard and season with salt and black pepper. Cook, stirring occasionally, until the sauce has reduced by at least a quarter, about 4 minutes. Taste and adjust the seasoning, if desired.
4. Remove the pan from the heat, add the meatballs to the sauce, and toss to coat. Let the meatballs sit until they have warmed through, about 3 minutes. Serve immediately.

Salsa Verde Chicken

Prep time: 20 minutes | Cook time: 4 hours

Serves 4

1 to 1½ pounds (454 to 680 g) boneless, skinless chicken breast

¼ teaspoon ground cumin

¼ teaspoon sea salt

¼ teaspoon black pepper

2 cups quartered husked tomatillos (4 to 5)

2 poblano peppers, stems removed and quartered

½ cup diced onion

2 tablespoons sliced garlic

2 cups chopped fresh cilantro

Juice of ½ lime

½ teaspoon salt

1. Place the chicken breasts and ¼ cup water in a slow cooker. Sprinkle with the cumin, salt, and pepper. Add the tomatillos, poblano peppers, onion, and garlic.
2. Cover and cook on low for 4 hours or on high for 2 hours.
3. Transfer the chicken to a platter with a slotted spoon; cover and keep warm. Transfer the tomatillos, peppers, onion, and garlic to a blender or food processor. Add the cilantro, lime juice, and salt. Cover and blend or process until almost smooth. Chop or shred the chicken, stir into the sauce, and serve over cooked riced vegetables or veggie noodles.

Grapefruit Chicken

Prep time: 10 minutes | Cook time: 2 hours
Serves 4

1 tablespoon plus 2½ teaspoons kosher salt
1½ teaspoons freshly ground black pepper
1 teaspoon granulated garlic
1 teaspoon dried marjoram
1 teaspoon paprika
¼ teaspoon cayenne pepper
1 whole chicken (about 4 pounds / 1.8 kg)
4 tablespoons extra-
virgin olive oil
¾ cup fresh grapefruit juice (reserve one of the juiced halves)
3 large carrots, halved lengthwise and cut into thirds
3 cups quartered red potatoes (about 1 pound / 454 g)
1 medium yellow onion, cut into 8 wedges
5 garlic cloves

1. In a small bowl, stir together 1 tablespoon plus 1½ teaspoons of the salt, 1 teaspoon of the black pepper, the granulated garlic, marjoram, paprika, and cayenne. Set aside.
2. Put the chicken on a baking sheet or large plate and coat the skin with 1 tablespoon of the olive oil. Sprinkle the spice blend on all sides of the chicken to liberally and evenly coat. Cover the chicken and refrigerate for at least 2 hours or up to overnight.
3. When ready to cook the chicken, preheat the oven to 350ºF (180ºC). Line a baking sheet with parchment paper.
4. Set the chicken on the lined baking sheet.
5. In a small bowl, stir together the grapefruit juice and 2 tablespoons of the olive oil. Set aside.
6. In a medium bowl, combine the carrots, potatoes, onion, and garlic cloves with the remaining 1 tablespoon olive oil, 1 teaspoon salt, and ½ teaspoon black pepper and toss to coat evenly. Distribute the vegetables evenly on the baking sheet around the chicken. Fold the juiced grapefruit half and stuff it inside the chicken.
7. Bake the chicken for 30 minutes, then baste it with the grapefruit juice mixture.

Return it to the oven and bake for a total time of 80 to 90 minutes (or 20 minutes per pound), basting every 15 minutes. If the chicken becomes too brown, loosely cover it with aluminum foil.
8. Serve.

Rosemary Whole Chicken

Prep time: 5 minutes | Cook time: 45 minutes
Serves 2 to 4

1 (2½- to 3-pound / 1.1- to 1.4-kg) whole chicken
1 tablespoon coarsely chopped fresh
rosemary
Kosher salt and freshly ground black pepper, to taste

1. Preheat the oven to 425ºF (220ºC). Line a 4-inch-deep roasting pan with parchment paper.
2. Pat the chicken very dry with paper towels. Using sharp kitchen shears or a sharp knife, cut along one side of the backbone, leaving the other side attached. Lay the chicken breast-side up on a cutting board and press down on the breastbone with your hands to flatten the chicken. Liberally season the chicken all over with the rosemary and salt and pepper. Transfer the chicken breast-side up to the prepared roasting pan.
3. Roast on the bottom rack of the oven for 40 to 45 minutes, until the thickest part of the thigh registers 165ºF (74ºC) on an instant-read thermometer. Use a turkey baster or large spoon to baste the chicken with the juices from the pan.
4. Set the oven to broil, but keep the chicken on the bottom rack (putting the parchment paper closer to the broiler could cause it to catch fire). Broil for 4 to 5 minutes, until the skin is golden brown and crispy.
5. Transfer the chicken to a grooved cutting board to catch any juices and let it rest for 5 to 10 minutes before carving and serving.

Butter Chicken

Prep time: 5 minutes | Cook time: 15 minutes

Serves 4

1½ pounds (680 g) boneless, skinless chicken thighs	lemon juice
	1 tablespoon finely chopped garlic
2 teaspoons kosher salt	2 teaspoons paprika
1 teaspoon freshly ground black pepper	1 teaspoon red pepper flakes
¼ cup plus 2 tablespoons extra-virgin olive oil	¼ cup plus 1 tablespoon clarified butter
2 tablespoons fresh	3 tablespoons hot sauce

1. Spread the chicken out in a shallow container good for marinating. Season with 1 teaspoon of the salt and ½ teaspoon of the black pepper. Set aside.
2. In a small bowl, combine the remaining 1 teaspoon salt, remaining ½ teaspoon black pepper, ¼ cup of the olive oil, the lemon juice, garlic, paprika, and red pepper flakes and stir until combined well. Pour the mixture over the chicken, tossing to thoroughly coat. Cover and refrigerate for at least 2 hours or up to overnight, if you have the time.
3. When ready to cook, remove the chicken from the refrigerator and let it come to room temperature.
4. Heat a large, dry cast-iron skillet over high heat. Once hot, reduce the heat to medium and heat the remaining 2 tablespoons olive oil. When the oil is warm, add the chicken thighs to the skillet and cook until browned and crispy, about 4 minutes, then flip and cook until cooked through and browned, 5 to 7 minutes more, depending on the thickness of the thighs. Test for doneness. Set the pan aside.
5. In a small pan, melt the clarified butter over low heat. Transfer the butter to a blender, add the hot sauce, and blend until emulsified. Spoon the sauce over the chicken in the pan, coating the chicken thoroughly.
6. Serve immediately.

Lemon and Oregano Chicken with Parsnips

Prep time: 25 minutes | Cook time: 6 hours

Serves 4

2 teaspoons garlic powder	Food-compliant pitted green olives
2 teaspoons dried oregano	2 medium parsnips, peeled and sliced ½-inch thick
1 teaspoon salt	
½ teaspoon paprika	2 medium russet potatoes, peeled and sliced ½-inch thick
½ teaspoon black pepper	
8 boneless, skinless chicken thighs (about 2 pounds / 907 g total)	¼ cup melted clarified butter or ghee
1 lemon, thinly sliced	2 tablespoons tapioca flour
½ cup chopped Whole	

1. In a small bowl, combine the garlic powder, oregano, salt, paprika, and pepper. Sprinkle 2 teaspoons of the garlic seasoning over the chicken. Place the chicken in a slow cooker. Add ½ cup water, the lemon slices, and olives.
2. In a medium bowl, combine the parsnips and potatoes; sprinkle with the remaining garlic seasoning. Add to the slow cooker and pour the melted butter over all.
3. Cover and cook on low for 6 hours or on high for 3 hours. Transfer the chicken, potatoes, and parsnips to a platter; cover and keep warm.
4. Turn the slow cooker to high if using the low setting. In a small bowl, stir together the tapioca powder and ¼ cup water; add to the cooking liquid. Stir until the sauce is thickened, about 3 minutes. Serve the sauce over the chicken, potatoes, and parsnips.

Lemon and Herb Roast Chicken and Vegetables

Prep time: 30 minutes | Cook time: 6 hours
Serves 4

1 lemon, quartered
4 sprigs fresh herbs (rosemary, thyme, and/ or oregano); plus more for serving (optional)
1 whole chicken (3 to 3½ pounds / 1.4 to 1.6 kg)
1 tablespoon extra-virgin olive oil
1 tablespoon grated lemon zest
1½ teaspoons fresh

lemon juice
½ teaspoon salt
¼ teaspoon black pepper
2 large onions, cut into wedges
1 pound (454 g) baby Yukon Gold potatoes
6 medium carrots, peeled and cut into 1-inch slices
Lemon wedges (optional)

1. Place the lemon quarters and the herb sprigs in the cavity of the chicken. In a small bowl, combine the olive oil, lemon zest, lemon juice, salt, and pepper. Rub the mixture all over the chicken. Tie the legs together with cotton kitchen string.
2. In a slow cooker, combine the onions, potatoes, and carrots. Place the chicken, breast side up, on the vegetables. Cover and cook on low for 6 to 7 hours or on high for 3 to 3½ hours, or until the chicken is no longer pink and a thermometer registers 170°F (77°C) when inserted into a thigh.
3. Preheat the oven to broil.
4. Carefully transfer the chicken to a broiler-safe 13 × 6-inch baking pan. Remove and discard the lemon and herbs from the cavity. Use a slotted spoon to transfer the vegetables to the baking pan; discard the cooking liquid. Broil the chicken and vegetables until the chicken skin is golden brown and crispy, about 5 minutes. Serve the chicken with the vegetables. If desired, top with additional fresh herb leaves and/or serve with lemon wedges.

Slow-Cooker Five-Spice Chicken Wings

Prep time: 20 minutes | Cook time: 3 hours
Serves 4

3 pounds (1.4 kg) chicken wings
2 tablespoons Whole Food-compliant five-spice powder
1 teaspoon cayenne pepper
1 teaspoon salt
3 green onions, trimmed
½ cup unsweetened pineapple juice

2 tablespoons coconut aminos
1 tablespoon grated fresh ginger
1 tablespoon sesame seeds, toasted
½ to 1 teaspoon red pepper flakes
Whole Food-compliant creamy ranch dressing
Mixed salad greens (optional)

1. Use kitchen shears or a very sharp chef's knife to remove the tips of the chicken wings (discard the tips or save them for making stock). Cut along the edge of the drumette through the joint to separate the wingette and the drumette (you should have 8 of each). Place the chicken pieces in a large bowl.
2. In a small bowl, combine the five-spice powder, cayenne, and salt. Sprinkle over the chicken and toss to coat.
3. Slice and set aside the green tops of the green onions. Trim the root of the white ends. Add the white green onion ends, pineapple juice, coconut aminos, and ginger to a slow cooker. Add the wings and toss to coat.
4. Cover and cook on high for 3 hours. Using a slotted spoon, transfer the chicken to a large bowl and carefully toss with the sliced green onion tops, sesame seeds, and red pepper flakes. Discard the cooking liquid. Serve the wings with the ranch salad dressing for dipping and, if desired, drizzled over mixed greens.

Turkey Meatballs with Spaghetti Squash

Prep time: 30 minutes | Cook time: 5 hours

Serves 4

1 large egg
½ cup finely chopped onion
¼ cup almond flour
½ teaspoon fennel seeds, finely crushed
½ teaspoon ground coriander
1 teaspoon salt
¼ teaspoon black pepper
1 pound (454 g) ground turkey
2 cups Whole Food-compliant canned crushed tomatoes, undrained
⅓ cup finely chopped drained Whole Food-compliant roasted red

peppers
¼ cup Whole Food-compliant tomato paste
3 cloves garlic, minced
1 bay leaf
1 spaghetti squash (about 2 pounds / 907 g), halved lengthwise and seeds removed
1 tablespoon extra-virgin olive oil
⅓ cup coarsely chopped Whole Food-compliant pitted green olives
2 tablespoons fresh lemon juice
½ cup chopped flat-leaf parsley

1. Preheat the oven to 400°F (205°C).
2. In a large bowl, whisk the egg together with 2 tablespoons water. Stir in the onion, almond flour, fennel seeds, coriander, ¾ teaspoon of the salt, and the pepper. Add the turkey and mix well. Shape into 12 meatballs and place in a foil-lined rimmed baking pan. Bake for 10 minutes.
3. Meanwhile, in a medium bowl, stir together the crushed tomatoes, roasted peppers, tomato paste, garlic, and bay leaf. Pour about half of the sauce into a slow cooker. Place the squash halves, cut sides down, on the sauce. (If necessary to fit in the slow cooker, cut squash halves in half.) Place the meatballs around and on top of the squash. Spoon the remaining sauce over the meatballs.
4. Cover and cook on low for 5 hours or on high for 2½ hours. Use a large spoon to transfer the squash halves to a cutting board; cool for about 10 minutes. Use a

fork to scrape the strands into a large bowl. Drizzle the squash strands with the olive oil and sprinkle with the remaining ¼ teaspoon salt. Toss to coat.
5. Remove and discard the bay leaf. Gently stir the olives and lemon juice into the sauce and meatballs. Serve the meatballs and sauce over the squash. Sprinkle with parsley.

Onion Chicken Meatballs

Prep time: 20 minutes | Cook time: 15 minutes

Serves 2

1 pound (454 g) ground chicken thigh
1 large egg, beaten
¼ onion, finely chopped
2 cloves garlic, minced
2 teaspoons minced fresh oregano, (or

1 teaspoon dried oregano)
1 teaspoon salt
½ teaspoon black pepper
2 tablespoons cooking fat, plus more if needed

1. Preheat the oven to 350°F (180°C). Line a baking sheet with parchment paper.
2. Thoroughly mix the chicken, egg, onion, garlic, oregano, salt, and pepper in a large bowl. Roll into 15 to 20 meatballs, each about the size of a golf ball.
3. Melt the cooking fat in a large skillet over medium-high heat. When the fat is hot, add the meatballs (depending on the size of your pan, you may have to do this in batches). Cook for about 30 seconds per side, turning to prevent burning, until browned all over, about 5 minutes. Reduce the heat and add more cooking fat if the pan begins to smoke.
4. Transfer the meatballs to the prepared baking sheet. Transfer to the oven to finish cooking for 8 to 10 minutes, until the internal temperature reaches 160°F (71°C). Let the meatballs rest for 5 minutes and serve.

Turmeric Chicken Thighs

Prep time: 5 minutes | Cook time: 1 hour | Serves 4

1 tablespoon hot paprika
1 tablespoon ground coriander
1 tablespoon smoked paprika
1 tablespoon Aleppo pepper
1 tablespoon caraway seeds
1 tablespoon ground sumac
¼ cup grated fresh ginger
¼ cup grated fresh turmeric

12 bone-in, skin-on chicken thighs (about 3½ pounds / 1.6 kg total)
3 teaspoons kosher salt
1 cup full-fat unsweetened coconut milk, blended
⅓ cup extra-virgin olive oil
3 tablespoons fresh lime juice
6 garlic cloves, chopped
Chopped fresh parsley, for garnish

1. In a small bowl, stir together the hot paprika, coriander, smoked paprika, Aleppo pepper, caraway seeds, and sumac. Measure out 3 tablespoons of the spice blend for this recipe and set aside. Save the remainder for another day.
2. Squeeze the juice from the grated ginger into a bowl, discarding the pulp. Set aside. Do the same with the grated turmeric and set aside.
3. Arrange the chicken thighs in a shallow container and sprinkle with 1½ teaspoons of the salt. Set aside.
4. In a medium bowl, stir together the coconut milk, olive oil, lime juice, ginger and turmeric juices, garlic, and the remaining 1½ teaspoons salt. Stir in the reserved 3 tablespoons spice blend. Set aside about ½ cup of the marinade and refrigerate, then pour the remaining marinade over the chicken. Cover the chicken and refrigerate for at least 3 hours or up to overnight, if you have the time.
5. When ready to cook the chicken, preheat the oven to 350ºF (180ºC). Line a large baking sheet with parchment paper. Remove the marinated chicken from the refrigerator and let it come to room temperature.
6. Put the chicken, with its marinade, on the prepared baking sheet and bake for 30 minutes, or until starting to turn golden. Remove the baking sheet from the oven.
7. Without disturbing the chicken, carefully pour the juices from the pan into a small bowl. Baste the chicken by spooning the juices over, then return the chicken to the oven and bake for 15 minutes more, or until it starts to turn golden brown, then baste again with the juices, and if needed, carefully pour off any excess juices once more into the bowl. Increase the oven temperature to 375ºF (190ºC) and bake for 5 to 10 minutes, until golden brown and bubbly and the bones of the thighs begin to stick through the skin. If you like the skin crispier, turn on the convection function, or turn up the oven temperature to 400ºF (205ºC) if you don't have a convection oven, and bake for 5 minutes.
8. Pour the reserved marinade into a small saucepan and simmer over medium heat until it has reduced by half.
9. Serve the chicken drizzled with the reduced sauce and sprinkled with parsley.

Smoky Spanish Chicken Meatballs

Prep time: 30 minutes | Cook time: 6 hours
Serves 6

1 (15-ounce / 425-g) can Whole Food-compliant tomato sauce
1 (14½-ounce / 411-g) can Whole Food-compliant diced fire-roasted tomatoes
¼ cup fresh orange juice
1 teaspoon Spanish (sweet) paprika
½ teaspoon smoked paprika
⅓ cup almond meal
1 large egg, lightly beaten
2 tablespoons chopped Whole Food-compliant green olives

1 serrano chile pepper, seeded and finely chopped
½ teaspoon grated orange zest
2 cloves garlic, minced
½ teaspoon salt
1½ pounds (680 g) ground chicken
1 tablespoon extra-virgin olive oil
2 packages (10 ounces / 283 g each) frozen riced butternut squash, prepared according to package directions
Chopped fresh parsley, for serving

1. In a slow cooker, combine the tomato sauce, tomatoes, orange juice, Spanish paprika, and smoked paprika. In a medium bowl, combine the almond meal, egg, olives, serrano, orange zest, garlic, and salt. Add the chicken and, using wet hands, mix well. Shape into 1½-inch meatballs. Arrange the meatballs over the sauce in the cooker. Drizzle with the olive oil. Cover and cook on low for 6 hours or on high for 3 hours.
2. Serve the meatballs and sauce over the riced squash. Sprinkle with parsley.

Braised Chicken with Artichoke and Olives

Prep time: 20 minutes | Cook time: 6 hours
Serves 4

2 teaspoons garlic powder
1 teaspoon salt
½ teaspoon black pepper
8 chicken legs, skin removed
2 medium white onions, roughly chopped
2 (14-ounce / 397-g) cans Whole Food-compliant whole artichoke hearts, drained and

halved
1½ cups pitted Whole Food-compliant Kalamata olives
1 lemon, cut into wedges
3 sprigs fresh thyme, plus additional leaves for garnish

1. In a small bowl, combine the garlic powder, salt, and pepper. Rub the chicken with the seasoning. Place the onions, artichoke hearts, and olives in a slow cooker. Add the chicken. Top with lemon wedges and thyme sprigs.
2. Cover and cook on low for 6 to 7 hours or on high for 3 to 3½ hours. Remove and discard the lemon wedges and thyme. Serve the chicken with the artichokes, onions, and olives. Sprinkle with additional thyme.

Balsamic Turkey Tenderloins with Peppers

Prep time: 15 minutes | Cook time: 35 minutes
Serves 4

1½ pounds (680 g) turkey tenderloins
½ teaspoon salt
½ teaspoon black pepper
2 tablespoons extra-virgin olive oil
4 cups sliced sweet mini peppers
1 serrano chile pepper, halved, seeded, and

thinly sliced
1 medium onion, sliced
3 cloves garlic, minced
1 pint cherry or grape tomatoes
¼ cup balsamic vinegar
2 tablespoons torn fresh basil

1. Preheat the oven to 425ºF (220ºC).
2. Season the turkey with the salt and black pepper. Heat the oil in an ovenproof skillet over medium-high heat. Add the turkey and cook until browned, 2 to 3 minutes per side.
3. Remove the turkey from the skillet. Add the bell peppers, chile, onion, and garlic to the skillet and cook, stirring occasionally, until just softened, 3 to 5 minutes. Stir in the tomatoes and vinegar.
4. Return the turkey to the skillet and transfer to the oven. Roast until the turkey is cooked through, 25 to 30 minutes. Let the turkey rest 5 minutes then cut into slices. Top with the basil and serve.

Chicken Stir Fry

Prep time: 10 minutes | Cook time: 10 minutes
Serves 2

3 tablespoons cooking fat
1 pound (454 g) chicken breast or thighs
(boneless, skinless)
1 clove garlic, minced
1 tablespoon ginger, grated
1 head broccoli florets
2 cups mushrooms, sliced

2 carrots, julienned
½ pound (227 g) green beans, cut into 1-inch
pieces
2 green onions, minced
½ lime, juiced
1 tablespoon minced fresh cilantro

1. Heat 2 tablespoons of the cooking fat in a large skillet over medium heat, swirling to coat the bottom of the pan. Place the chicken in the pan and sear until the outside is browned and it lifts easily from the bottom of the skillet, about 3 minutes on each side. Add the garlic and ginger. Cook and stir until aromatic, about 1 minute. Remove the chicken from the pan and slice into thin strips. Set the sliced chicken aside.
2. Wipe the pan clean and dry.
3. Heat the remaining 1 tablespoon of cooking fat in the skillet over medium-high heat. Add the broccoli, mushrooms, carrots, and green beans and quickly stir-fry until the vegetables begin to soften, 2 to 3 minutes. Add the chicken strips to the pan; mix, and continue to cook for 2 to 3 minutes until everything is heated through.
4. Top with the green onions, lime juice, and cilantro. Serve immediately.

Italian-Style Chicken with Fennel

Prep time: 10 minutes | Cook time: 4 hours
Serves 4

¼ cup Whole Food-compliant tomato paste
5 cloves garlic, minced
1 teaspoon dried oregano
¾ teaspoon salt
¼ teaspoon black pepper
8 bone-in chicken thighs, skin removed
1 bulb fennel, cored and cut into thin wedges

1 medium red, orange, or yellow bell pepper, cut into 1-inch pieces
1 (14½-ounce / 411-g) can Whole Food-compliant fire-roasted diced tomatoes
¼ cup Whole Food-compliant capers, drained
Chopped fresh flat-leaf parsley, for serving

1. In a slow cooker, stir together the tomato paste, garlic, oregano, salt, and pepper. Add the chicken and turn to coat. Place the fennel under the chicken. Top the chicken with the bell pepper and tomatoes.
2. Cover and cook on low for 4 to 5 hours or on high for 2 to 2½ hours. Serve the chicken and vegetables topped with the capers and fresh parsley.

Turkey Stuffed Bell Peppers

Prep time: 30 minutes | Cook time: 2½ hours
Serves 4

Peppers:

4 medium red, green, or yellow bell peppers
1 pound (454 g) ground turkey
2 cups chopped button mushrooms
1 stalk celery, thinly sliced
½ cup chopped onion
3 cloves garlic, minced

1 teaspoon paprika
½ teaspoon ground coriander
½ teaspoon coarse salt
¼ to ½ teaspoon cayenne pepper
1 large Roma (plum) tomato, finely chopped

Guacamole:

1 medium avocado, halved, pitted, and peeled
1 tablespoon fresh lemon juice
1 clove garlic, minced

½ teaspoon coarse salt
⅛ teaspoon black pepper
2 tablespoons chopped flat-leaf parsley

1. Make the peppers: Place a small rack in a slow cooker. Add ¼ cup water to the slow cooker. Cut a thin slice across the top of each pepper to remove the stem. Use a small sharp knife to cut out the seeds and membranes, keeping the pepper intact. Set the peppers, cut sides up, on the rack in the cooker.
2. In a large skillet over medium heat, cook the turkey, mushrooms, celery, and onion, stirring occasionally and breaking up the meat with a wooden spoon, until the turkey is browned. Drain off the fat. Add the 3 cloves minced garlic, the paprika, coriander, ½ teaspoon salt, and the cayenne pepper. Cook, stirring, over medium heat for 30 seconds. Remove from the heat. Stir in the tomato. Spoon the turkey mixture into the peppers.
3. Cover and cook on low for 2½ to 3 hours. Carefully transfer the stuffed peppers to serving plates.

4. Make the guacamole: In a medium bowl combine the avocado, lemon juice, 1 clove minced garlic, ½ teaspoon salt, and the black pepper. Mash with a fork or potato masher until almost smooth. Stir in the parsley. Top the peppers with the guacamole and serve.

Stir-Fried Chicken and Bok Choy

Prep time: 15 minutes | Cook time: 10 minutes

Serves 4

1 pound (454 g) chicken breast stir-fry strips
¼ teaspoon salt
¼ teaspoon black pepper
2 tablespoons extra-virgin olive oil
1 tablespoon finely chopped fresh lemongrass
1 tablespoon minced fresh ginger

4 cloves garlic, minced
½ teaspoon red pepper flakes
4 heads baby bok choy, coarsely chopped
¼ cup roasted salted cashews, finely chopped
¼ cup chopped fresh cilantro

1. Season the chicken with the salt and black pepper. Heat 1 tablespoon of the olive oil in a large skillet over medium-high heat. Add the chicken and cook, stirring occasionally, until the chicken is almost cooked through, about 5 minutes.
2. Add the lemongrass, ginger, garlic, and pepper flakes to the skillet. Cook, stirring, for 1 minute. Add the remaining 1 tablespoon olive oil. Add the bok choy and cook, stirring, until beginning to soften but still crisp, 2 to 3 minutes. Remove the skillet from the heat. Top with the cashews and cilantro and serve.

Garlic Chicken Primavera

Prep time: 15 minutes | Cook time: 27 minutes

Serves 2

2 tablespoons cooking fat
½ cup diced onions
2 cloves garlic, minced
1 teaspoon minced fresh oregano
1 teaspoon fresh thyme
3 cups diced seeded tomatoes (about 3 large tomatoes)
1 pound (454 g) boneless, skinless chicken

thighs, 1-inch diced
2 cups green beans, cut into 1-inch pieces
1½ cups medium-diced zucchini
1½ cup medium-diced yellow squash
¼ teaspoon red pepper flakes
1 teaspoons salt
½ teaspoon black pepper
1 to 2 tablespoons minced fresh basil leaves

1. In a large pot or Dutch oven, heat the cooking fat on medium-high heat and swirl to coat the bottom of the pan. Add the onions, garlic, oregano, and thyme and cook until the onions are translucent and the garlic is fragrant, 2 to 3 minutes.
2. Add the tomatoes and chicken to the pot and cook, stirring occasionally, until the tomatoes have softened, 3 to 4 minutes. Add the green beans, zucchini, and squash and cook, stirring occasionally, until the vegetables are crisp-tender and the chicken is cooked through (with no pink remaining in the center), 5 to 6 minutes. Add the red pepper flakes, salt, and pepper, sprinkle on the basil, stir for 30 seconds to incorporate, and serve immediately.

Chapter 11: Fish and Shellfish

Broiled Shrimp with Pine Nuts

Prep time: 15 minutes | Cook time: 5 minutes
Serves 2

12 ounces (340 g) shrimp (medium or jumbo size), peeled and deveined, tails removed
Extra-virgin olive oil, for brushing
⅛ teaspoon coarse salt
⅛ teaspoon black pepper
⅓ cup pine nuts, chopped
2 cloves garlic, minced
1 teaspoon grated lemon zest
2 tablespoons snipped fresh parsley
Lemon wedges, for serving

1. Preheat the broiler to high. Line a large rimmed baking sheet with aluminum foil.
2. Rinse the shrimp and pat them dry with paper towels. Use a sharp knife to split the shrimp horizontally, cutting almost through to the opposite sides, but leaving the shrimp halves attached.
3. Open the shrimp so they lay flat. Arrange the shrimp, flat sides down, on the prepared baking sheet and brush lightly with olive oil. Sprinkle with the salt and pepper.
4. In a small bowl, combine the pine nuts, garlic, lemon zest, and 1 tablespoon olive oil.
5. Broil the shrimp, 4 to 5 inches from the heat, until almost completely opaque, 4 to 5 minutes for jumbo shrimp or 2 to 3 minutes for medium shrimp. Carefully flip each shrimp. Spoon the pine nut mixture evenly on the shrimp. Broil for 1 minute more.
6. To serve, divide the shrimp between two serving plates. Sprinkle with the parsley and serve with lemon wedges for squeezing over the shrimp.

Pan-Seared Scallops with Orange Sauce

Prep time: 5 minutes | Cook time: 20 minutes
Serves 4

1 pound (454 g) large sea scallops
⅛ teaspoon plus ¼ teaspoon kosher salt
⅛ teaspoon freshly ground black pepper
6 tablespoons clarified butter
1 teaspoon finely grated orange zest
3 tablespoons fresh orange juice
1 teaspoon finely chopped garlic
1 tablespoon minced fresh tarragon leaves

1. Rinse the scallops in cold water, then place between two towels and let dry for 10 minutes. When the scallops are completely dry, season them with ⅛ teaspoon of the salt and the pepper. Set aside.
2. In a small saucepan, melt 5 tablespoons of the clarified butter over medium-low heat. Add the garlic and stir, cooking for 1 minute until fragrant. Add the orange zest, orange juice, tarragon, and remaining ¼ teaspoon salt and stir to combine. Remove from the heat and set aside.
3. In a medium cast-iron pan, melt the remaining 1 tablespoon clarified butter over high heat. Reduce the heat to medium-high and add the scallops to the pan. Cook until lightly browned on the bottom, about 2½ minutes. Flip to the other side and cook until just cooked through, about 1½ minutes more. Transfer the scallops to a serving dish and set aside.
4. Pour the mixture from the small saucepan into the skillet. Warm the sauce over low heat, stirring and scraping up any caramelized bits from the bottom of the pan, for 30 seconds, then pour the sauce over the scallops.
5. Serve immediately.

Cod in Tomato and Pepper Sauce

Prep time: 10 minutes | Cook time: 4 hours

Serves 4

2 medium yellow bell peppers, sliced
3 medium shallots, sliced
3 cloves garlic, minced
1 (14½-ounce / 411-g) can Whole Food-compliant diced tomatoes
4 cod fillets (5 to 6 ounces / 142 to 170 g each)
¼ teaspoon salt
¼ teaspoon black pepper
1 tablespoon chopped fresh flat-leaf parsley
1 tablespoon Whole Food-compliant capers, drained
1 teaspoon grated lemon zest
1 tablespoon extra-virgin olive oil

1. In a slow cooker, combine the bell peppers, shallots, garlic, and tomatoes. Cover and cook on low for 4 to 5 hours or on high for 2 to 2½ hours.
2. If on low, turn the slow cooker to the high setting. Place the fish fillets on the sauce. Sprinkle with the salt and pepper. Cover and cook just until the fish starts to flake with a fork, 30 to 40 minutes.
3. Top the cod with the parsley, capers, lemon zest, and olive oil, and serve.

Lemon Dill Salmon

Prep time: 25 minutes | Cook time: 1 hour | Serves 4

4 salmon fillets (4 to 6 ounces / 113 to 170 g each), skin removed
½ teaspoon salt
½ teaspoon black pepper
2 Meyer lemons or regular lemons, sliced and seeded, plus additional lemon wedges for serving
1 tablespoon chopped fresh dill, plus more for serving
1 cup diced English cucumber
1 medium red bell pepper, diced
2 teaspoons cider vinegar
1 garlic clove, minced

1. Line a slow cooker with parchment paper. Sprinkle the salmon with the salt and pepper and place on the parchment. Top with the lemon slices and dill.
2. Cover and cook on high for 1 hour.
3. Meanwhile, in a small bowl, combine the cucumber, bell pepper, vinegar, and garlic. Cover and refrigerate until serving.
4. Remove the salmon from the slow cooker; discard the lemon slices. Top the salmon with the cucumber salad and additional chopped dill and serve with lemon wedges.

Cod en Papillote

Prep time: 20 minutes | Cook time: 2 hours

Serves 4

1 pound (454 g) haricot verts or slender green beans, trimmed
2 red or yellow bell peppers, thinly sliced (3 cups)
1 small onion, thinly sliced (1 cup)
2 cloves garlic, minced
1 teaspoon smoked
paprika
1½ teaspoons black pepper
1 teaspoon salt
2 tablespoons plus 2 teaspoons extra-virgin olive oil
4 cod or halibut fillets (5 to 6 ounces / 142 to 170 g each)

1. In a large bowl, combine the green beans, bell peppers, onion, garlic, smoked paprika, 1 teaspoon of the pepper, and ½ teaspoon of the salt. Drizzle with 2 tablespoons of the olive oil and toss to combine. Cut four 15-inch squares of parchment paper. Divide the vegetable mixture into 4 portions and place one in the center of each piece of parchment.
2. Lightly drizzle the fish with the remaining 2 teaspoons olive oil and season with the remaining ½ teaspoon each salt and pepper. Place the fillets over the vegetable mixture on the parchment. Bring up two opposite edges of paper and fold several times over the fish. Fold in the ends.
3. Place the packets in an oval slow cooker. Cover and cook on high for 2 to 3 hours, or until the fish flakes easily with a fork.

Sweet and Sour Snapper

Prep time: 10 minutes | Cook time: 20 minutes

Serves 4

4 (6-ounce / 170-g) red snapper fillets
1 teaspoon kosher salt
½ teaspoon freshly ground black pepper
½ teaspoon ground coriander
½ teaspoon ground ginger
¼ cup extra-virgin olive oil
3 medium carrots, finely julienned
6 garlic cloves,

pressed
½ cup fresh orange juice
1 tablespoon red curry paste
2 tablespoons puréed mango
2 tablespoons coconut aminos
2 tablespoons fresh lemon juice
1 tablespoon fresh lime juice

1. Preheat the oven to warm.
2. Season each piece of fish with the salt and black pepper. Then season with the coriander and ginger.
3. In a large sauté pan, heat the olive oil over high heat. When the oil is warm, reduce the heat to medium. Add the fish to the pan, skin-side down, and cook until just cooked through, turning once, about 6 minutes total (or longer, if your fillets are on the thicker side). Transfer the fish to an oven-safe plate and keep warm in the oven.
4. In the same pan, cook the carrots and garlic over medium-high heat, stirring and scraping the bottom of the pan to loosen the fish bits, until brown and caramelized, about 3 minutes. Reduce the heat to medium.
5. In a medium bowl, stir together the orange juice and red curry paste. Add the mixture to the pan and stir. Add the mango purée, coconut aminos, lemon juice, and lime juice and cook, stirring to combine well, until thoroughly warmed.
6. To serve, scoop some of the carrots out of the sauce to use as the base on your plate. Put the fish on top of the carrots and spoon the sauce over.

Shrimp and Fish Cakes

Prep time: 15 minutes | Cook time: 20 minutes

Serves 4

1 pound (454 g) shrimp, peeled and deveined
½ pound (227 g) white-fleshed fish, such as cod, haddock, or halibut
¾ cup finely chopped green beans
¾ cup thinly sliced scallions
¾ cup diced carrots
Juice from 3 tablespoons grated

fresh ginger
3 tablespoons finely chopped lemongrass
1 large egg, beaten
1½ tablespoons coconut aminos
½ teaspoon ground white pepper
1½ teaspoons kosher salt
2 tablespoons extra-virgin olive oil
2 cups sugar snap peas, blanched

1. In a food processor, combine the shrimp and fish and pulse for just 3 seconds, making sure to keep them somewhat chunky so the fish cakes hold together when cooked. Transfer the mixture to a medium bowl.
2. Add the greens beans, scallions, carrots, ginger juice, lemongrass, egg, coconut aminos, white pepper, and salt and mix to combine well with the seafood. Using a food scale, make 3-inch patties weighing 3 ounces / 85 g each. Set aside.
3. In a large stainless steel skillet, heat the olive oil over medium to medium-low heat. Working in batches if needed, add the fish patties to the hot oil and fry until a golden brown crust forms on the bottom, about 4 minutes. Gently flip the patties and fry for 1 minute, then cover the pan and cook the patties until the shrimp is cooked through in the middle, about 3 minutes more. Remove from the heat and set aside.
4. For each serving, put some of the sugar snap peas in a bowl and top with 2 fish cakes.

Baked Fish en Papillote

Prep time: 15 minutes | Cook time: 15 minutes

Serves 2

1 cup chopped seeded tomato	(5 to 6 ounces / 142 to 170 g each)
1 small shallot, thinly sliced	⅛ teaspoon black pepper
2 cloves garlic, minced	8 Kalamata or oil-cured black olives, pitted and halved
2 tablespoons extra-virgin olive oil	
1½ teaspoons herbes de Provence	1 tablespoon chopped fresh parsley
¼ teaspoon salt	Lemon wedges, for serving
2 halibut or cod fillets	

1. Preheat the oven to 425°F (220°C).
2. Combine the tomato, shallot, garlic, 1 tablespoon of the olive oil, herbes de Provence, and ⅛ teaspoon of the salt in a medium bowl; mix well.
3. Cut two 12 × 15-inch squares of parchment paper. Rinse the fish and pat dry with paper towels. Place a fillet on each piece of parchment about 4 inches from the edge of the shorter sides. Sprinkle the fish with the remaining ⅛ teaspoon salt and the pepper. Spoon the tomato mixture on top of the fish and drizzle with the remaining 1 tablespoon olive oil.
4. Working with one packet at a time, fold the parchment over the fish, making the edges of the parchment even with each other. Starting at the bottom of the fold, tightly crimp the edges of the parchment to seal, making a half-moon-shaped packet.
5. Arrange the packets on a large baking sheet. Bake for about 12 minutes, until the fish just barely starts to flake when pulled apart with a fork (carefully open the packets to check doneness).
6. To serve, place each packet on a dinner plate; carefully open the packets. Top with the olives and parsley. Serve with lemon wedges.

Jamaican Jerk Salmon with Mango Salsa

Prep time: 10 minutes | Cook time: 10 minutes

Serves 4

Salsa:

1 ripe mango, pitted, peeled, and chopped	chopped fresh cilantro leaves
1 ripe avocado, halved, pitted, peeled, and chopped	1 small fresh jalapeño, seeded and finely chopped
½ cup chopped red bell pepper	1 tablespoon fresh lime juice
½ cup roughly	Salt, to taste

Fish:

1½ teaspoons dried thyme, crushed	cinnamon
½ teaspoon garlic powder	4 skinless salmon fillets (6 to 8 ounces / 170 to 227 g each), about 1 inch thick
½ teaspoon salt	
½ teaspoon ground allspice	1 tablespoon extra-virgin olive oil
¼ teaspoon cayenne pepper	6 cups fresh baby spinach
¼ teaspoon ground	

1. Make the salsa: In a medium bowl, gently combine the mango, avocado, bell pepper, cilantro, jalapeño, and lime juice. Season with salt. Cover and refrigerate for up to 2 hours.
2. Make the fish: Grease the grill rack. Preheat the grill to medium heat. In a small bowl, combine the thyme, garlic powder, salt, allspice, cayenne, and cinnamon; set aside. Rinse the fish; pat dry with paper towels. Brush both sides of the fish with the olive oil. Sprinkle with the spice blend and rub it in with your fingers. Grill the fish over direct heat for 8 to 12 minutes, turning once, until it barely starts to flake when pulled apart with a fork.
3. To serve, divide the spinach leaves between two plates. Top with the grilled salmon and mango salsa.

Citrus-Ginger Glazed Halibut

Prep time: 10 minutes | Cook time: 20 minutes
Serves 2

Glaze:

½ cup apple cider
Grated zest and juice of 2 lemons
Juice of 1 orange

½ tablespoon grated fresh ginger (or ½ teaspoon ground ginger)

Fish:

3 tablespoons cooking fat
2 halibut fillets (5 ounces / 142 g each)

1 teaspoon salt
½ teaspoon black pepper

1. Preheat the oven to 400ºF (205ºC).
2. For the glaze: Cook the apple cider in a small saucepan over medium-high heat until reduced to about 1 tablespoon, 4 to 6 minutes. Add the lemon juice, orange juice, and ginger and cook until reduced by half, 3 to 5 minutes. Remove the pan from the heat and add the lemon zest. Set aside.
3. For the fish: Heat 2 tablespoons of the cooking fat in a large skillet over high heat, swirling to coat the bottom of the pan. While the fat is heating, season the halibut with the salt and pepper. When the fat is hot, place the fish top-side-down in the pan and sear for 2 to 3 minutes. While the fish is searing, melt the remaining 1 tablespoon cooking fat (if necessary), line a baking sheet with parchment paper, and brush half of the fat on the paper.
4. Remove the halibut from the pan and transfer seared-side-up to the greased, lined baking sheet. Brush the remaining cooking fat over the top of the halibut. Bake in the oven for 10 to 12 minutes, until the flesh is just barely firm and flakes easily with a fork. Transfer the fish to a serving dish or individual plates and spoon the glaze over the top just before serving.

Baked Cod with Mushrooms

Prep time: 10 minutes | Cook time: 15 minutes
Serves 2

1 pound (454 g) cod
½ teaspoon salt
¼ teaspoon black pepper
2 tablespoons cooking fat
¼ onion, finely chopped
2 teaspoons grated

fresh ginger (or ½ teaspoon ground ginger)
2 cloves garlic, minced
1 pint (2 cups) button, cremini, or portabella mushrooms, sliced
1 cup roasted red peppers, chopped

1. Preheat the oven to 350ºF (180ºC). Line a baking pan or glass baking dish with parchment paper.
2. Cut the fish into portions and gently pat dry with a paper towel. Season evenly with ¼ teaspoon of the salt and ⅛ teaspoon of the pepper and place in the baking pan. Bake for 12 to 15 minutes, until the flesh in the center of the fish no longer appears wet or spongy in texture when you pierce it with a fork. It's done when it just barely starts to flake when pulled apart.
3. While the fish is cooking, add the cooking fat to a large skillet over medium heat. When the fat is hot, add the onion and cook, stirring, until the onion is translucent, 2 to 3 minutes. Add the ginger and stir for 30 seconds. Add the garlic and stir until aromatic, about 1 minute. Add the mushrooms and continue to cook, stirring, for 1 to 2 minutes. The mushrooms will release moisture, bringing the flavors together, and then become more dry in appearance. Add the roasted red peppers and the remaining ¼ teaspoon salt and ⅛ teaspoon pepper and stir for 2 minutes, allowing the peppers to warm. Remove the pan from the heat and hold covered to keep warm.
4. Remove the fish from the oven, spoon the mushroom and pepper mixture generously over the top of the fish, and serve immediately.

Harissa Salmon Fillets

Prep time: 10 minutes | Cook time: 10 minutes

Serves 2

2 tablespoons Whole Food-compliant harissa paste
2 teaspoons coriander seeds, crushed
2 teaspoons grated lemon zest
2 skin-on salmon fillets (6 to 8 ounces / 170 to 227 g each)
2 tablespoons extra-virgin olive oil
1 small yellow onion, cut into slivers
1 small red bell pepper, seeded and cut into matchsticks
1 small green bell pepper, seeded and cut into matchsticks
1 tablespoon fresh lemon juice
1 large ripe tomato, seeded and chopped
1 clove garlic, thinly sliced
¼ teaspoon sea salt, plus more as needed
Black pepper, to taste
¼ cup snipped fresh cilantro

1. Preheat the oven to 450ºF (235ºC).
2. In a small bowl, mix together the harissa, coriander, and lemon zest. Place the salmon fillets, skin side down, in a shallow baking pan. Wearing plastic or rubber gloves, spoon the harissa mixture on top of the salmon and rub it in with your fingers. Let the salmon stand while you prepare the salad.
3. Heat the olive oil in a large skillet over medium heat. Add the onion and bell peppers and cook, stirring, for 5 minutes. Add the lemon juice, tomato, garlic, salt, and black pepper to taste and cook, stirring, until the tomato begins to soften, about 3 minutes. Remove the skillet from the heat and top with the cilantro. Let the salad stand while you roast the salmon.
4. Roast the salmon for 4 to 6 minutes per ½-inch thickness, until the fish just barely starts to flake when pulled apart with a fork. Season with salt. Serve the salmon with the warm salad.

Basil Roasted Salmon with Broccoli

Prep time: 15 minutes | Cook time: 25 minutes

Serves 2

½ cup fresh basil leaves
½ cup fresh parsley leaves
6 tablespoons extra-virgin olive oil
1 tablespoon fresh lemon juice
1 teaspoon salt
1 teaspoon black pepper
½ teaspoon grated lemon zest
¼ cup almond flour
2 salmon fillets (6 ounces / 170 g each)
3 small heads broccoli with the stems attached (about 1 pound / 454 g total)
½ cup sliced almonds, toasted

1. Preheat the oven to 400ºF (205ºC).
2. Combine the basil, parsley, 4 tablespoons of the oil, lemon juice, ½ teaspoon of the salt, ½ teaspoon of the pepper, and the lemon zest in a blender or food processor. Cover and pulse until smooth. Pour the herb mixture into a bowl and stir in the almond flour.
3. Place the salmon fillets in a large roasting pan or on a rimmed baking sheet. Pack the herb mixture on the top of each fillet.
4. Trim the broccoli stems to about 3 inches below the florets. Slice the broccoli heads lengthwise into 1-inch-thick slabs (two or three slabs per head), cutting from the bottom of the stems through the crown to preserve the shape of the broccoli. Brush both sides of each broccoli slice with the remaining 2 tablespoons olive oil and sprinkle with the remaining ½ teaspoon salt and ½ teaspoon pepper. Arrange the broccoli in a single layer in the pan around the salmon.
5. Roast the broccoli and salmon for 25 minutes, until the salmon just barely starts to flake when pulled apart with a fork and the broccoli is lightly browned, turning the broccoli once halfway through roasting. Sprinkle the broccoli with the toasted almonds before serving.

Mexican Tuna Boats

Prep time: 10 minutes | Cook time: 0 minutes
Serves 2

1 avocado, pitted and peeled
2 (5-ounce / 142-g) cans tuna, drained
3 green onions, thinly sliced
Juice of 1½ limes
½ jalapeño, minced
1 tablespoon minced

fresh cilantro
½ teaspoon chili powder
½ teaspoon salt
⅛ teaspoon black pepper
1 head endive, separated into leaves

1. In a medium sized bowl, mash the avocado with a fork, leaving it slightly chunky. Add the tuna to the bowl, flaking it apart with a fork, and mix to combine with the avocado. Add the onions, juice of 1 lime, jalapeño, cilantro, chili powder, salt, and pepper and mix well.
2. Spoon the tuna mixture into the endive leaves. Sprinkle a dusting of chili powder. Squeeze the juice from the remaining ½ lime over the top and serve.

Ahi Tuna Steaks with Mango Salsa

Prep time: 15 minutes | Cook time: 5 minutes
Serves 2

Salsa:

1 mango, pitted, peeled, and diced
1 medium tomato, seeded and diced
2 green onions, minced
1 avocado, halved, pitted, peeled, and diced

¼ cup roughly chopped fresh cilantro
½ jalapeño, seeded and minced
Juice of 1 lime
⅛ teaspoon salt
⅛ teaspoon black pepper

Tuna:

2 ahi tuna steaks (4 to 6 ounces / 113 to 170 g each), about 1 inch thick

Avocado oil
1 teaspoon black sesame seeds
1 teaspoon white

sesame seeds
¼ teaspoon salt

¼ teaspoon black pepper

1. Make the salsa: In a medium bowl, combine all the salsa ingredients and toss to mix.
2. Make the tuna: Brush both sides of the tuna with a small amount of avocado oil. Season both sides with the sesame seeds, salt, and black pepper.
3. Heat a large ceramic nonstick skillet or cast-iron skillet over medium-high heat. Add the tuna and sear for 2 minutes on one side. Turn the tuna over and sear the other side for 2 minutes, until browned and crusty on the outside and rare inside. Serve the salsa with the tuna steaks.

Asian Shrimp Zucchini Noodles

Prep time: 25 minutes | Cook time: 10 minutes
Serves 4

¼ cup rice vinegar
3 tablespoons coconut aminos
3 cloves garlic, minced
1 tablespoon minced fresh ginger
¼ teaspoon salt
1½ tablespoons olive oil
1 large yellow onion, slivered
1½ pounds (680 g)

peeled and deveined medium shrimp
3 medium red and/or green bell peppers, cut into matchsticks
2 (10.7-ounce / 303-g) packages zucchini noodles; or 3 medium zucchini, spiralized, long noodles snipped if desired
3 green onions, sliced

1. In a small bowl, mix together the vinegar, coconut aminos, garlic, ginger, and salt.
2. Heat the olive oil in an extra-large skillet or wok over medium-high heat. Add the onion and cook, stirring, until it just starts to become tender, about 2 minutes. Stir in the vinegar mixture and cook until slightly reduced, about 1 minute. Add the shrimp, bell pepper, and zucchini noodles. Cook, stirring, until the shrimp are opaque and the vegetables are crisp-tender, 5 to 8 minutes. Top with the green onions and serve.

Shrimp Mashed Potatoes

Prep time: 15 minutes | Cook time: 50 minutes
Serves 4

1 tablespoon plus 3½ teaspoons kosher salt
2 pounds (907 g) small white potatoes
7 tablespoons clarified butter
¾ cup chicken stock
1 to 2 teaspoons red pepper flakes
1 tablespoon coarsely ground black pepper
1 tablespoon extra-virgin olive oil
¼ cup plus 2 tablespoons chopped

shallots
2 pounds (907 g) cherry tomatoes, halved
1 (8-ounce / 227-g) jar Whole Food-compliant clam juice
1 pound (454 g) rock shrimp or small wild-caught shrimp, peeled and deveined (if possible)
Chopped fresh parsley, for garnish (optional)

1. Preheat the oven to 175ºF (79ºC).
2. Fill a medium pot with water, add 1 tablespoon of the salt, and bring to a boil over high heat. Add the potatoes and boil until soft, about 20 minutes. Drain the potatoes and transfer them to a large bowl.
3. Add 1½ teaspoons of the salt and 3 tablespoons of the clarified butter to the bowl with the potatoes and smash and mix using a potato masher. Add the stock and stir to combine. Cover the potatoes and transfer to the oven to keep warm.
4. Heat a large sauté pan over medium heat. Dry-roast the red pepper flakes in the pan for just a few seconds, then add the black pepper and dry-roast it for a few seconds, or until fragrant. Add the olive oil and 1 tablespoon of the clarified butter and cook, stirring, until the butter has melted and combined with the oil and spices. Add the shallots and 1 teaspoon of the salt. Stir to combine and cook, stirring, until the shallots are translucent, 1 to 2 minutes. Add the tomatoes and clam juice and stir to combine. Cook for 10 minutes, then reduce the heat to medium-low and simmer until the tomatoes break down to form a luscious

sauce, 15 to 20 minutes, depending on how firm your tomatoes are.
5. Add the remaining 3 tablespoons clarified butter and stir to combine. Add the shrimp and remaining 1 teaspoon salt and cook, stirring occasionally, until the shrimp are just cooked through, about 3 minutes.
6. Spoon the potatoes onto a plate. Top with the shrimp and tomato sauce and serve garnished with parsley, if desired.

Pineapple Salmon

Prep time: 5 minutes | Cook time: 15 minutes
Serves 4

2 tablespoons clarified butter or ghee
4 pineapple rings, halved
1 teaspoon minced fresh ginger
½ teaspoon black or white sesame seeds
4 skin-on salmon fillets

(5 to 6 ounces / 142 to 170 g each)
½ teaspoon salt
¼ teaspoon black pepper
1 tablespoon coconut oil
Chopped green onion (optional)

1. In a large nonstick skillet, heat the butter over medium-high heat. Add the pineapple, ginger, and sesame seeds and cook, turning once, until the pineapple is golden, 6 to 8 minutes. Transfer to a plate and cover to keep warm. Carefully wipe out the skillet.
2. Sprinkle the salmon with the salt and pepper. Heat the same pan over medium heat until very hot. Add the coconut oil and heat until you see ripples across the surface. Place the salmon in the skillet, skin side down. Cook, without touching, until the salmon has cooked about three-fourths of the way up the fillets, 4 to 5 minutes. Using a spatula, carefully turn the salmon over. Cook until the salmon just barely starts to flake when pulled apart with two forks, 2 to 3 minutes longer.
3. Serve the salmon with the caramelized pineapple and drizzle any pan juices over the top. If desired, top with green onion.

Fish Vegetable Stir-Fry

Prep time: 15 minutes | Cook time: 10 minutes
Serves 2

Fish:

2 skinless cod or sea bass fillets, cut about ½ inch thick (5 to 6 ounces / 142 to 170 g each)
⅛ teaspoon coarse salt
⅛ teaspoon black pepper
¼ cup almond meal
¼ cup unsweetened flaked coconut
¼ cup finely chopped shallots
1 tablespoon coconut oil, melted

Vegetables:

1 tablespoon coconut oil
1 bunch fresh broccolini, trimmed, or 1 cup fresh broccoli florets
¾ cup halved and thinly sliced yellow summer squash
¼ cup sliced quartered onion
1 cup coarsely shredded napa cabbage
8 snow peas, trimmed and halved lengthwise
2 teaspoons minced fresh ginger
1 clove garlic, minced
1 tablespoon olive oil
1 tablespoon coconut aminos
1 tablespoon Whole Food-compliant rice vinegar
2 teaspoons sesame seeds, toasted (optional)

1. Preheat the oven to 425ºF (220ºC).
2. Make the fish: Line a baking sheet with parchment paper. Rinse the fish; pat dry with paper towels. Place the fish on the prepared baking sheet. Sprinkle the fish with the salt and pepper. In a small bowl, combine the almond meal, flaked coconut, and shallots. Add the coconut oil to the coconut mixture and mix well. Spoon the coconut mixture evenly on top of the fish fillets.
3. Bake the fish for 8 to 11 minutes, until the topping is browned and the fish just barely starts to flake when pulled apart with a fork.
4. Make the vegetables: Heat the coconut oil in a wok or large nonstick skillet over medium heat. Add the broccolini; cover and cook for 2 minutes. Uncover and cook, stirring, for 2 minutes more. Add the squash and onion. Cook, stirring, until the vegetables are crisp-tender, 3 to 5 minutes. Add the cabbage, snow peas, ginger, and garlic. Cook, stirring, for 2 minutes. Add the olive oil, coconut aminos, and rice vinegar. Cook, stirring, for 1 minute.
5. Divide the vegetable stir-fry between two serving plates. Top with the fish. Sprinkle with sesame seeds, if desired.

Garlic Mussels in Spicy Tomato Sauce

Prep time: 20 minutes | Cook time: 10 minutes
Serves 4

2 tablespoons extra-virgin olive oil
4 medium shallots, finely chopped
4 cloves garlic, minced
1 (28-ounce / 794-g) can Whole Food-compliant diced tomatoes
½ to 1 teaspoon red pepper flakes
½ teaspoon salt
½ teaspoon black pepper
2 pounds (907 g) mussels, scrubbed and debearded
2 medium yellow summer squash, trimmed and shaved into ribbons
2 tablespoons fresh lemon juice
½ cup chopped fresh basil

1. Heat 1 tablespoon of the olive oil in an extra-large skillet over medium heat. Add the shallots and garlic and cook, stirring, just until softened, about 2 minutes. Add the tomatoes, pepper flakes, salt, and pepper and bring to a boil. Add the mussels. Cover and cook until the mussels are just starting to open, 3 to 4 minutes.
2. Stir in the squash ribbons. Continue to cook, stirring occasionally, until the mussels have opened and the squash is crisp-tender, 1 to 2 minutes. Discard any mussels that do not open. Drizzle the lemon juice and remaining 1 tablespoon olive oil over the mussels and squash, top with the basil, and serve.

per with Shiitake Mushrooms

Prep time: 10 minutes | Cook time: 15 minutes

Serves 2

1½ teaspoons olive oil
1¼ cups sliced shiitake mushroom caps (3 to 4 ounces / 85 to 113 g)
2½ teaspoons grated lemon zest
Salt and black pepper, to taste
1 cup chicken bone broth, Whole Food-compliant chicken broth, or water
2 teaspoons coconut aminos

2 red snapper fillets (6 ounces / 170 g each)
1 tablespoon thinly sliced fresh ginger
2 teaspoons avocado oil
1 clove garlic
½ teaspoon black or white sesame seeds
4 cups sliced bok choy
Lemon wedges, for serving
Fresh chives, snipped (optional)

1. Heat 1 teaspoon of the olive oil in a large skillet over medium heat. Add 1 cup of the mushrooms and cook, stirring, until tender, 3 to 4 minutes. Stir in ½ teaspoon of the lemon zest. Season with salt and pepper. Remove the mushroom mixture from the pan and keep warm.
2. Combine the remaining ¼ cup mushrooms, the broth, remaining 2 teaspoons lemon zest, the coconut aminos, and ¼ teaspoon of the olive oil in the same skillet. Bring to a boil. Reduce the heat to keep the liquid at a low simmer. Carefully add the fish. Sprinkle the fish lightly with salt and place the ginger slices on top. Cover and cook until the fish barely starts to flake when pulled apart with a fork, 4 to 5 minutes. Remove the fish from the skillet and cover to keep warm. Discard the poaching liquid and wipe out the skillet with a paper towel.
3. Heat the avocado oil in the skillet over medium heat. Add the garlic and sesame seeds and cook, stirring, for 1 minute. Stir in the bok choy and cook, covered, stirring occasionally, until the stems are crisp-tender and the leaves are wilted, 3 to 5 minutes. Remove the skillet from the heat and lightly season the bok choy with salt;

drizzle with the remaining ¼ teaspoon olive oil.
4. Spoon the bok choy onto two dinner plates. Top each with a fish fillet and spoon sautéed mushrooms onto the fish. Serve with lemon wedges and sprinkle with chives, if desired.

Thai Red Curry Shrimp

Prep time: 20 minutes | Cook time: 15 minutes

Serves 4

1 tablespoon coconut oil
1 small onion, chopped
2 cloves garlic, minced
2 teaspoons minced fresh ginger
1 (14-ounce / 397-g) can Whole Food-compliant coconut milk
2 tablespoons Whole Food-compliant Thai red curry paste
1 tablespoon coconut aminos
1 pound (454 g)

peeled and deveined large shrimp
4 cups fresh baby spinach
1 tablespoon fresh lime juice, plus lime wedges for serving
1 (16-ounce / 454-g) package cauliflower crumbles, or 4 cups raw cauliflower rice
Torn fresh basil, for serving
Lime wedges, for serving

1. In a large skillet, heat the oil over medium heat. Add the onion and cook, stirring occasionally, until tender, 3 to 4 minutes. Add the garlic and ginger and cook, stirring, until fragrant, about 1 minute. Stir in the coconut milk, curry paste, and coconut aminos. Bring to a boil, then reduce the heat and simmer for 5 minutes. Add the shrimp and cook, stirring occasionally, until opaque, about 5 minutes. Remove from the heat and stir in the spinach and lime juice.
2. Meanwhile, prepare the cauliflower crumbles according to the package directions. Serve the shrimp curry over the cauliflower rice. Top with the fresh basil and serve with lime wedges.

Salmon with Cauliflower and Spinach Salad

Prep time: 30 minutes | Cook time: 15 minutes

Serves 4

Salad:

1 small head cauliflower, broken into large florets
2 tablespoons extra-virgin olive oil
2 cups baby spinach or kale (not packed)

1 cup grape tomatoes, halved
⅓ cup thinly sliced fresh basil leaves
⅓ cup sliced almonds, toasted

Vinaigrette:

⅓ cup extra-virgin olive oil
3 tablespoons champagne vinegar, white wine vinegar, or apple cider vinegar
1 tablespoon finely chopped shallots

1 teaspoon Whole Food-compliant Dijon mustard
¼ teaspoon salt
¼ teaspoon black pepper

Fish:

4 skinless salmon fillets (6 to 8 ounces / 170 to 227 g each)
Extra-virgin olive oil

Salt and black pepper, to taste
2 tablespoons chopped fresh chives
Lemon wedges, for serving

1. Grease a grill rack and preheat the grill to medium heat.
2. Make the salad: In a food processor, pulse the cauliflower (in batches) until the pieces are the size of couscous. In a large skillet, cook the cauliflower couscous in the olive oil, stirring occasionally, until tender and just beginning to brown, about 5 minutes. Transfer to a large bowl. Add the spinach, tomatoes, basil, and almonds and toss to combine.
3. Make the vinaigrette: In a small bowl, whisk together the olive oil, vinegar, shallots, and mustard. Season with the salt and pepper. Drizzle the couscous salad with the vinaigrette and toss to coat.
4. Make the salmon: Brush the salmon with olive oil and season with salt and pepper. Close the grill lid and grill the salmon until it is nicely seared, crispy, and releases easily from the grill, about 6 minutes. Turn the salmon and grill until it barely starts to flake when pulled apart with a fork, about 2 minutes. Remove the salmon from the grill and let rest for 3 minutes.
5. Sprinkle the salmon with the chives and serve with the cauliflower couscous salad and lemon wedges.

Easy Shrimp Scampi

Prep time: 10 minutes | Cook time: 10 minutes

Serves 2

2 tablespoons finely chopped garlic (about 3 large cloves)
1 tablespoon ghee
1 tablespoon extra-virgin olive oil
¾ pound (340 g) raw jumbo shrimp, peeled, tails on, and deveined
1 teaspoon red pepper flakes (optional)

⅓ cup chicken stock
1 tablespoon fresh lemon juice
Kosher salt and freshly ground black pepper, to taste
¼ cup loosely packed fresh parsley leaves, finely chopped

1. In a large stainless-steel or nonstick skillet, combine the garlic, ghee, and olive oil. Cook over medium-high heat, stirring, until the garlic is fragrant, about 2 minutes. Pat the shrimp very dry with a paper towel. Add them to the pan and cook, stirring, until slightly pink, about 2 minutes per side. Add the red pepper flakes (if using) and cook, stirring, for 1 minute.
2. Add the stock and lemon juice and cook until the liquid has reduced by about a quarter, about 2 minutes. Taste the sauce and season with salt and black pepper. Remove the pan from the heat and stir in the parsley. Serve immediately.

Citrus Almond Cod with Spinach

Prep time: 5 minutes | Cook time: 25 minutes
Serves 4

2½ teaspoons kosher salt, plus a pinch
1 teaspoon freshly ground black pepper
1 teaspoon finely grated lemon zest
4 (6-ounce / 170-g) pieces cod
½ cup almond meal, for dusting
¼ cup extra-virgin olive oil
1 cup quartered grape or cherry tomatoes

¼ cup clarified butter
1 tablespoon fresh lemon juice
1 tablespoon fresh orange juice
1 tablespoon coconut aminos
1 tablespoon Whole Food-compliant capers
2 tablespoons chicken stock
2 cups chopped spinach

1. Preheat the oven to 200°F (93°C).
2. In a small bowl, stir together the salt, black pepper, and lemon zest. Set aside.
3. Pat the cod dry with a paper towel. Sprinkle each piece thoroughly with the spice blend, then dust them on all sides with the almond meal.
4. In a large sauté pan, heat the olive oil over medium-high heat. Add the cod to the pan, then immediately reduce the heat to medium. Cook the cod until golden and just cooked through, about 3 minutes per side, or a bit longer for thicker pieces. Transfer the fish to a baking sheet and put it in the oven to keep warm.
5. Wipe out the pan and set it over medium heat. Combine the tomatoes, clarified butter, lemon juice, orange juice, coconut aminos, capers, and a pinch of salt in the pan, stir, and bring to a boil. Reduce the heat to medium and simmer until the tomatoes begin to soften, about 1 minute. Add the spinach and the stock and cook, stirring to combine well, until the spinach has wilted, about 1 minute.
6. Remove the fish from the oven. Use some of the spinach and the tomatoes from the sauce as a base on each serving plate. Then put the cod pieces on the spinach and tomatoes and top with the sauce to serve.

Sea Scallops with Ginger-Blueberry Sauce

Prep time: 10 minutes | Cook time: 10 to 15 minutes
Serves 2

Ginger-Blueberry Sauce:
1 cup fresh or frozen blueberries
Scallops:
¾ pound (340 g) sea scallops, patted dry
½ teaspoon salt

1½ teaspoons finely chopped fresh ginger
¼ teaspoon salt

½ teaspoon black pepper
3 tablespoons cooking fat

1. Make the ginger-blueberry sauce: Defrost your blueberries (if necessary), then combine with 1 cup of water in a small saucepan over medium-high heat. Let the mixture reach a boil, then add the ginger and salt. Reduce the heat to medium and cook for 5 minutes, letting the blueberries burst and release their juice and the ginger steep.
2. The sauce can be left chunky, but it looks prettier if you blend it in a food processor or with an immersion blender to a smooth consistency. Just return it to the pan after blending to keep warm.
3. Make the scallops: Season both sides evenly with the salt and pepper. Heat the cooking fat in a large skillet over medium-high heat. When the fat is hot, add the scallops in a single layer (you may need to cook them in batches). Cook until the scallops begin to pull away from pan and brown, 2 to 3 minutes. Using kitchen tongs, turn the scallops and repeat the searing on the other side, for another 2 minutes.
4. Transfer the scallops to a serving dish or individual plates. Top with ¼ to ½ cup of the blueberry sauce. Serve warm or at room temperature.

Cassava Crusted Calamari

Prep time: 10 minutes | Cook time: 20 minutes
Serves 4

1 pound (454 g) calamari, cut into ½-inch rounds
1 teaspoon kosher salt
½ teaspoon freshly ground black pepper
½ teaspoon cayenne pepper

4 large eggs, beaten
2 cups cassava flour
1 cup coconut oil

1. Preheat the oven to 200ºF (93ºC). Line a baking sheet with parchment.
2. Put the calamari in a medium bowl, sprinkle with the salt, black pepper, and cayenne, and toss thoroughly to coat.
3. Put the beaten eggs in a shallow bowl and the cassava flour in a second shallow bowl. Working in batches and using your left hand for the cassava flour and your right hand for the egg, put 3 or 4 calamari pieces into the egg mixture. Stick your right index finger into the center of the calamari tubes and spin them around to thoroughly coat the inside as well as outside with egg. Pick up the pieces and allow the excess egg to drip off, then put them in the flour and, using your dry hand, sprinkle the flour over the calamari to coat. Stick your left index finger in the center of the calamari tubes and spin them around to ensure they are completely coated inside and out. Shake off any excess flour and set the coated pieces aside on a plate. Repeat to coat the remaining calamari.

4. In a large sauté pan, melt ½ cup of the coconut oil over medium-high heat. When the oil is hot, working in batches, add the coated calamari to the pan and fry until golden and crispy, about 1 minute, then flip and fry on the second side for 1 minute. Use a slotted spoon to transfer the calamari to the prepared baking sheet and keep warm in the oven. Repeat until you have cooked half the calamari, then carefully discard the used cooking oil. Add the remaining ½ cup coconut oil to the pan, heat it over medium-high heat, and cook the remaining calamari (in batches, as needed). Serve.

Cod with Olive Relish and Pilaf

Prep time: 10 minutes | Cook time: 20 minutes
Serves 4

Relish:

½ cup pitted green olives
½ cup extra-virgin olive oil
1 shallot, minced
2 tablespoons fresh orange juice

2 teaspoons fresh thyme leaves
1 teaspoon ground ancho chile
½ teaspoon grated orange zest

Fish:

4 cod fillets (5 to 6 ounces / 142 to 170 g each)
2 tablespoons extra-virgin olive oil
½ teaspoon dried thyme

½ teaspoon salt
½ teaspoon black pepper

Pilaf:

1 head cauliflower, cut into florets
2 tablespoons olive oil
1 small poblano pepper, seeded and finely chopped
1 shallot, minced

½ teaspoon salt
½ teaspoon black pepper
¼ cup sliced almonds, toasted
2 tablespoons fresh lemon juice

1. For the relish: In a food processor, combine all the ingredients for the relish. Pulse until the mixture is very finely chopped and forms a loose paste. Transfer the olive relish to a bowl and set aside.
2. For the fish: Preheat the oven to 400°F (205°C). Arrange the fish on a rimmed baking sheet. Drizzle with the olive oil. Sprinkle with the dried thyme, salt, and black pepper. Roast for 20 minutes, until the fish just barely starts to flake when pulled apart with a fork.
3. For the pilaf: Place half the cauliflower in a food processor and pulse into a rice-like consistency, 15 to 20 pulses. Transfer to a bowl and repeat with the remaining cauliflower. In a large skillet, heat the olive oil over medium heat. Add the poblano and shallot and cook, stirring, until just tender, about 5 minutes. Add the cauliflower, salt, and black pepper. Cook, stirring frequently, until the cauliflower is just tender and beginning to brown, about 5 minutes. Stir in the almonds and lemon juice.
4. Serve the fish over the pilaf and top with the olive relish. Store leftover relish in an airtight container in the refrigerator for up to 3 days.

Chapter 12: Sauces and Dressings

Italian Dressing

Prep time: 5 minutes | Cook time: 0 minutes
Makes 1 cup

¼ cup red wine vinegar
2 tablespoons minced fresh oregano (or 2 teaspoons dried)
1 clove garlic, minced
1 teaspoon mustard powder
¾ cup extra-virgin olive oil
½ teaspoon salt
¼ teaspoon black pepper

1. Mix together the vinegar, oregano, garlic, and mustard powder in a small bowl. Add the olive oil in a steady stream while whisking to emulsify. Adjust the seasoning with salt and pepper and whisk until fully incorporated.

Sunflower Seed Curry Sauce

Prep time: 5 minutes | Cook time: 5 minutes
Makes 1 cup

⅓ cup sunflower seed butter
3 tablespoons coconut aminos
1 tablespoon coconut oil
1 tablespoon finely chopped sulfite-free dried apricot
½ to 1 teaspoon curry powder, to taste
1 clove garlic, minced

1. Whisk together ¼ cup water, the sunflower seed butter, coconut aminos, coconut oil, apricot, curry powder, and garlic in a small saucepan. Cook over medium-low heat, stirring, until bubbly and the sauce is smooth except for the fruit and garlic pieces, 5 minutes.
2. Use immediately or cool to room temperature and store in an airtight container in the refrigerator for up to 4 days.

Balsamic Vinaigrette

Prep time: 5 minutes | Cook time: 0 minutes
Makes 1 cup

¼ cup balsamic vinegar
2 cloves garlic, minced
2 teaspoons mustard powder
¾ cup extra-virgin olive oil
1 teaspoon minced fresh cilantro (or ¼ teaspoon dried)
Salt and black pepper, to taste

1. Mix together the vinegar, garlic, and mustard powder in a small bowl. Add the olive oil in a steady stream while whisking to emulsify. Add the cilantro, adjust to taste with salt and pepper, and whisk until fully incorporated.

Avocado Green Goddess Dressing

Prep time: 10 minutes | Cook time: 0 minutes
Makes 1 cup

½ avocado, pitted and peeled
¼ cup minced fresh parsley
¼ cup fresh lemon juice
2 tablespoons Whole Food-compliant mayonnaise
2 tablespoons extra-virgin olive oil
1 tablespoon snipped fresh chives
2 to 3 teaspoons minced fresh tarragon
2 cloves garlic, minced
½ teaspoon salt
⅛ teaspoon black pepper

1. In a blender or food processor, combine all the ingredients. Cover and blend or process until smooth.
2. Use immediately or place in an airtight container and store in the refrigerator for up to 24 hours.

Cumin and Tomato Pineapple Sauce

Prep time: 5 minutes | Cook time: 20 minutes
Makes 2 cups

1 teaspoon cumin seeds	g) can Whole Food-compliant tomato sauce
1 tablespoon extra-virgin olive oil	3 tablespoons pineapple juice
3 tablespoons finely chopped onion	½ teaspoon salt
1 tablespoon chili powder	1 to 2 teaspoons Whole Food-compliant hot sauce
1 (15-ounce / 425-	

1. Toast the cumin seeds in a small heavy saucepan over medium heat until fragrant, about 2 minutes. Transfer to a mortar and pestle, spice grinder, or a cutting board and coarsely crush, grind, or chop the seeds.
2. Heat the oil in the saucepan over medium heat. Add the onion and cook, stirring occasionally, until softened and beginning to brown, about 5 minutes. Stir in the cumin seeds and chili powder and cook, stirring, for 1 minute. Stir in the tomato sauce, pineapple juice, and salt. Bring to a boil, then reduce the heat and simmer, uncovered, for 10 minutes. Stir in the hot sauce.
3. Use immediately, or store in an airtight container in the refrigerator for up to 1 week.

Cashew Cauliflower Alfredo

Prep time: 15 minutes | Cook time: 15 minutes
Makes 2 cups

1 cup chopped raw cashews	2 teaspoons fresh lemon juice
4 or 5 cloves garlic, chopped	1 teaspoon salt
2 tablespoons clarified butter or ghee	½ teaspoon black pepper
1 cup cauliflower florets	Chopped fresh parsley and/or basil (optional)

1. Place the cashews in a small bowl and add enough boiling water to cover. Let stand for 10 minutes. Drain and rinse.
2. In a large skillet, cook the garlic in the butter over medium heat, stirring, until softened, about 2 minutes. Add the drained cashews, cauliflower, and 1 cup water. Increase the heat and bring to a simmer. Cover, reduce the heat, and simmer until the cauliflower is very tender, about 8 minutes.
3. Transfer the cauliflower mixture to a blender and add the lemon juice, salt, and black pepper. Let cool briefly and then blend until smooth, 2 to 3 minutes. Stir in the fresh parsley and/or basil, if desired.
4. Use immediately, or store in an airtight container in the refrigerator for up to 24 hours.

Herb and Garlic Chimichurri Sauce

Prep time: 10 minutes | Cook time: 10 minutes
Makes 1¼ cups

2 bulbs garlic, separated into cloves but not peeled	olive oil
	2 teaspoons grated lemon zest
1 cup packed fresh parsley	1 tablespoon Whole Food-compliant capers, drained
1 cup packed fresh basil	½ teaspoon salt
¾ cup extra-virgin	

1. In a cast-iron skillet or other heavy skillet, roast the garlic cloves over medium heat, removing small cloves as they soften, until the skins are toasted and cloves have softened, 10 to 15 minutes. Cool slightly, then remove and discard the skins.
2. Place the cloves in a food processor. Add the parsley, basil, olive oil, lemon zest, capers, and salt and process until nearly smooth.
3. Use immediately, or store in an airtight container in the refrigerator for up to 24 hours.

Carrot and Tomato Sauce

Prep time: 15 minutes | Cook time: 1 hour | Makes 3 cups

1 tablespoon cooking fat
1 onion, finely chopped
2 celery stalks, finely chopped
1 carrot, peeled and finely chopped
2 cloves garlic, minced
1 (28-ounce / 794-g) can crushed tomatoes

1 teaspoon fresh thyme
1 teaspoon fresh oregano
1 bay leaf
1 teaspoon salt
1 teaspoon black pepper

1. Heat the cooking fat in a large pot over medium heat. When the fat is hot, add the onion, celery, and carrot and cook, stirring, until the onion becomes translucent, 2 to 3 minutes. Add the garlic and stir until aromatic, about 1 minute. Add the tomatoes, thyme, oregano, bay leaf, salt, and pepper.
2. Reduce the heat to a simmer, cover, and cook over low heat, stirring every 20 minutes, until the sauce is thick and smooth, about 1 hour. Discard the bay leaf.
3. Store in the refrigerator for up to 5 to 7 days.

Almond Lime Satay Sauce

Prep time: 10 minutes | Cook time: 0 minutes

Makes 1½ cups

½ cup almond butter
½ cup Whole Food-compliant coconut milk
2 tablespoons coconut aminos
1 tablespoon fresh lime juice

1 tablespoon minced fresh ginger
1 teaspoon Red Boat fish sauce
1 clove garlic, minced

1. In a blender or food processor, combine all the ingredients. Cover and blend or process until smooth.
2. Use immediately, or store in an airtight container in the refrigerator for up to 5 days.

Asian Orange Dressing

Prep time: 5 minutes | Cook time: 10 minutes

Makes 1 cup

2 tablespoons coconut oil
2 tablespoons minced fresh ginger
4 cloves garlic, minced
⅔ cup fresh orange juice

⅓ cup coconut aminos
¼ cup cider vinegar
2 teaspoons olive oil

1. Heat the coconut oil in a medium skillet over medium heat. Add the ginger and garlic and cook, stirring, for 1 minute. Add the orange juice, coconut aminos, and vinegar. Bring to a boil, then reduce the heat and simmer for 5 minutes. Remove from the heat and add the olive oil.
2. Use immediately, or store in an airtight container in the refrigerator for up to 1 week.

Hollandaise Sauce

Prep time: 15 minutes | Cook time: 0 minutes
Makes 2 cups

1½ cups clarified unsalted butter or ghee
4 large egg yolks
2 tablespoons lemon juice

1 teaspoon salt
⅛ teaspoon cayenne pepper (optional)

1. In a medium saucepan over low heat, melt the butter or ghee until warm but not bubbling.
2. Combine the egg yolks, lemon juice, salt, and cayenne pepper (if you like) in a food processor or blender and pulse 10 to 15 times to combine. Slowly drizzle in the warm butter or ghee while mixing on low speed, until the sauce emulsifies and thickens. If the sauce becomes too thick, blend in a tablespoon of warm water.
3. Serve the sauce immediately, or hold covered in a small saucepan on the lowest heat setting for up to an hour. Make your hollandaise fresh every time you serve it, as it doesn't store well in the refrigerator.

Cider-Mustard Vinaigrette

Prep time: 10 minutes | Cook time: 0 minutes
Makes 1¼ cups

3 tablespoons cider vinegar
2 tablespoons apple cider
2 teaspoons Whole Food-compliant Dijon or whole-grain mustard
1 clove garlic, minced

1 teaspoon chopped fresh thyme
½ teaspoon salt
¼ teaspoon black pepper
¾ cup extra-virgin olive oil

1. In a small bowl, combine the vinegar, cider, mustard, garlic, thyme, salt, and pepper. While whisking, drizzle in the olive oil until blended.
2. Use immediately, or store in an airtight container in the refrigerator for up to 3 days.

Lemon Dressing

Prep time: 5 minutes | Cook time: 0 minutes
Makes 1¼ cups

1 cup coconut aminos
1 tablespoon fresh lemon juice
1 tablespoon Whole Food-compliant spicy brown mustard

2 cloves garlic, crushed
¼ teaspoon salt
¼ teaspoon black pepper

1. In a blender, combine all the ingredients. Cover and blend until fully combined and frothy.
2. Use immediately, or store in an airtight container in the refrigerator for up to 1 week.

Buffalo Sauce

Prep time: 5 minutes | Cook time: 2 minutes

Makes 2 cups

½ cup coconut oil
½ cup ghee or clarified butter
1 cup hot sauce

2 tablespoons apple cider vinegar
1 clove garlic, minced

1. In a small saucepan, gently melt the coconut oil and ghee over medium-low heat until completely liquefied.
2. Combine the hot sauce, vinegar, and garlic in a medium mixing bowl and whisk until thoroughly blended. While whisking, drizzle in the melted coconut oil and ghee. The sauce should have a smooth, consistent texture.
3. Store this sauce in an airtight container in the fridge for up to 7 days. (Note, the coconut oil and ghee will solidify in the cold, so pull it out of the fridge and let it come back to room temperature before serving.)

Ginger Curry Sauce

Prep time: 15 minutes | Cook time: 15 minutes | Makes 2 cups

1 tablespoon cooking fat
½ onion, diced
1½ teaspoons minced fresh ginger
1 clove garlic, minced
1½ teaspoons yellow curry powder

½ teaspoon red curry powder
2 cups full-fat coconut milk
Grated zest and juice of ½ lime
½ teaspoon salt
¼ teaspoon black pepper

1. Heat the cooking fat in a medium skillet over medium heat. When the fat is hot, add the onion and cook until translucent, 2 to 3 minutes. Add the ginger and cook for 1 minute, stirring quickly. Add the garlic and cook for another minute while continuing to stir.
2. Add both curry powders and stir quickly for 30 seconds to open up the flavor of the spices. Once fragrant, add the coconut milk. Turn the heat down to low and allow the mixture to simmer (not boil) until the mixture thickens a bit, 8 to 10 minutes. (It will continue to thicken as it cools.) Season with the lime zest and juice, salt, and pepper.
3. Keep warm and serve right away, or let the flavors develop even further in the refrigerator; it'll keep for about 5 days. (Note, the coconut milk will solidify in the cold, so pull it out of the fridge and let it come back to room temperature before serving.)

Chapter 13: Basics

Homemade Mayonnaise

Prep time: 10 minutes | Cook time: 0 minutes
Makes 1½ cups

1¼ cups light olive oil	mustard
1 large egg	½ teaspoon salt
½ teaspoon dry	Juice of ½ lemon

1. Place ¼ cup of the olive oil, the egg, dry mustard, and salt in a blender, food processor, or mixing bowl. Blend, process, or mix thoroughly. While the food processor or blender is running (or while mixing in a bowl with an immersion blender), slowly drizzle in the remaining 1 cup olive oil until the mayonnaise has emulsified. Add the lemon juice and blend on low or stir to incorporate.

Basic Cauliflower Rice

Prep time: 5 minutes | Cook time: 5 minutes
Serves 4

1 large head cauliflower, cut into small pieces	virgin olive oil
	Kosher salt and freshly ground black pepper,
1 tablespoon extra	to taste

1. Place the cauliflower pieces in a food processor (depending on the size of your food processor, you will likely need to do this in 2 batches). Pulse the food processor until the cauliflower is the texture of rice, or "riced."
2. Heat the oil in a large skillet over medium-high heat. When shimmering, add the riced cauliflower and cook, stirring, until heated through, 3 to 5 minutes. Don't overcook the cauliflower rice, or it tends to get mushy. Season with salt and pepper to taste and serve as desired.

Beef Bone Broth

Prep time: 10 minutes | Cook time: 2½ hours
Makes 9 cups

3 to 4 pounds (1.4 to 1.8 kg) beef bones	5 or 6 fresh sprigs parsley
2 carrots, roughly chopped	1 sprig fresh thyme
3 stalks celery, roughly chopped	2 tablespoons cider vinegar
2 onions, roughly chopped	10 whole black peppercorns
	1 teaspoon salt

1. Preheat the oven to 400°F (205°C). Place the bones in a shallow roasting pan or rimmed baking sheet. Roast until the bones are golden-brown, about 35 minutes.
2. In an Instant Pot, place the bones, carrots, celery, onions, parsley, thyme, vinegar, peppercorns, and salt. Add enough water to reach 1 inch below the maximum fill line. Lock the lid in place.
3. Select Manual and adjust to high pressure for 120 minutes. Use natural release.
4. Strain the broth through a fine-mesh strainer set over a large bowl or clean pot. Discard the solids. Transfer the broth to multiple containers to speed up cooling, don't freeze or refrigerate it while it's hot! Allow the broth sit in the fridge, uncovered, for several hours, until the fat rises to the top and hardens. Scrape off the fat with a spoon and discard it.
5. Refrigerate the broth in airtight containers for 3 to 4 days or freeze for up to 6 months.

Creamy Ranch Dressing

Prep time: 10 minutes | Cook time: 0 minutes

Makes 1½ cups

1 cup Whole Food-compliant mayonnaise
½ cup Whole Food-compliant coconut milk
1 small clove garlic, minced
½ teaspoon onion powder

¼ teaspoon black pepper
1 tablespoon finely chopped fresh dill
1 tablespoon finely chopped chives
2 teaspoons fresh lemon juice

1. In a medium bowl, whisk together all the ingredients. Cover with plastic wrap and refrigerate for 1 hour.
2. Use immediately, or store in an airtight container in the refrigerator for up to 1 week.

Sriracha

Prep time: 15 minutes | Cook time: 10 minutes

Makes 1½ cups

1 pound (454 g) Fresno chiles, seeded and roughly chopped
5 cloves garlic, smashed and peeled
2 tablespoons apple cider vinegar
2 tablespoons Whole Food-compliant tomato

paste
1 medium dried Medjool date, pitted
2 tablespoons Whole Food-compliant fish sauce
½ teaspoon salt

1. In a high-power blender, combine all the ingredients and process until smooth.
2. Transfer to a small saucepan and bring to a boil. Reduce the heat and simmer, stirring occasionally, for 10 minutes. Taste the sauce and adjust for salt. If the sauce is too thick, add water, 1 tablespoon at a time, until it reaches the desired consistency. Let cool.
3. Use immediately, or store in an airtight container in the refrigerator for up to 1 week.

Ketchup

Prep time: 5 minutes | Cook time: 10 minutes

Makes 1 cup

1 cup Whole Food-compliant tomato paste
½ cup apple cider
½ cup cider vinegar

1 teaspoon garlic powder
½ teaspoon salt
⅛ teaspoon ground cloves (optional)

1. Heat a medium saucepan over medium heat. Add the tomato paste, apple cider, and vinegar. Stir to combine and let the mixture come to a simmer, but do not allow it to boil. Add the garlic powder, salt, and cloves (if using) and cook, stirring frequently to prevent scorching. You may need to turn the heat down to low or simmer here, until the ketchup has thickened enough to evenly coat the back of a spoon, 5 to 8 minutes. Remove from the heat and allow to cool.
2. Serve when cool, or store in an airtight container in the refrigerator for up to 2 weeks.

Clarified Butter

Prep time: 5 minutes | Cook time: 20 minutes
Makes 1½ cups

1 pound (4 sticks / 454 g) unsalted butter

1. Cut the butter into 1-inch cubes. In a small pot or saucepan, melt the butter over medium-low heat and let it come to a simmer without stirring. As the butter simmers, foamy white dairy solids will rise to the surface. With a spoon or ladle, gently skim the dairy solids off the top and discard, leaving just the pure clarified butter in the pan.
2. Once you've removed the majority of the milk solids, strain the butter through cheesecloth into a glass storage jar, discarding the milk solids and cheesecloth when you are done. Allow the butter to cool before storing.
3. Clarified butter can be stored in the refrigerator for up to 6 months or at room temperature for up to 3 months. (With the milk solids removed, clarified butter is shelf-stable for a longer period of time than regular butter.)

Chicken Bone Broth

Prep time: 15 minutes | Cook time: 1 hour 40 minutes
Makes 8 cups

Carcass from a roasted 3- to 4-pound (1.4- to 1.8-kg) chicken
2 carrots, roughly chopped
3 stalks celery, roughly chopped
2 onions, roughly chopped
5 or 6 sprigs fresh parsley
1 sprig fresh thyme
2 tablespoons cider vinegar
10 whole black peppercorns
1 teaspoon salt

1. In an Instant Pot, place the carcass, carrots, celery, onions, parsley, thyme, vinegar, peppercorns, and salt. Add enough water to reach 1 inch below the maximum fill line. Lock the lid in place.
2. Select Soup/Broth. Use natural release.
3. Strain the broth through a fine-mesh strainer set over a large bowl or clean pot. Discard the solids. Transfer the broth to multiple containers to speed up cooling, don't freeze or refrigerate it while it's hot! Allow the broth to sit in the fridge, uncovered, for several hours, until the fat rises to the top and hardens. Scrape off the fat with a spoon and discard it.
4. Refrigerate the broth in airtight containers for 3 to 4 days or freeze for up to 6 months.

Chapter 14: Drinks

Citrus Zinger

Prep time: 5 minutes | Cook time: 0 minutes
Serves 2

½ lemon, juiced
½ lime, juiced

1 teaspoon fresh ginger zest
12 ounces (340 g) sparkling water

1. Squeeze the lemon and lime into a glass and add ginger zest. Top with ice and the sparkling water. Give it a quick stir before serving.

Rosemary Raspberry Smash

Prep time: 5 minutes | Cook time: 0 minutes
Serves 2

¼ cup raspberries (fresh or frozen)
1 sprig fresh rosemary leaves

½ lemon, juiced
12 ounces (340 g) sparkling water

1. Muddle raspberries and rosemary leaves in a large glass. Add the lemon juice and sparkling water, and shake or mix thoroughly. Strain the mixture into a new glass, discarding the rosemary leaves. Add ice if desired.

Iced Mango Mint Green Tea

Prep time: 10 minutes | Cook time: 0 minutes
Serves 2

¼ cup fresh mint leaves
¾ cup simmering water
1 green tea bag
2 thin slices fresh ginger
¾ cup chopped fresh mango

¾ cup unsweetened coconut water
Ice
¾ cup sparkling water
Fresh mint sprigs, for garnish

1. Place the mint leaves in a mug and use a wooden spoon to gently bruise them. Add the simmering water, tea bag, and ginger. Cover and steep for 5 minutes. Remove the tea bag, squeezing gently. Chill the tea for 30 minutes. Strain the tea and discard the mint and ginger.
2. Meanwhile, in a blender, combine the mango and coconut water. Cover and blend until smooth. Pour the mixture through a fine-mesh sieve or through a nut milk bag into a 1-quart glass measuring cup, pressing with the back of a large spoon or squeezing the bag to remove all the liquid. Discard the pulp.
3. Stir the chilled tea into the mango liquid. Fill two tall glasses halfway with ice. Pour the tea mixture over the ice. Add sparkling water and stir gently. Garnish with fresh mint sprigs. Serve immediately.

Blood Orange Paloma

Prep time: 5 minutes | Cook time: 0 minutes
Serves 2

1 blood orange, juiced
½ lime, juiced

12 ounces (340 g) sparkling water

1. Add the blood orange and lime into a glass. Top with ice and the sparkling water.

White Tea Sangria

Prep time: 5 minutes | Cook time: 0 minutes
Serves 2

1 white tea bag
1 ginger tea bag
1 cup boiling water
¼ cup halved white grapes

¼ cup diced golden delicious apple
8 ounces (227 g) sparkling water
Lemon slices, for garnish

1. Heat 1 cup of water to boiling, let it cool for 5 minutes. Add the tea bags to the hot water and steep for 7 to 10 minutes; remove and discard the tea bags. Chill in the refrigerator for 25 minutes.
2. Place the fruit into a large glass and add ice if desired. Pour tea over the fruit and top with sparkling water. Garnish with lemon slices.

Basil Peach Agua Fresca

Prep time: 10 minutes | Cook time: 0 minutes
Serves 4

4 cups ripe cubed, peeled peaches (about 4 peaches)
2 cups fresh orange juice
2 tablespoons fresh lemon juice

1¼ cups water
8 large fresh basil leaves, torn, plus whole leaves for serving
Orange slices, for serving

1. Combine the peaches, orange juice, and lemon juice in a blender. Cover and blend until smooth. Pour the peach mixture into a pitcher. Stir in the water. Add the torn basil leaves. Cover and steep in the refrigerator for at least 2 hours.
2. To serve, remove and discard the torn basil leaves. Serve in ice-filled glasses with orange slices and whole basil leaves.

Appendix 1 Measurement Conversion Chart

VOLUME EQUIVALENTS(DRY)

US STANDARD	METRIC (APPROXIMATE)
1/8 teaspoon	0.5 mL
1/4 teaspoon	1 mL
1/2 teaspoon	2 mL
3/4 teaspoon	4 mL
1 teaspoon	5 mL
1 tablespoon	15 mL
1/4 cup	59 mL
1/2 cup	118 mL
3/4 cup	177 mL
1 cup	235 mL
2 cups	475 mL
3 cups	700 mL
4 cups	1 L

VOLUME EQUIVALENTS(LIQUID)

US STANDARD	US STANDARD (OUNCES)	METRIC (APPROXIMATE)
2 tablespoons	1 fl.oz.	30 mL
1/4 cup	2 fl.oz.	60 mL
1/2 cup	4 fl.oz.	120 mL
1 cup	8 fl.oz.	240 mL
1 1/2 cup	12 fl.oz.	355 mL
2 cups or 1 pint	16 fl.oz.	475 mL
4 cups or 1 quart	32 fl.oz.	1 L
1 gallon	128 fl.oz.	4 L

TEMPERATURES EQUIVALENTS

FAHRENHEIT(F)	CELSIUS(C) (APPROXIMATE)
225 °F	107 °C
250 °F	120 °C
275 °F	135 °C
300 °F	150 °C
325 °F	160 °C
350 °F	180 °C
375 °F	190 °C
400 °F	205 °C
425 °F	220 °C
450 °F	235 °C
475 °F	245 °C
500 °F	260 °C

WEIGHT EQUIVALENTS

US STANDARD	METRIC (APPROXIMATE)
1 ounce	28 g
2 ounces	57 g
5 ounces	142 g
10 ounces	284 g
15 ounces	425 g
16 ounces (1 pound)	455 g
1.5 pounds	680 g
2 pounds	907 g

Appendix 2 Recipe Index

A

Ahi Mango Poke   35
Ahi Tuna Steaks with Mango Salsa   119
Almond Chicken and Sweet Potato Stew   43
Almond Green Beans   59
Almond Lime Satay Sauce   129
Apple Pork Chops and Spinach   85
Applesauce Pork Chops   79
Apricot Stuffed Pork Chops   80
Asian Beef with Mushrooms and Snow Peas 71
Asian Beef Zoodle Soup   60
Asian Chicken Curry   94
Asian Orange Dressing   129
Asian Shrimp Zucchini Noodles   119
Authentic Picadillo   72
Avocado Green Goddess Dressing   127

B

Bacon, Spinach, and Tomato Breakfast Salad 22
Baked Cod with Mushrooms   117
Baked Fish en Papillote   116
Balsamic Peach Arugula Salad   32
Balsamic Roast Beef and Veggies   74
Balsamic Roasted Root Vegetables   53
Balsamic Turkey Tenderloins with Peppers   110
Balsamic Vinaigrette   127
Banger Sausage Patties with Sweet Potatoes   92
Basic Cauliflower Rice   132
Basil Peach Agua Fresca   136
Basil Pork and Cauliflower Curry   84
Basil Roasted Salmon with Broccoli   118
Basil Sirloin Medallions with Carrots   62
Beef and Broccoli Salad   37
Beef and Broccoli Stir-Fry   67
Beef and Pepper Soup   42
Beef and Vegetable Stew   44
Beef Bone Broth   132
Beef Brisket Braised with Potatoes   75
Beef Short Ribs Braised with Mushrooms   64
Beef Stroganoff with Coconut Cream   76
Beef Stuffed Bell Peppers   61
Beef, Zucchini, and Mushroom Stir-Fry   62
Beet and Red Cabbage Salad   52

Bistro Endive and Egg Salad   21
Black Pepper Beef and Cabbage Stir-Fry   64
Blood Orange Paloma   136
Braised Chicken with Artichoke and Olives   109
Broiled Shrimp with Pine Nuts   113
Buffalo Sauce   131
Butter Chicken   105
Butternut Squash Apple Soup   48

C-D

Carne Asada Salad   39
Carrot and Tomato Sauce   129
Carrots with Fennel and Shallots   58
Cashew Cauliflower Alfredo   128
Cassava Crusted Calamari   125
Catalina Beef Tacos   69
Cauliflower Soup with Sausage and Spinach   45
Chicken and Artichoke Stew   96
Chicken and Carrot Stew   40
Chicken Avocado Soup   49
Chicken Bone Broth   134
Chicken Cacciatore   102
Chicken Meatballs with Creamy Tomato Sauce   103
Chicken Romaine Salad   36
Chicken Stir Fry   110
Chicken Taco Salad   29
Chicken with Mushrooms and Sweet Potatoes   97
Chile Lime Roasted Sweet Potatoes   53
Chili Verde Pork   93
Chimichurri Pork and Cabbage Salad   35
Chipotle Chicken Thighs with Tomatoes   99
Cider Pulled Pork   81
Cider-Brined Roasted Pork   90
Cider-Mustard Vinaigrette   130
Cilantro-Lime Pork Salad   29
Citrus Almond Cod with Spinach   124
Citrus Zinger   135
Citrus-Ginger Glazed Halibut   117
Clarified Butter   134
Classic Borscht   68
Cod en Papillote   114

Cod in Tomato and Pepper Sauce 114
Cod with Olive Relish and Pilaf 126
Comforting Chicken Fricassée 96
Coriander Crusted Pork Tenderloin 87
Creamy Broccoli Soup 58
Creamy Ranch Dressing 133
Creamy Spinach Artichoke Chicken 95
Crispy Chicken Schnitzel 102
Cuban-Style Beef and Peppers 75
Cucumber and Tomato Salad 31
Cumin and Tomato Pineapple Sauce 128
Curried Carrot Sweet Potato Soup 54
Curried Chicken Salad 31
Dukkah Brussels Sprouts 57

E-F

Easy Shrimp Scampi 123
Easy Zucchini Noodles 50
Eggs Florentine 23
Fattoush Salad 30
Fish Vegetable Stir-Fry 121
Fried Eggs with Green Beans and Mushrooms 24
Fruity Chicken Salad 34

G

Garlic and Herb Stuffed Portobello Mushrooms 51
Garlic Chicken Primavera 112
Garlic Herb Chicken and Veggies 98
Garlic Kale 50
Garlic Mussels in Spicy Tomato Sauce 121
Garlicky Green Beans with Almonds 52
Ginger Curry Sauce 131
Grapefruit Chicken 104
Greek Lemon Chicken and Potatoes 99
Greek Lemon Potatoes 55
Greek Turkey Meatball Salad 38
Green Chile Chicken Stew 101
Green Chile Pork 81
Green Omelet 26
Green Pork Curry with Asparagus 82
Grilled Pork Chops with Watermelon Salad 86
Grilled Romaine with Lemon Tahini Dressing 56
Grilled Skirt Steak 70
Grilled Steaks with Garlic-Shallot Purée 65
Ground Beef Taco Salad 37

H

Harissa Salmon Fillets 118
Hasselback Zucchini with Basil 57
Hearty Hamburger Soup 65

Herb and Garlic Chimichurri Sauce 128
Hollandaise Sauce 130
Homemade Mayonnaise 132
Hot and Sour Shrimp Soup 41
Hot Roast Beef 73

I-J

Iced Mango Mint Green Tea 135
Indian Pepper Steak Stir-Fry 70
Italian Chicken Sausage Soup 41
Italian Chicken Vegetable Soup 42
Italian Dressing 127
Italian-Style Chicken with Fennel 111
Jamaican Jerk Salmon with Mango Salsa 116

K

Kale and Bacon Frittata 21
Kale and Butternut Squash Salad 54
Kale and Chicken Sausage Stew 43
Ketchup 133

L

Lamb Loaves with Apricots and Cauliflower 72
Lemon and Herb Roast Chicken and
Vegetables 106
Lemon and Oregano Chicken with Parsnips 105
Lemon Dill Salmon 114
Lemon Dressing 130
Lemon Mediterranean Chicken Salad 32
Lemon-Tarragon Grilled Pork Rib Chops 85
Lemony Chicken with Green Beans 101
Lime-Garlic Zucchini Ribbons 52
Lush Pork Loin Stew 43

M

5-Minute Sugar Snap Peas 50
Mango and Shrimp Salad 36
Mashed Sweet Potatoes 51
Mexican Chicken Soup 47
Mexican Pork Shoulder Stew 40
Mexican Tuna Boats 119
Mici 68
Mojo Roast Chicken 95
Mongolian Beef and Mixed Greens 69
Mushroom and Spinach Frittata 22
Mushroom Stuffed Beef Roulade 77
Mustard Brussels Sprout Slaw 55

O

Onion Chicken Meatballs 107
Onion-Braised Beef Brisket 63

Orange Tuna, Snow Pea, and Broccoli Salad 33
Oregano Chicken and Kale Salad 31

P

Pan-Seared Scallops with Orange Sauce 113
per with Shiitake Mushrooms 122
Pesto-Pepper Frittata with Butternut Squash 27
Pineapple Beef Kabobs 61
Pineapple Salmon 120
Piri Piri Chicken 100
Pistachio Kale Salad 55
Pork and Bell Pepper Stir-Fry 88
Pork and Green Chile Stew 46
Pork and Napa Cabbage Soup 47
Pork Carnitas 79
Pork Chops with Mashers and Pepita Pesto 89
Pork Chops with Parsnip Purée 82
Pork Greek Salad 34
Pork Lettuce Wraps with Peach Salsa 80
Pork Scaloppini with Mushrooms 83
Pork with Sweet Potato Colcannon 88
Potato and Green Soup 45
Potato, Sausage, and Kale Soup 86

R

Red Cabbage with Bacon and Apple 56
Red Potato Salad with Chicken Sausage 34
Roasted Brussels Sprouts with Lemon Tahini 53
Roasted Cauliflower 51
Roasted Parsnips with Lemon and Dill 54
Roasted Pepper Chicken 98
Roasted Pork with Butternut Squash 87
Rosemary Beef Eye of Round Roast 73
Rosemary Pork Chops with Red Potatoes 83
Rosemary Raspberry Smash 135
Rosemary Whole Chicken 104
Russian Beef Stew 60

S

Salmon Potato Salad 33
Salmon with Cauliflower and Spinach Salad 123
Salsa Verde Chicken 103
Sausage and Mushroom Frittata 23
Sausage Potato Hash 84
Sautéed Greens with Pine Nuts 59
Scrambled Egg Breakfast Tacos 28
Scrambled Eggs with Smoked Salmon 27
Sea Scallops with Ginger-Blueberry Sauce 125

Seared Sirloin Steak 78
Shakshuka 25
Shrimp and Fish Cakes 115
Shrimp Mashed Potatoes 120
Slow Cooker Beef Fajita Soup 41
Slow-Cooker Five-Spice Chicken Wings 106
Smoky Spanish Chicken Meatballs 109
Spanish Chicken Cauliflower Skillet 100
Spice-Crusted Roast Pork Tenderloin 91
Spiced Moroccan Meatball Stew 46
Spicy Chicken, Watermelon, and Spinach Salad 39
Spinach and Tomato Frittata 25
Sriracha 133
Steak Fajita Bowls with Vegetables 66
Steak Fajita Salad 30
Steak Salad with Charred Onions 38
Sticky Apricot Drumsticks 98
Stir-Fried Chicken and Bok Choy 112
Sunflower Seed Curry Sauce 127
Sweet and Sour Snapper 115
Sweet Potato and Chicken Hash 101
Sweet Potato Beef Chili 66
Sweet Potato Breakfast Stacks 24
Sweet Potato Cauliflower Mash 50
Sweet Potato Pork Stew 48

T

Tender Pot Roast 67
Thai Chicken Larb Salad 33
Thai Coconut Beef Curry with Green Beans 74
Thai Lemon Curry Chicken Bowls 97
Thai Red Curry Cauliflower 56
Thai Red Curry Shrimp 122
Thyme Chicken Zoodle Soup 42
Thyme Lamb Chops and Fingerlings 71
Tunisian Lamb and Squash Stew 63
Turkey Meatballs with Spaghetti Squash 107
Turkey Stuffed Bell Peppers 111
Turmeric Chicken Thighs 108
Turnip Leek Soup 49

V-W

Vegetable Soup with Basil Pesto 44
White Tea Sangria 136

Printed in Great Britain
by Amazon

65905411R00086